These photographs were all taken in the space of a few months in the City of London.
The images were manipulated using Magix video-editing software.

FUTURE ARKITEKT

A COLLECTION OF PHOTOGRAPHS

LEE GIBSON

PRINTED IN THE UK BY CREATESPACE/AMAZON

ISBN: 1517010411
ISBN-13: 978 - 1517010416

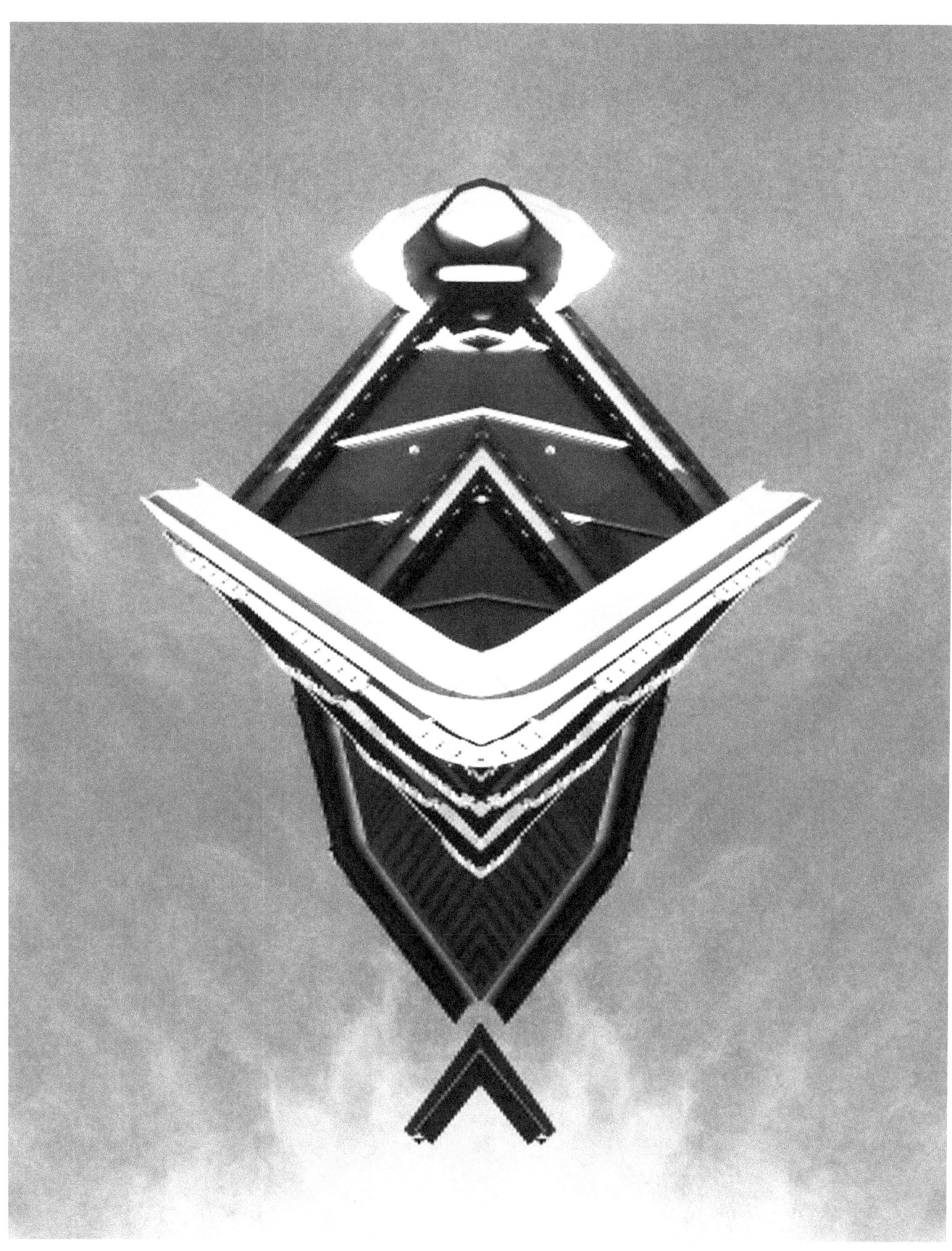

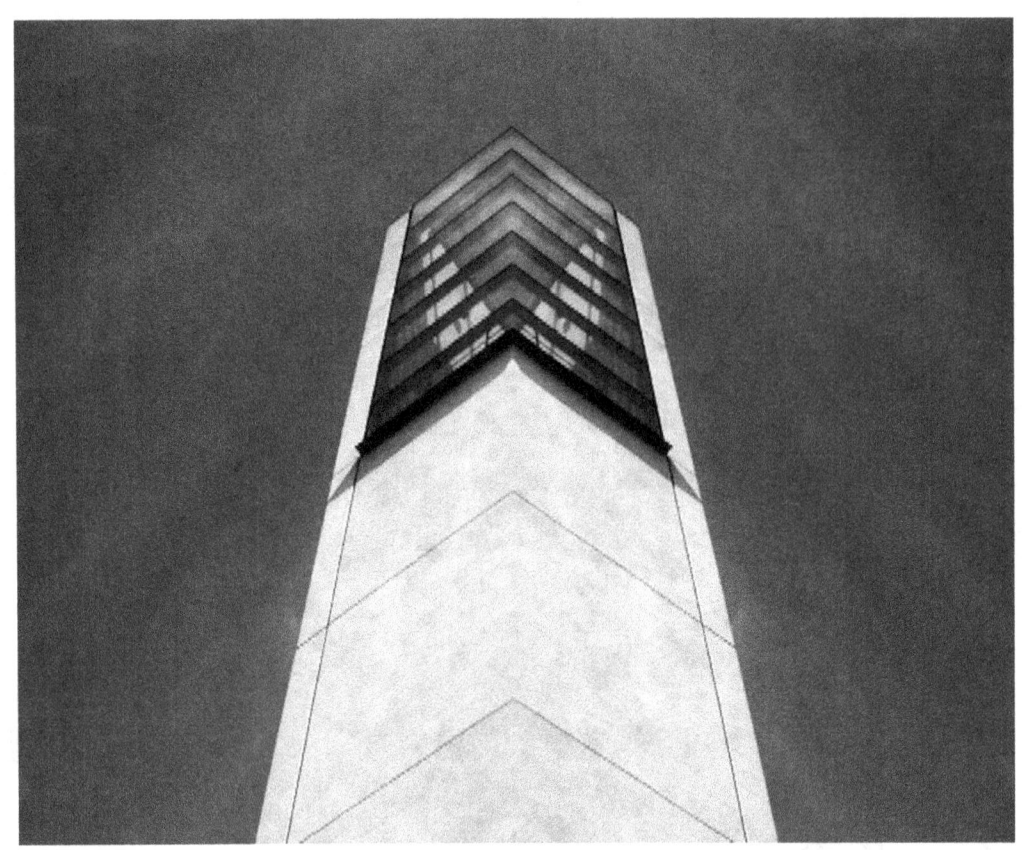

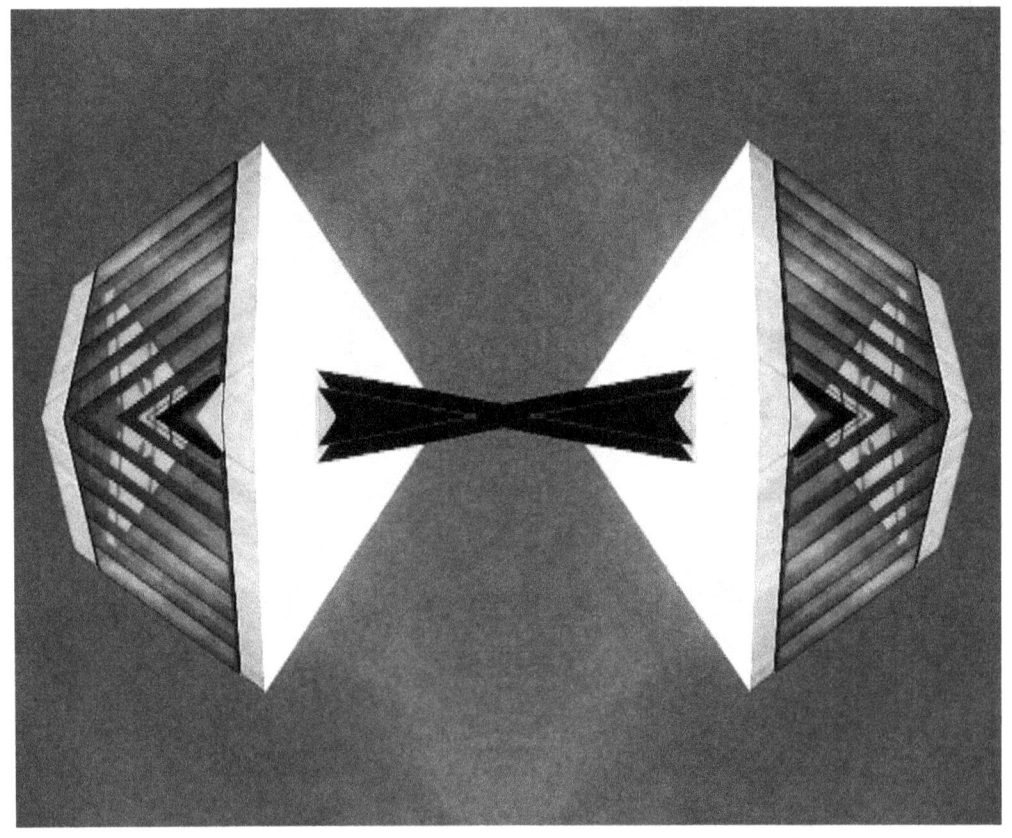

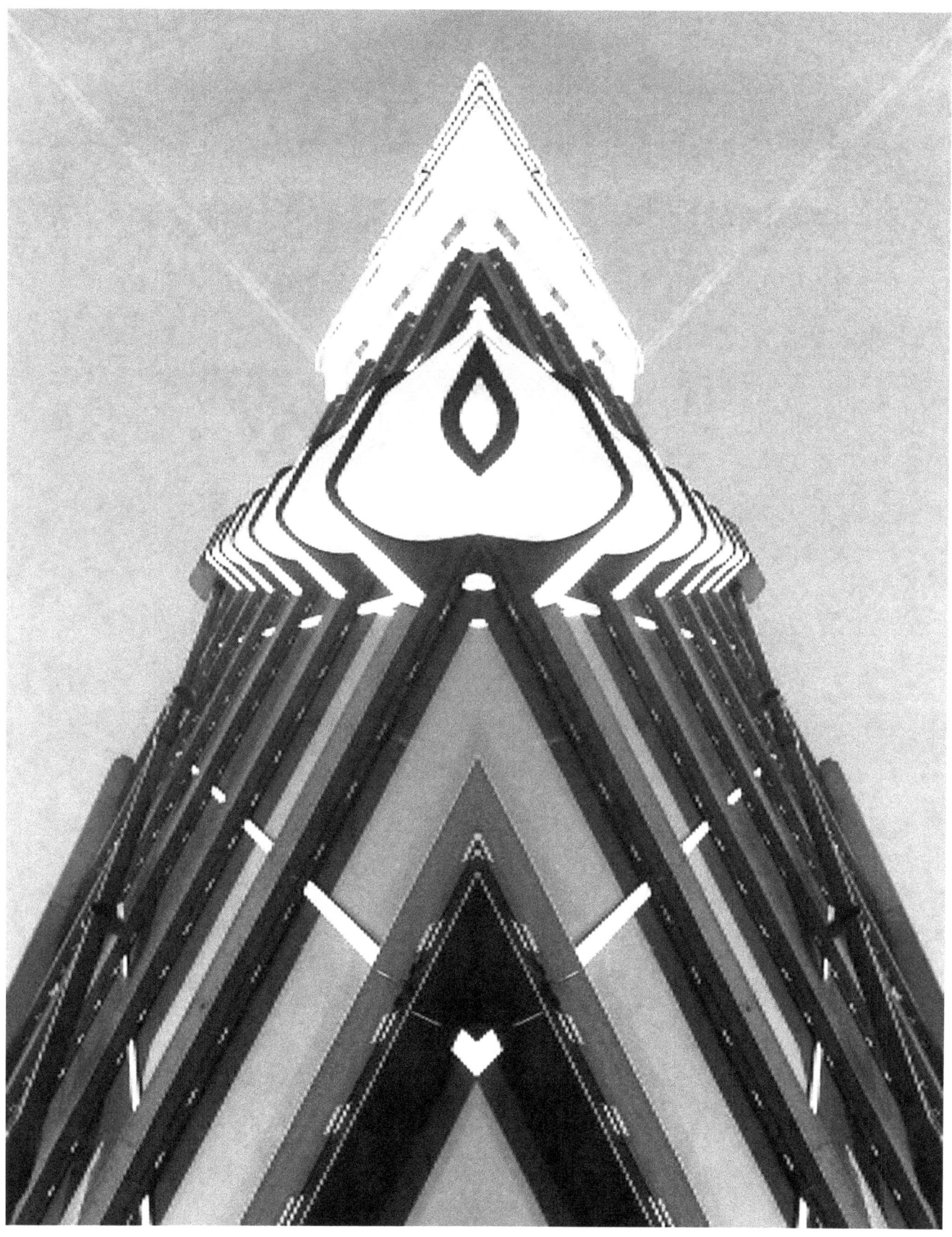

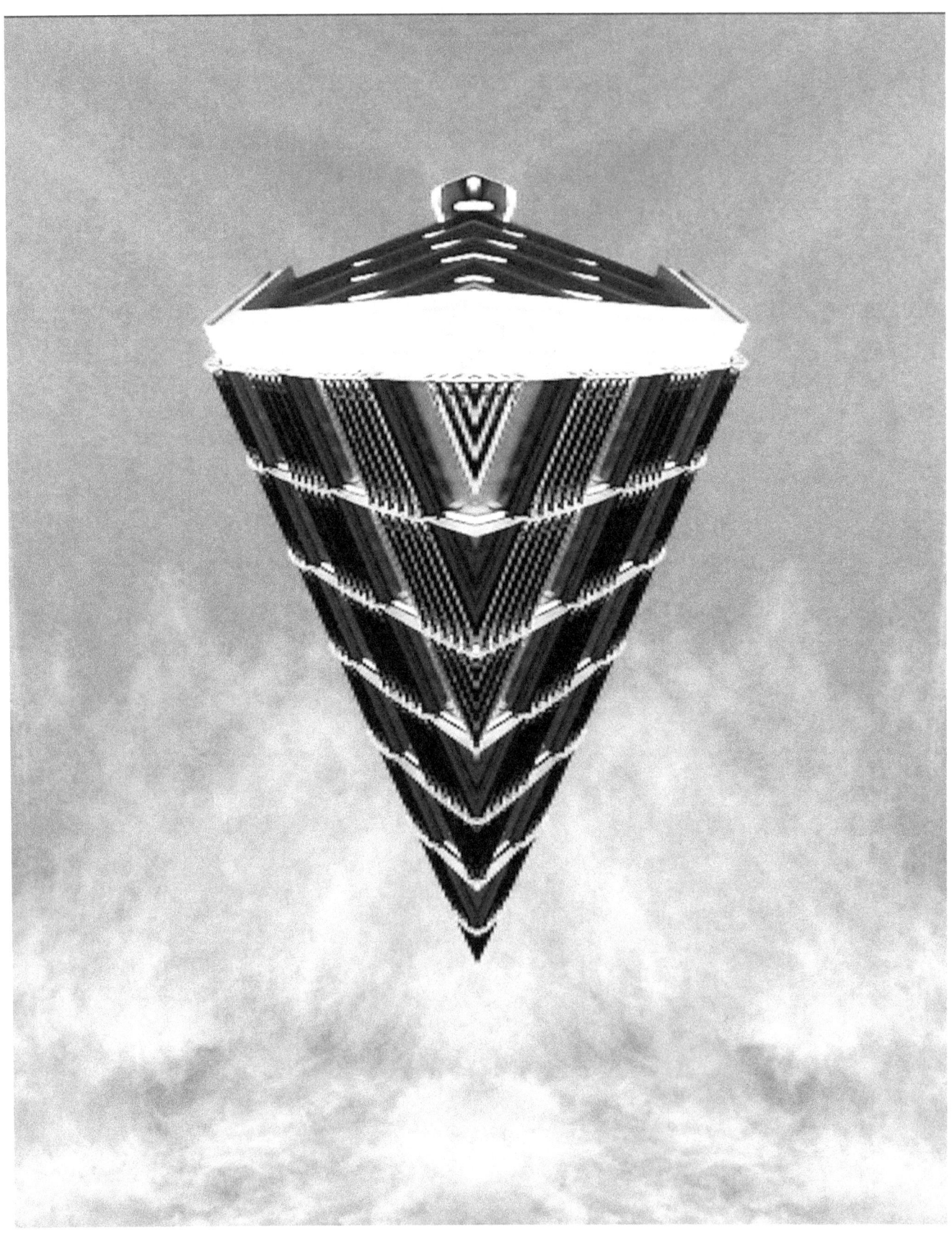

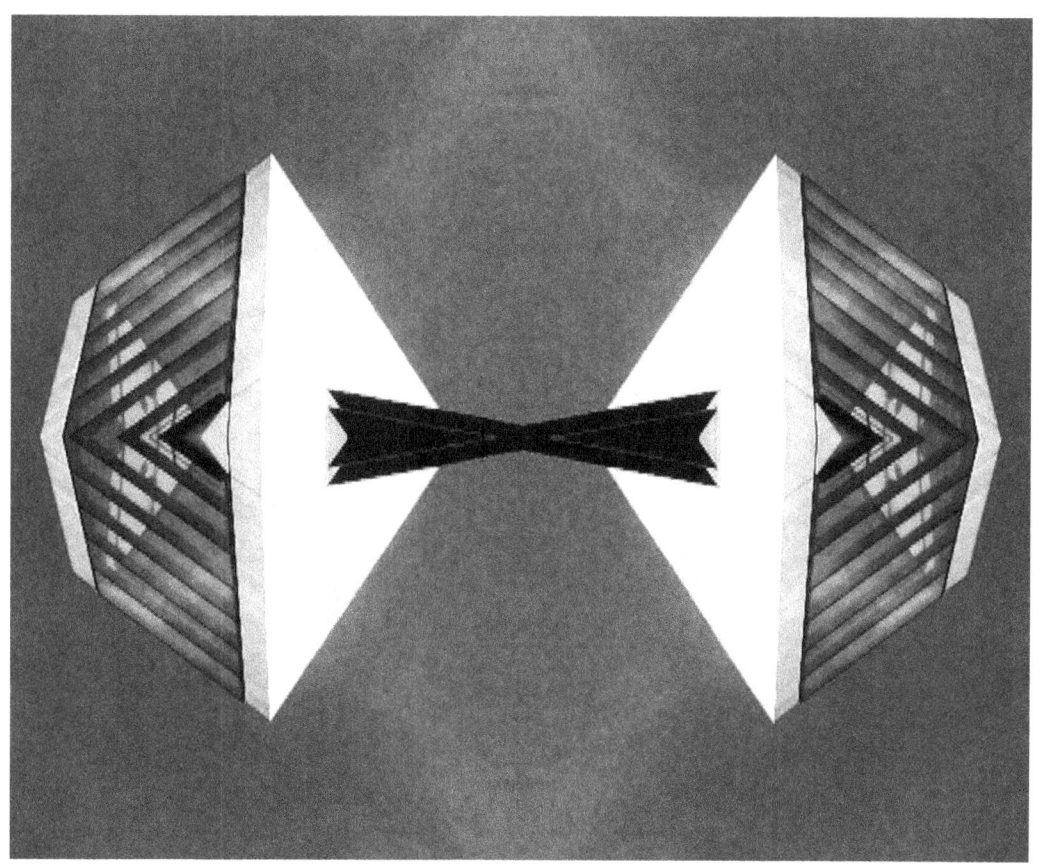

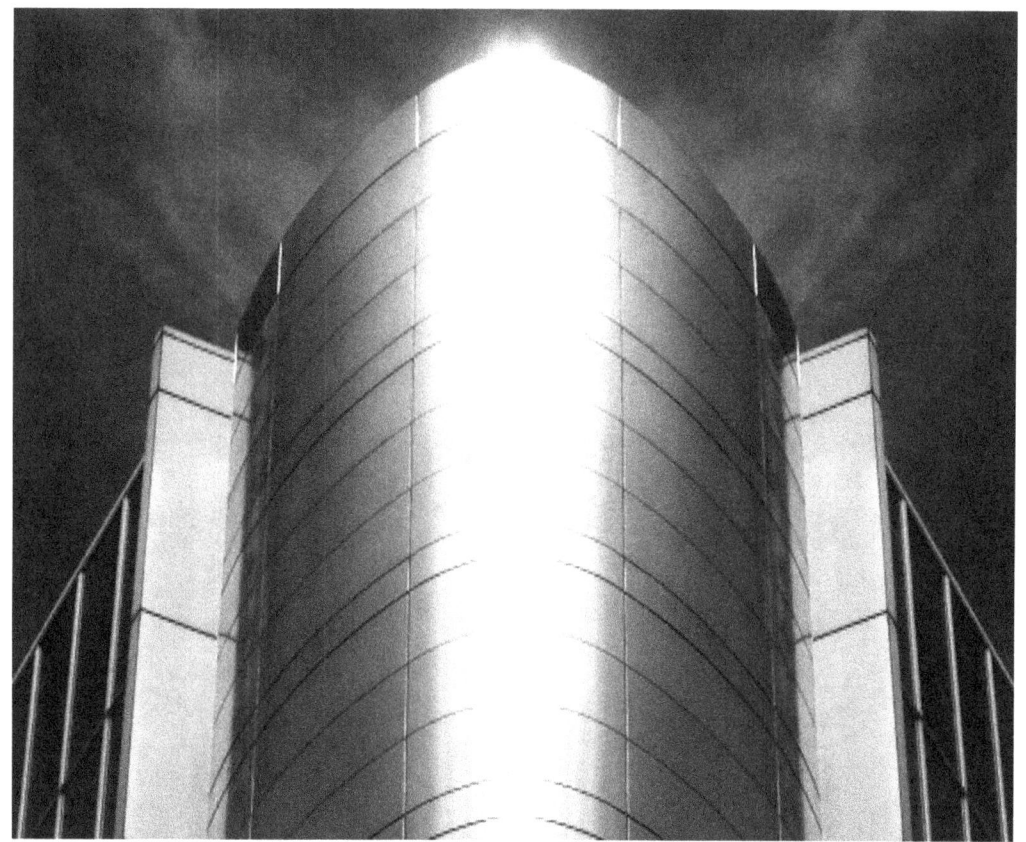

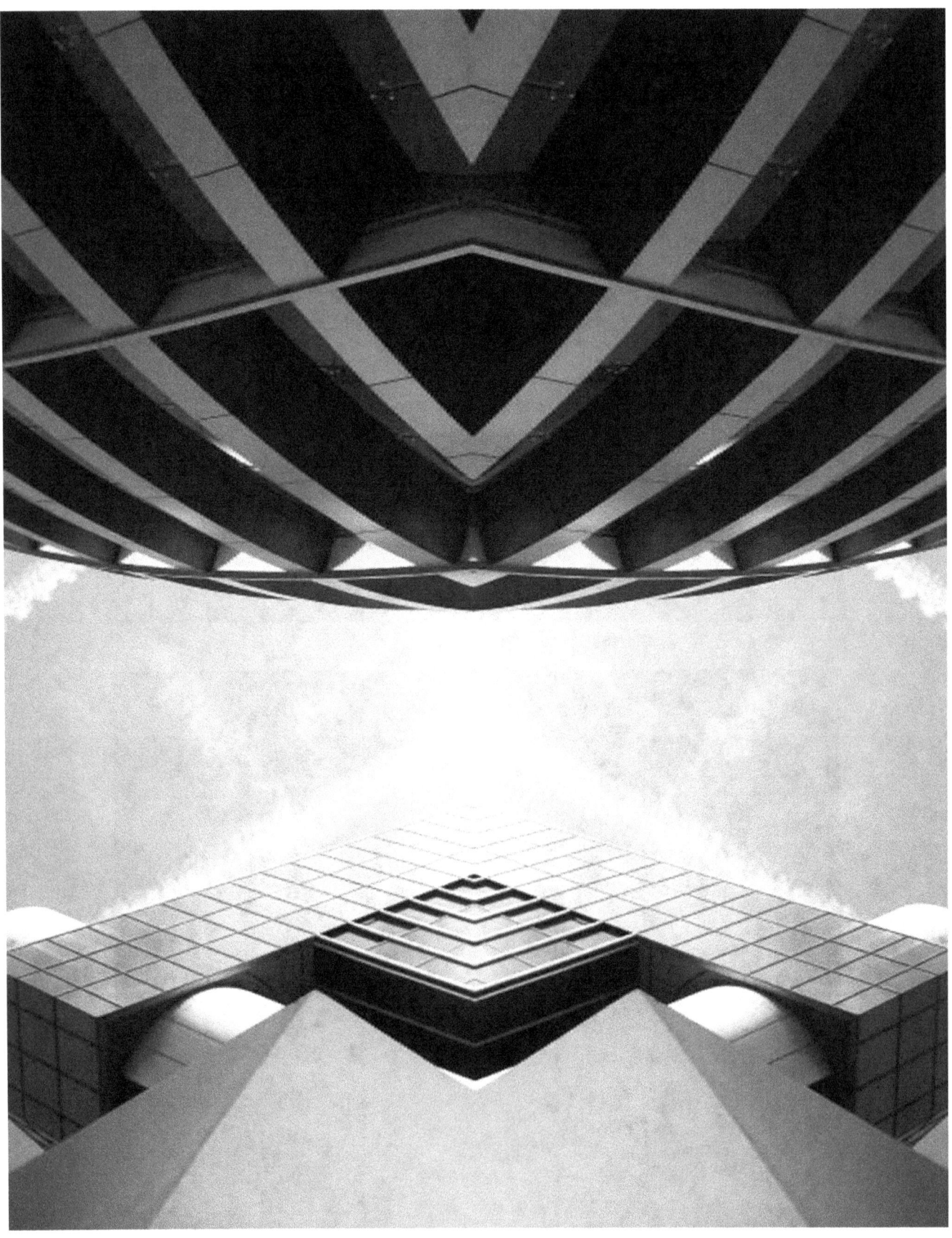

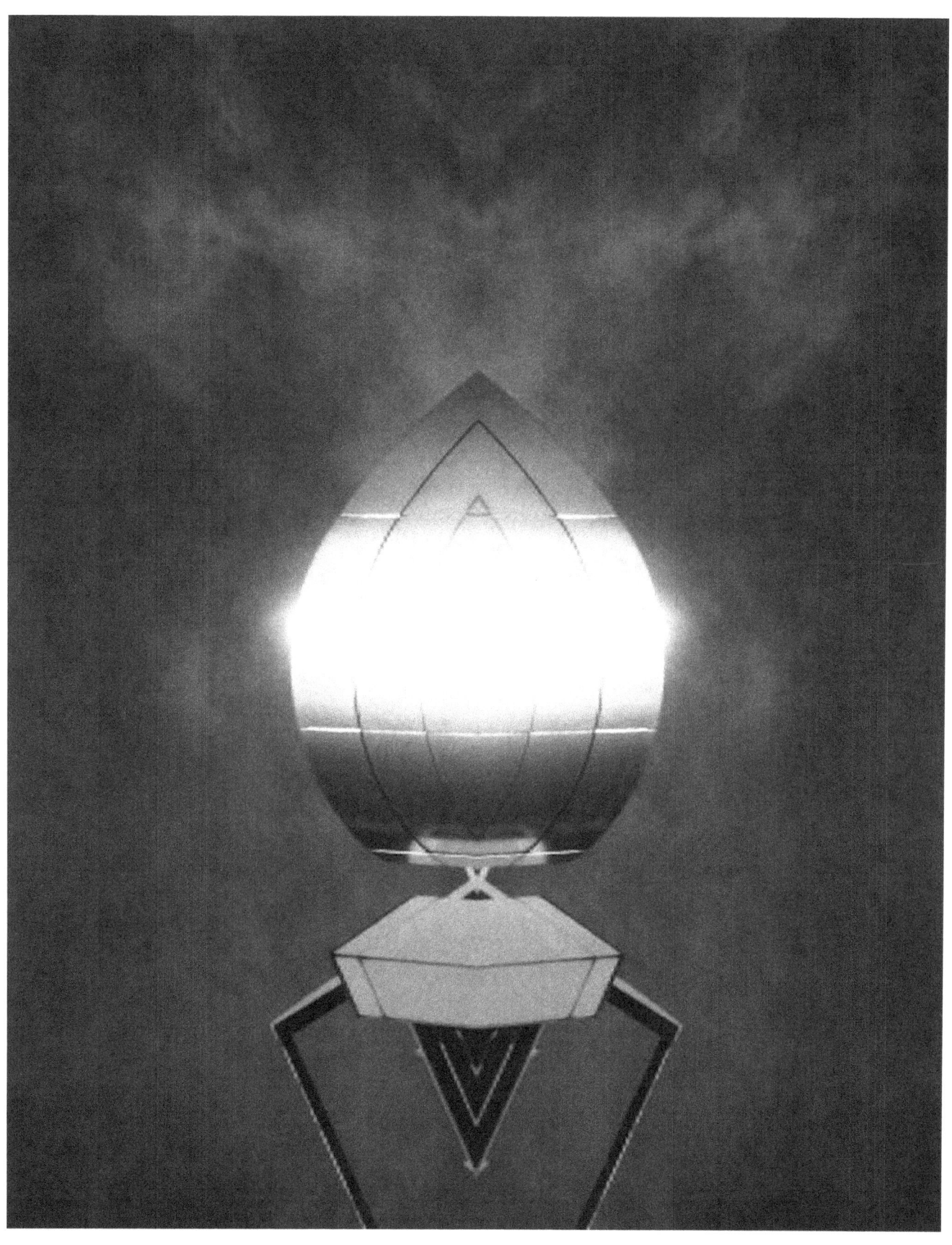

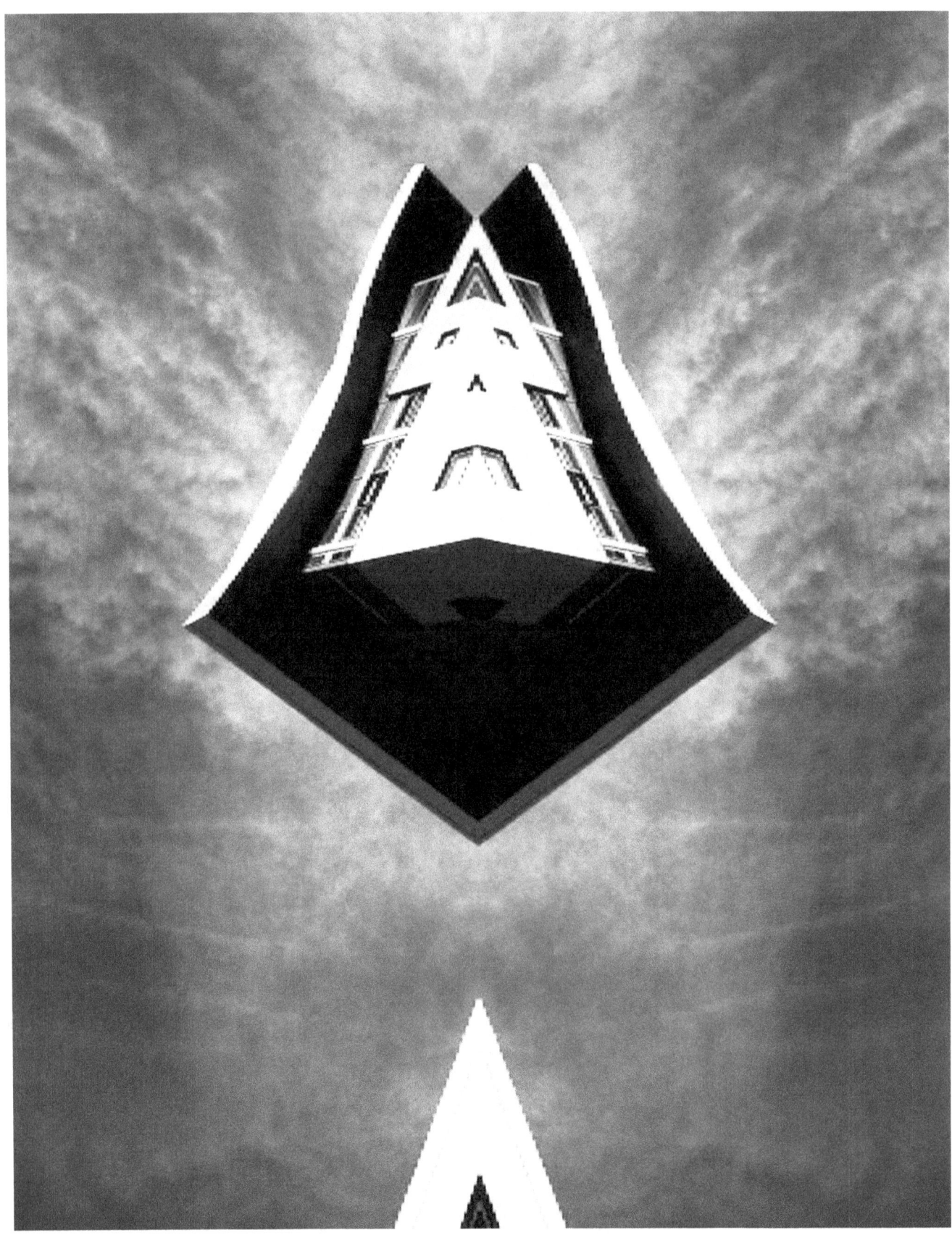

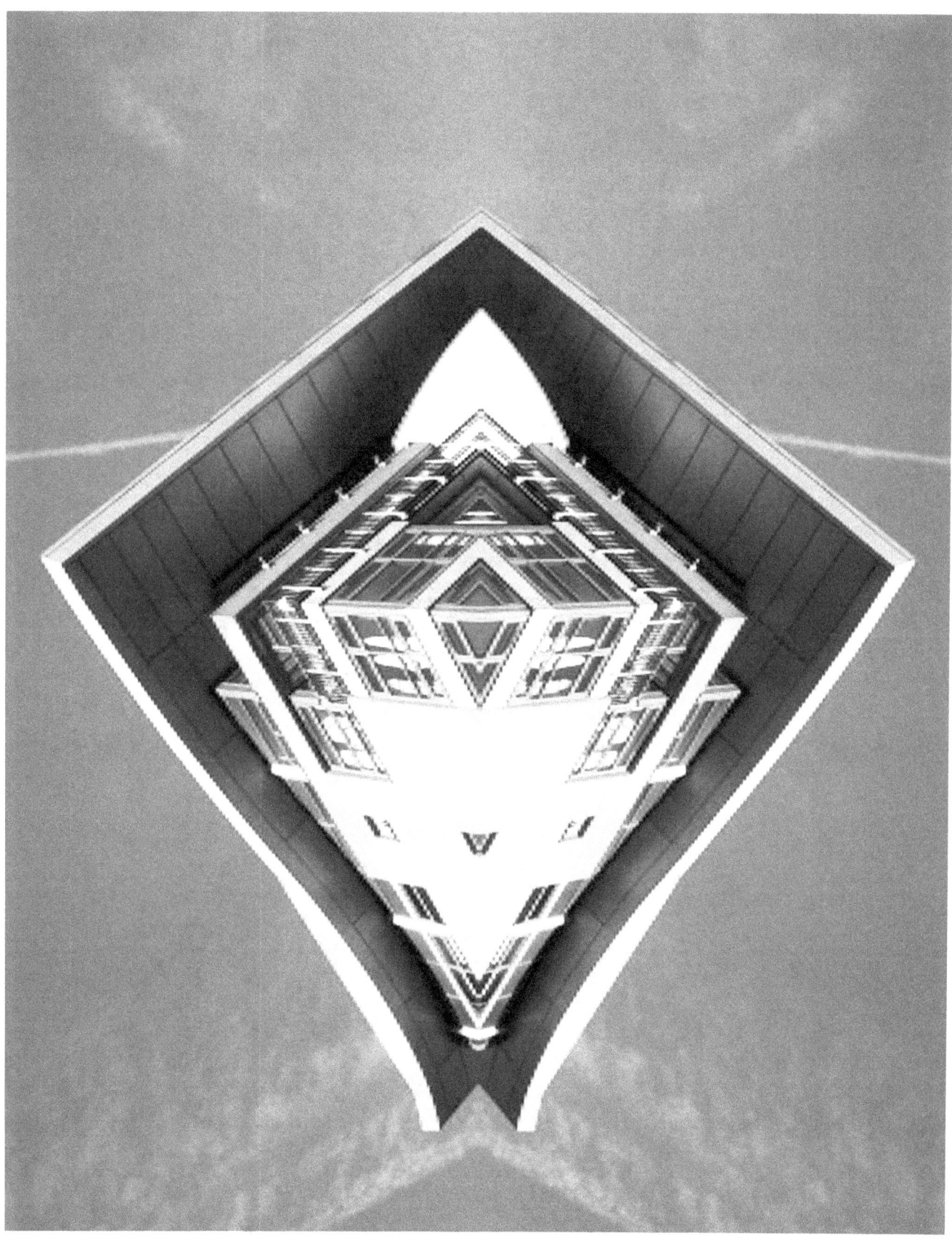

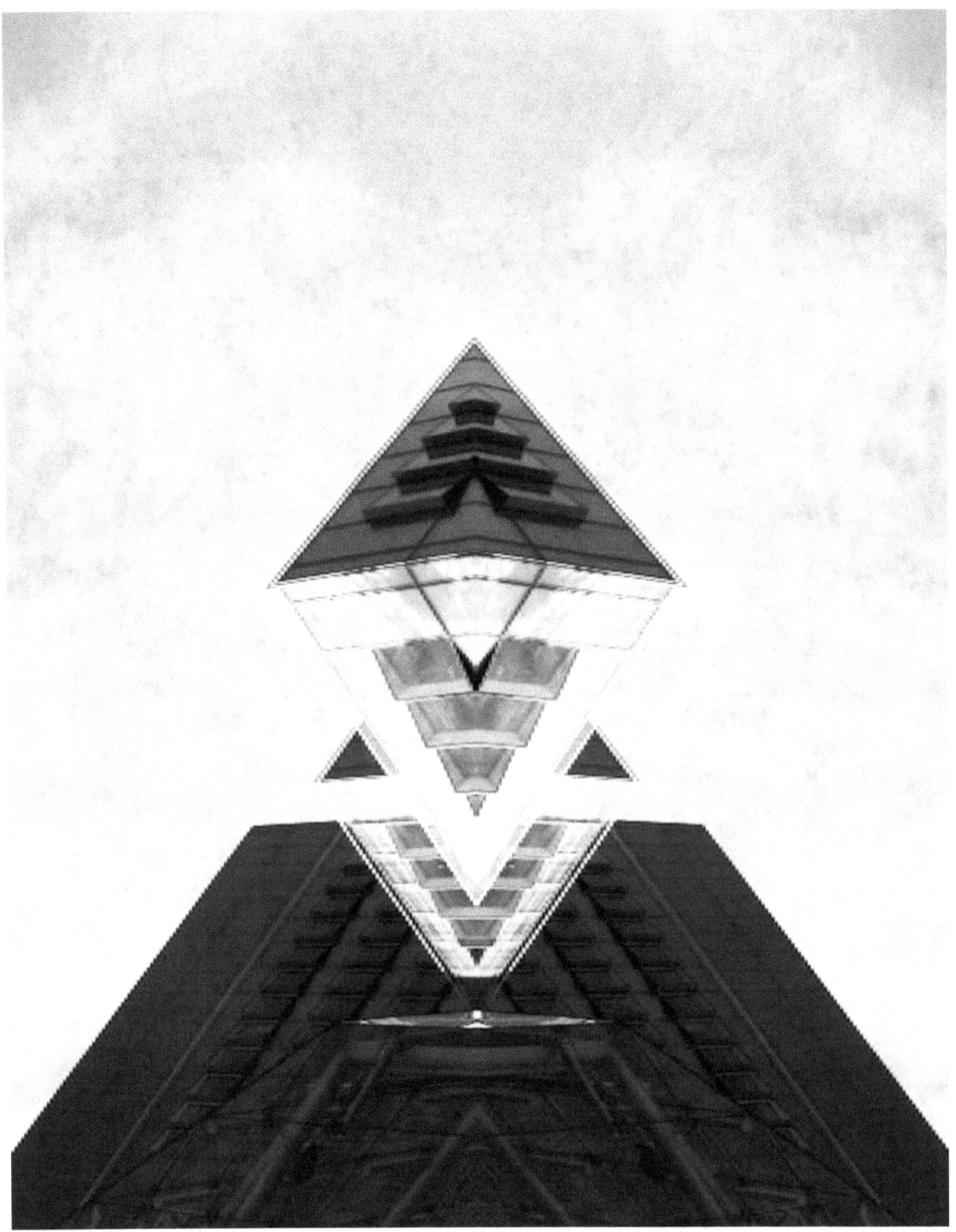

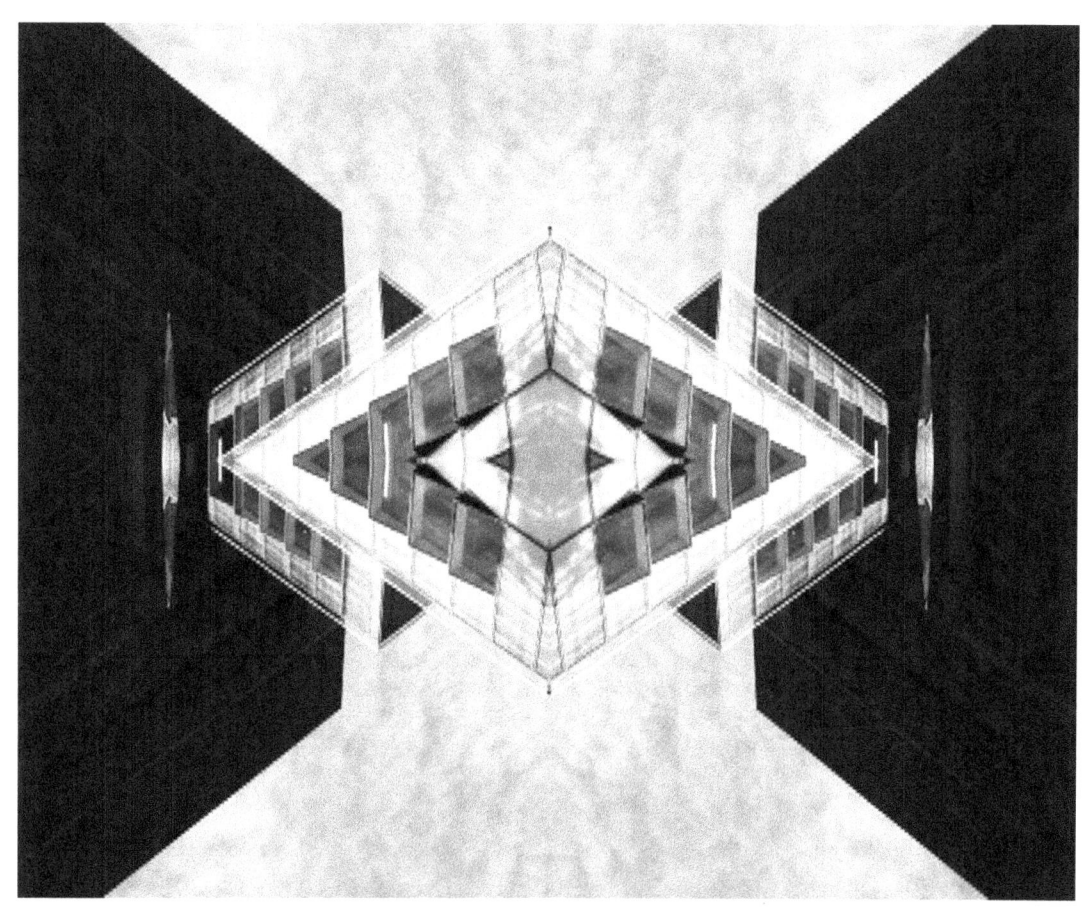

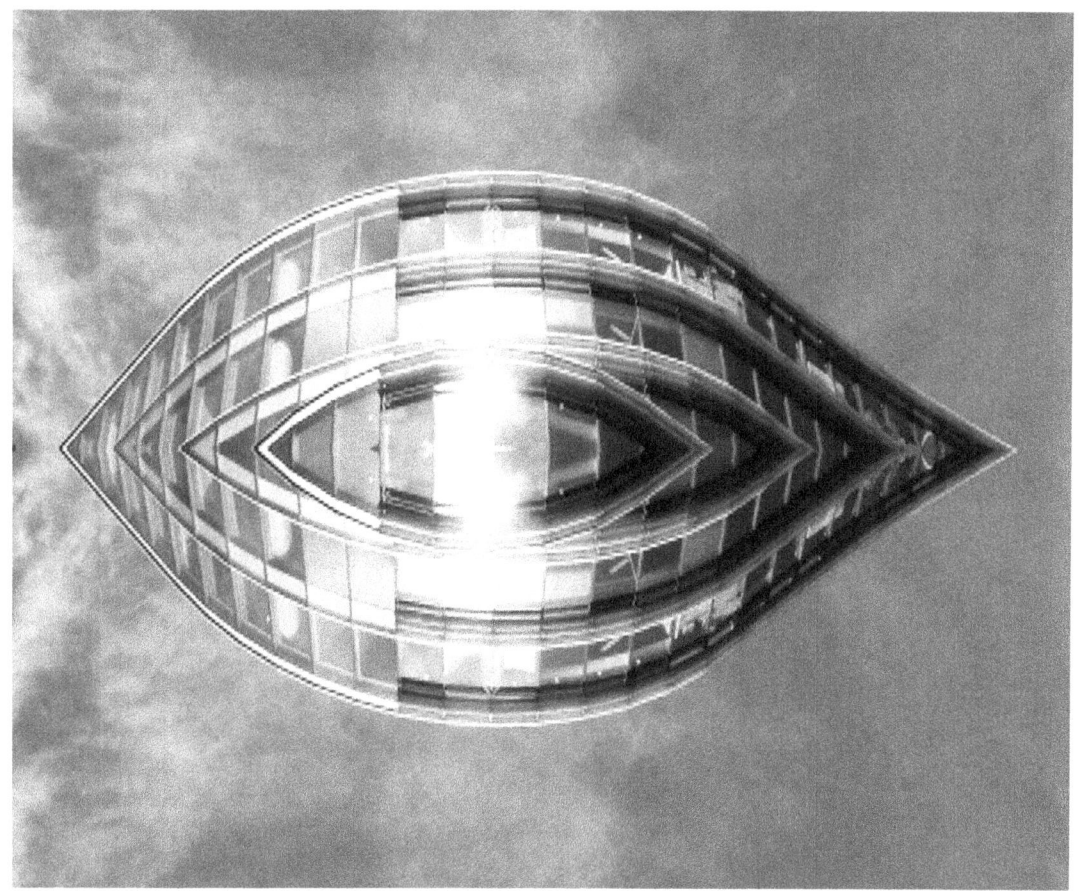

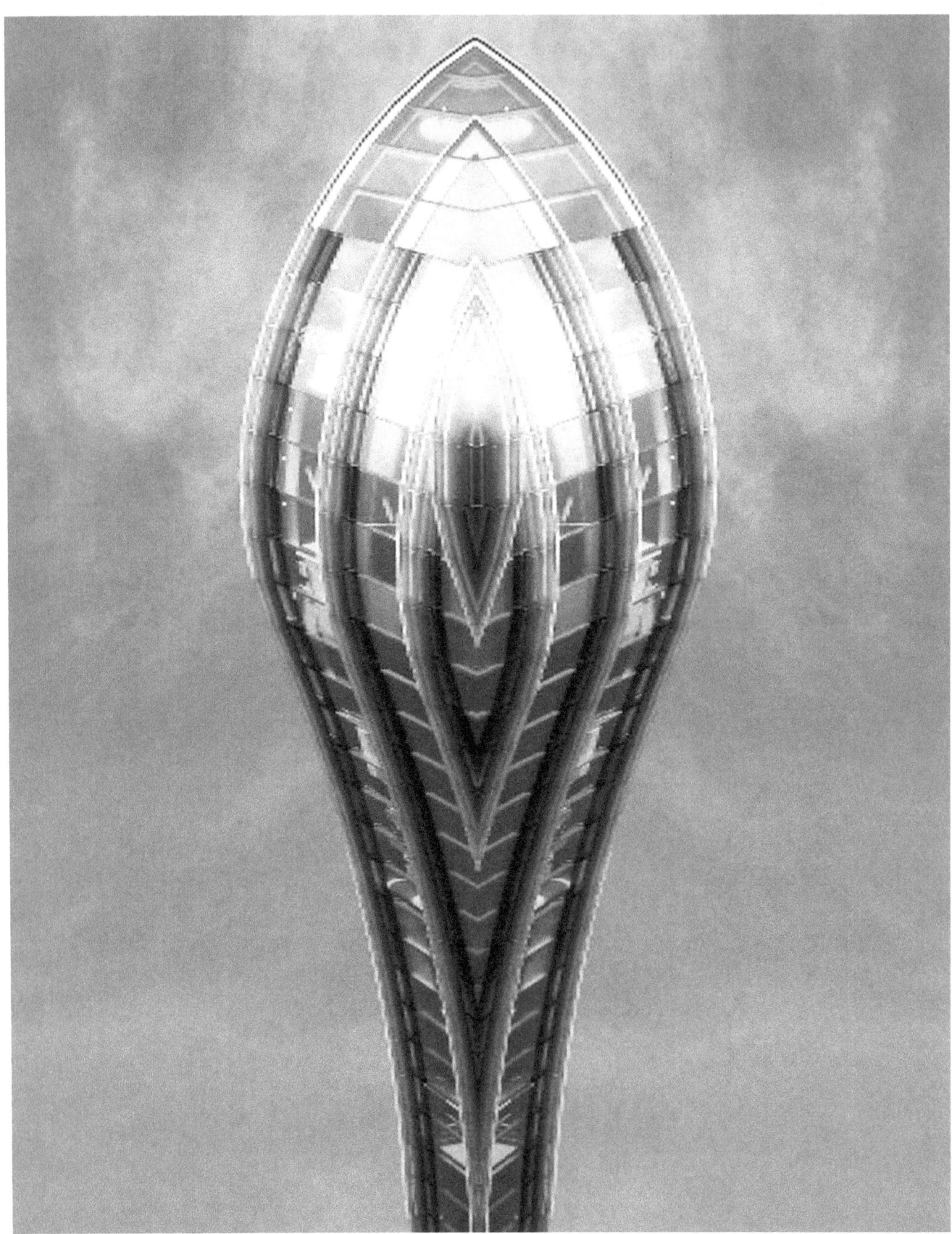

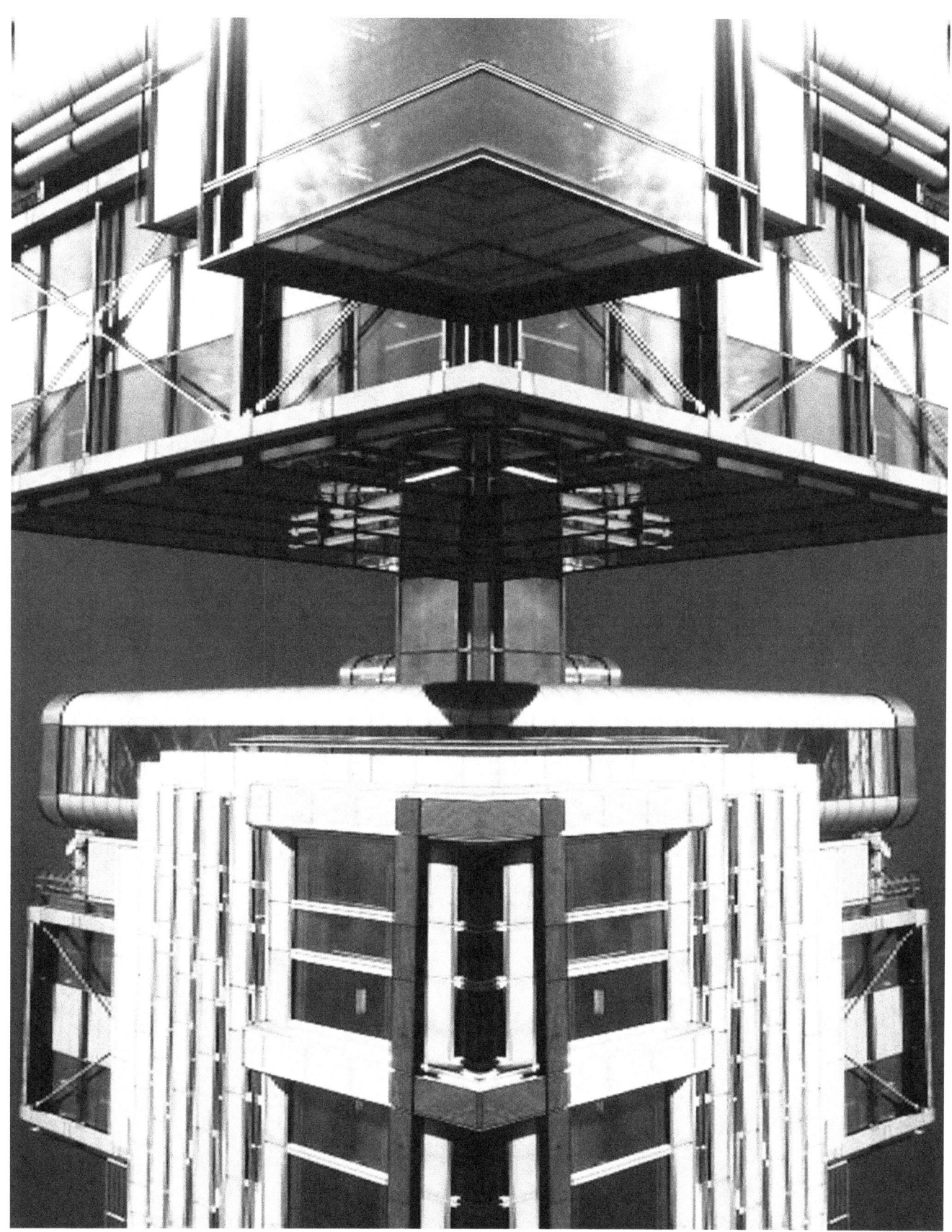

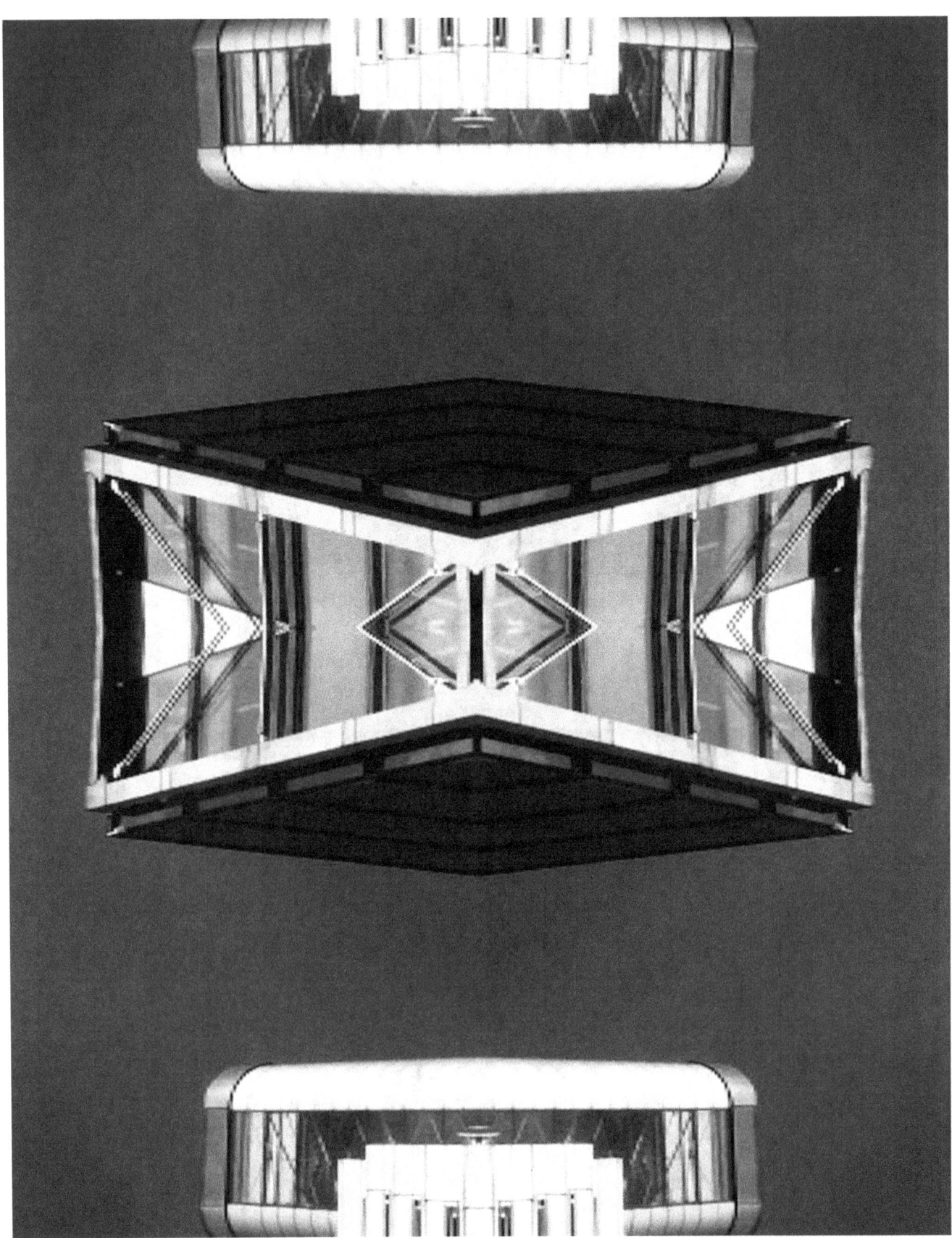

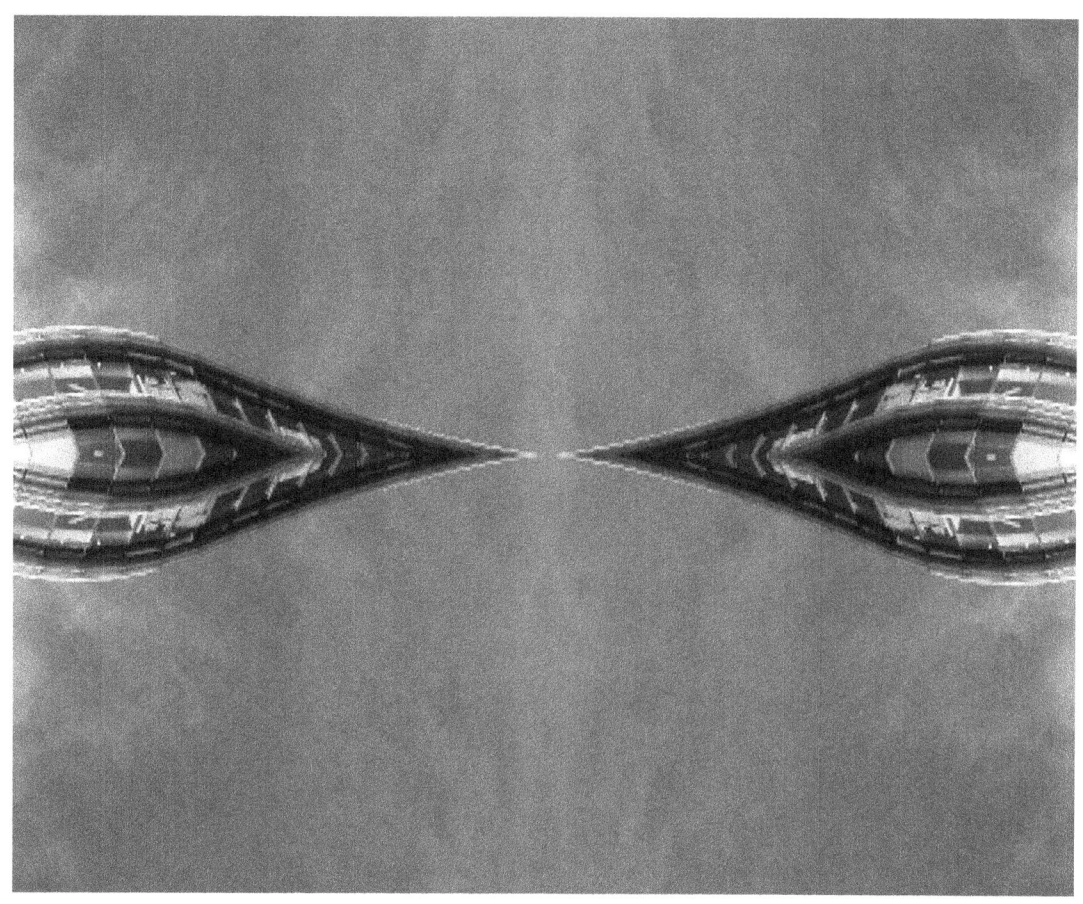

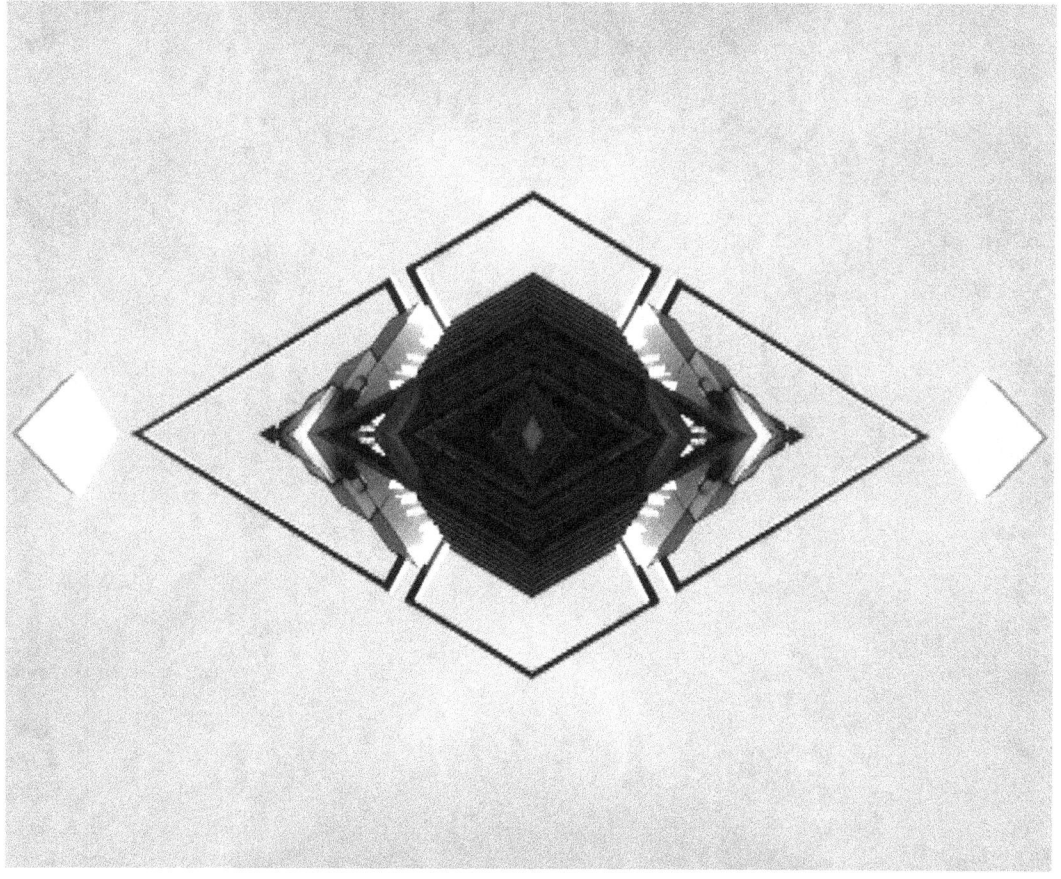

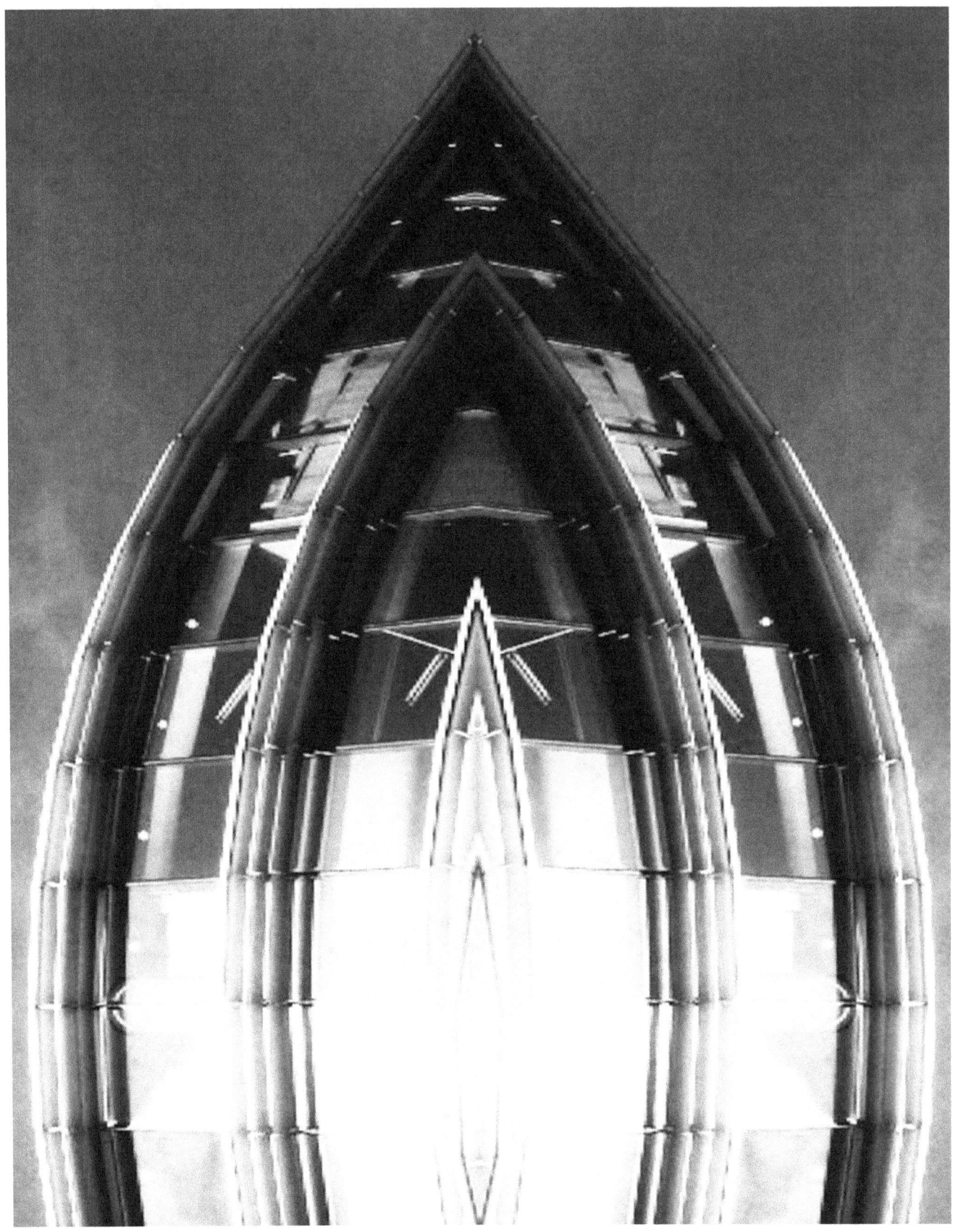

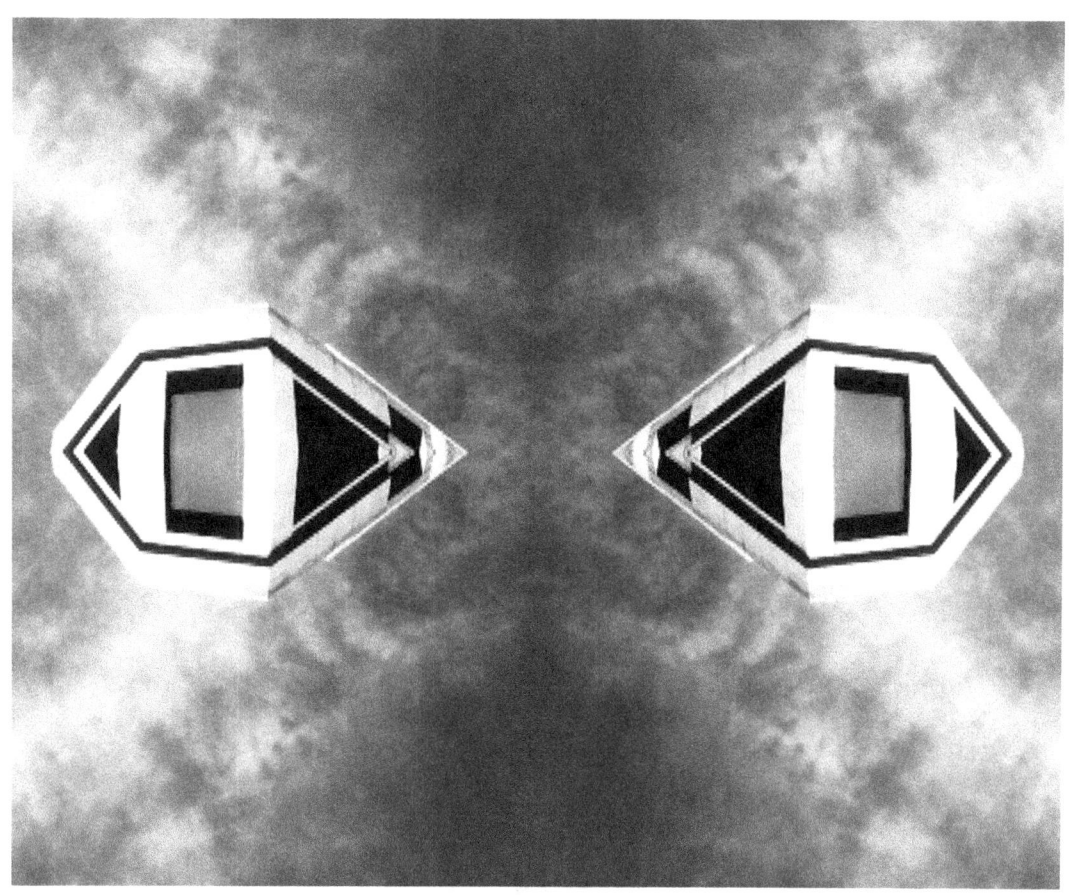

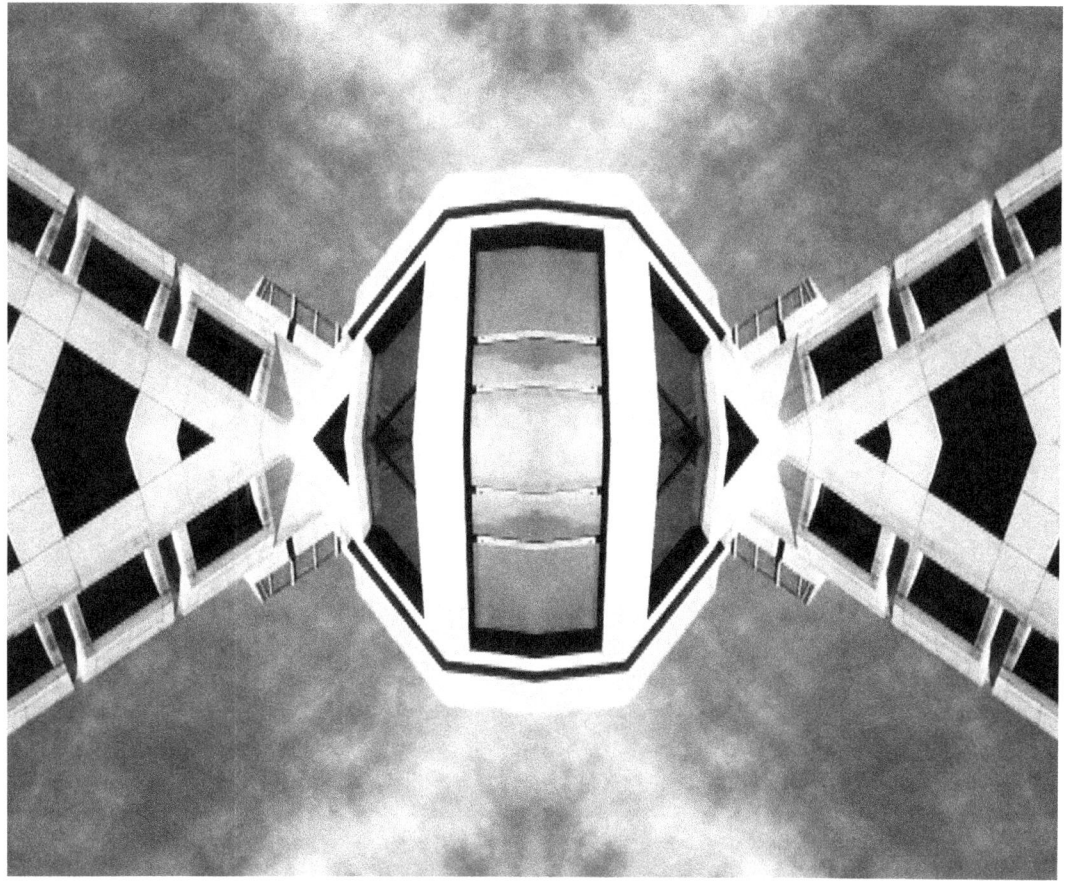

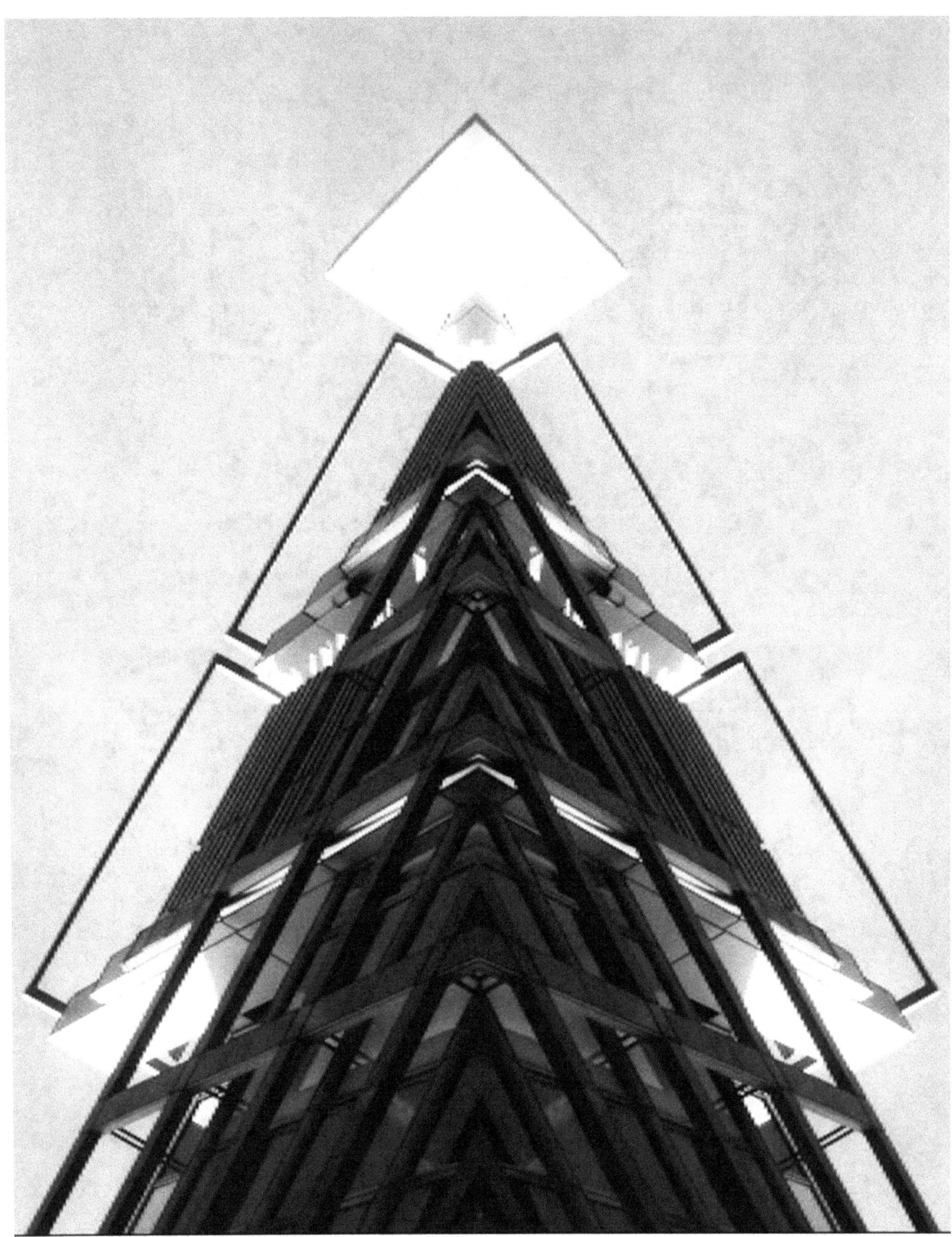

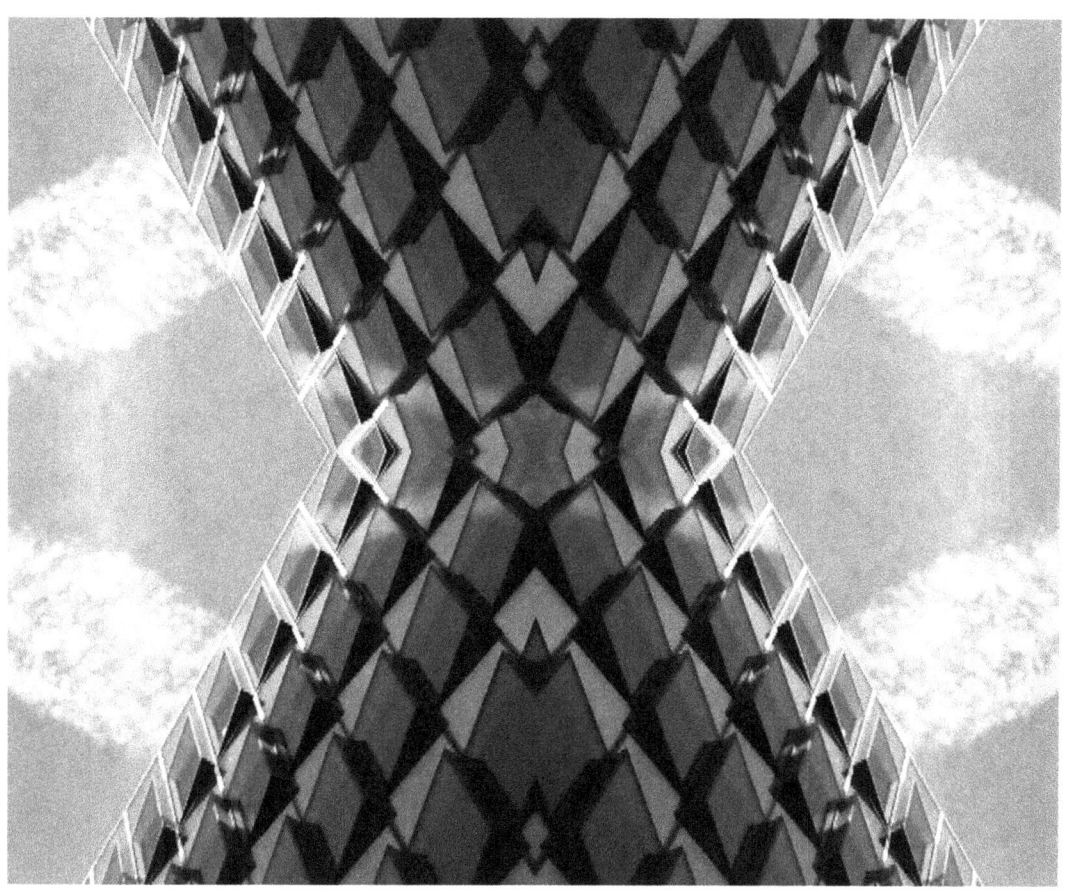

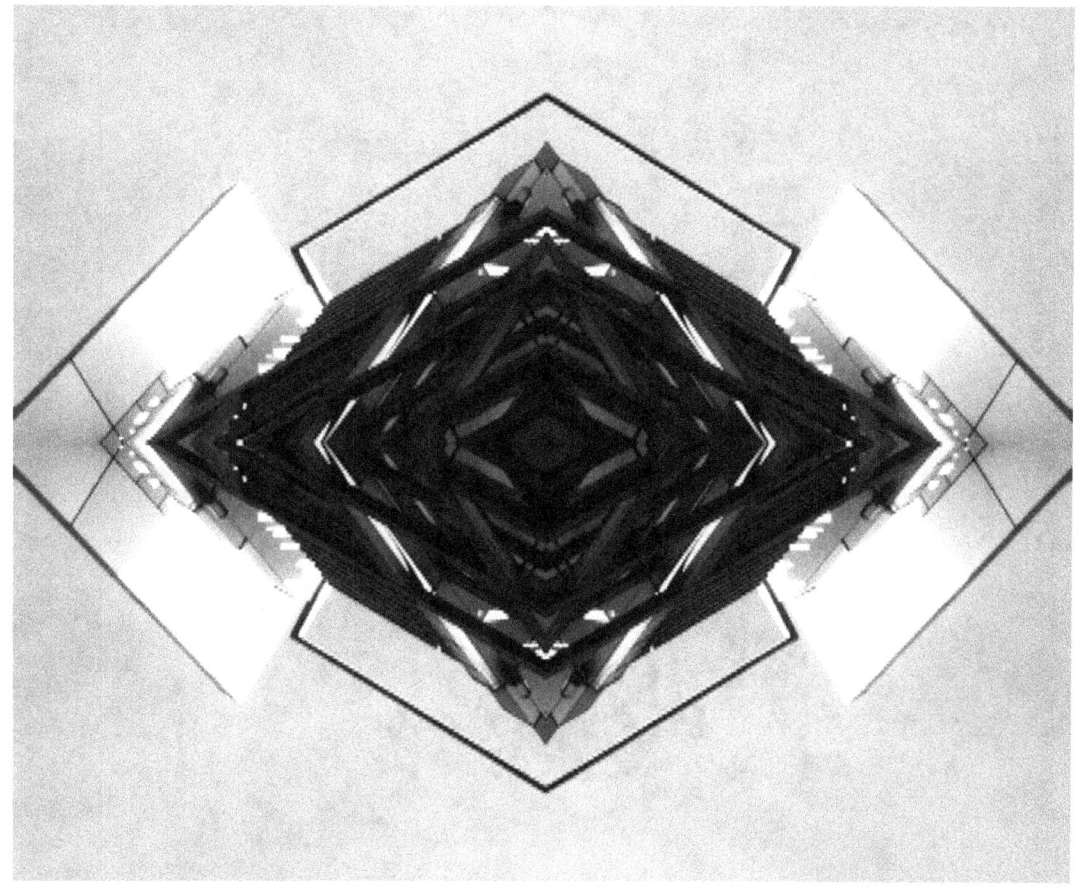

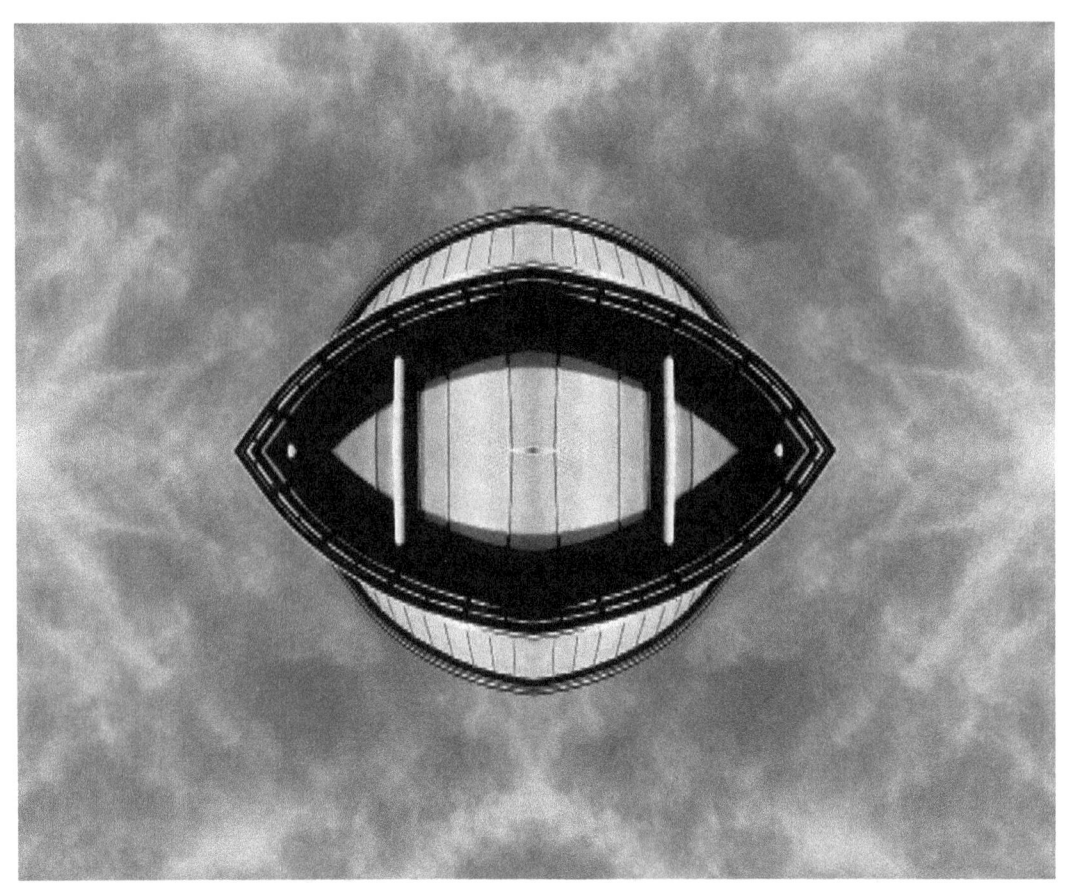

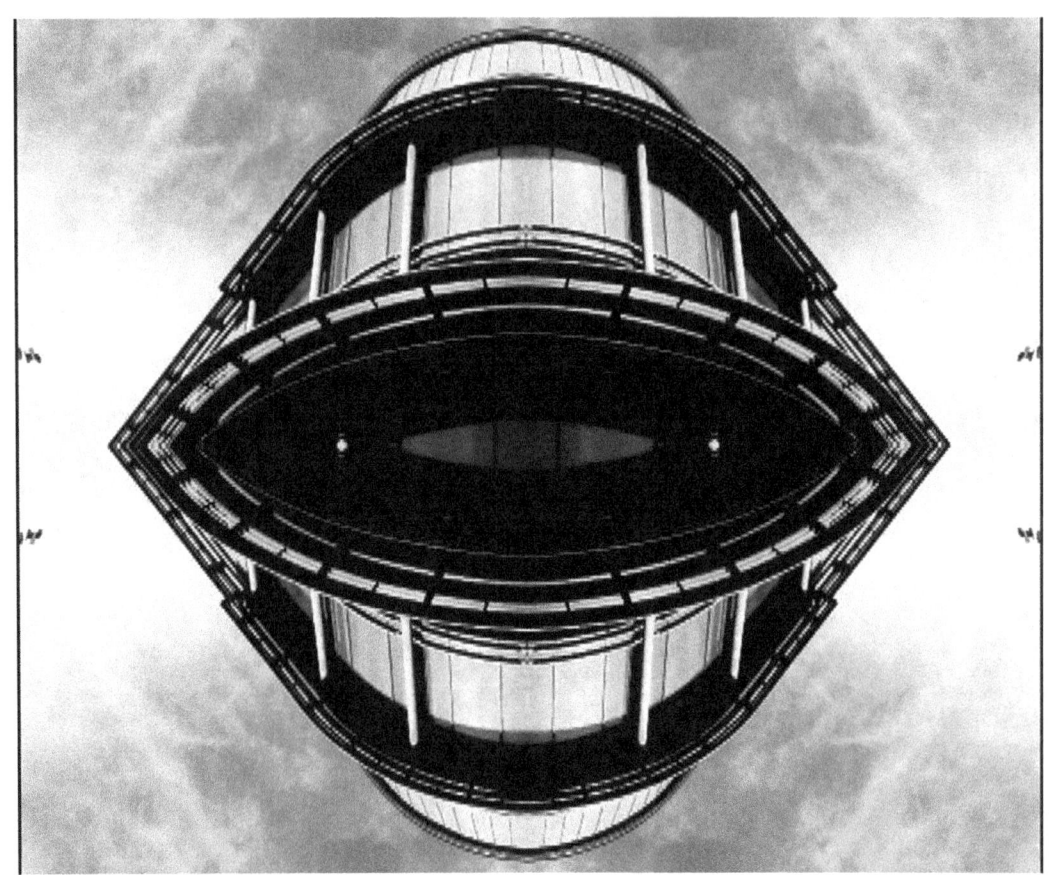

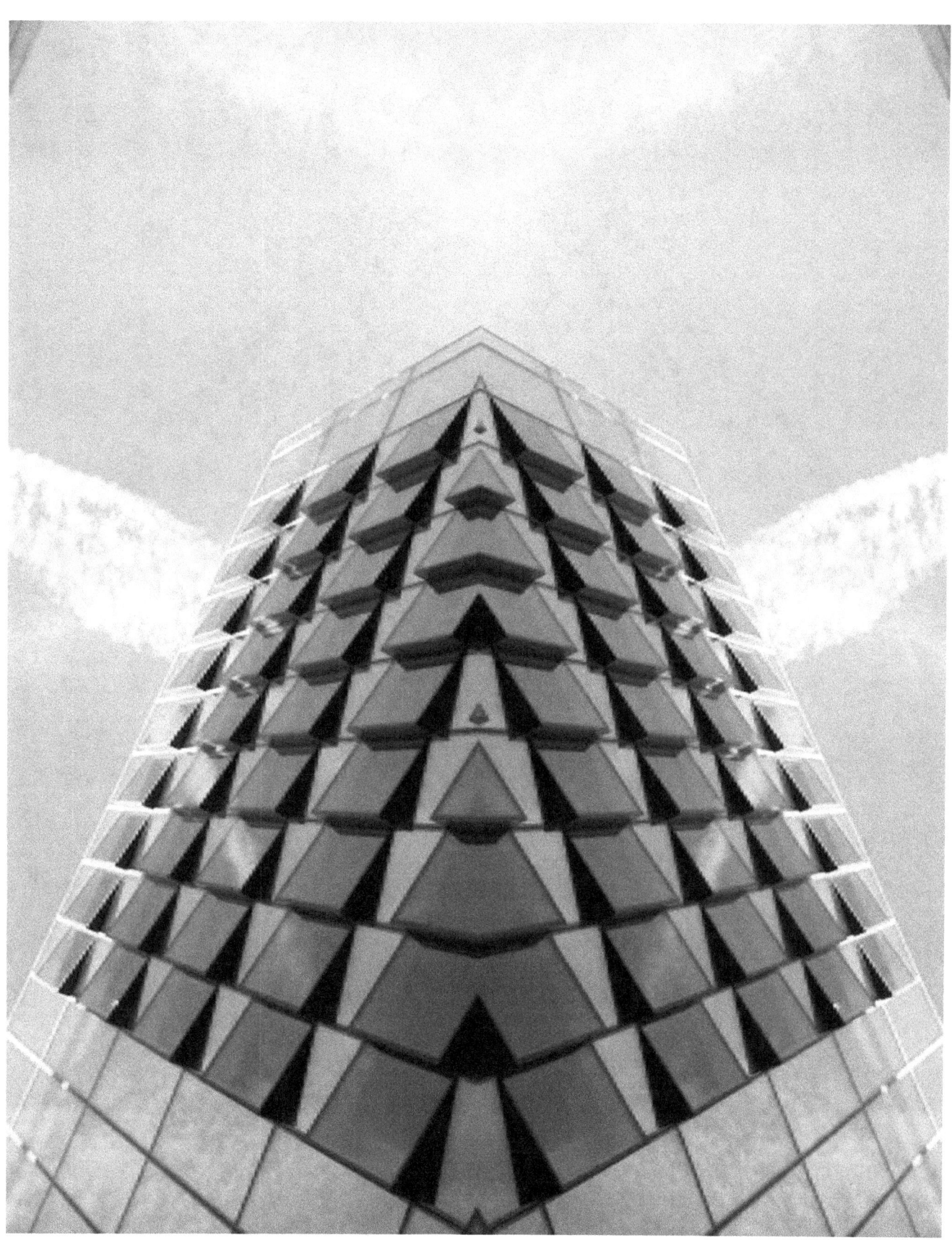

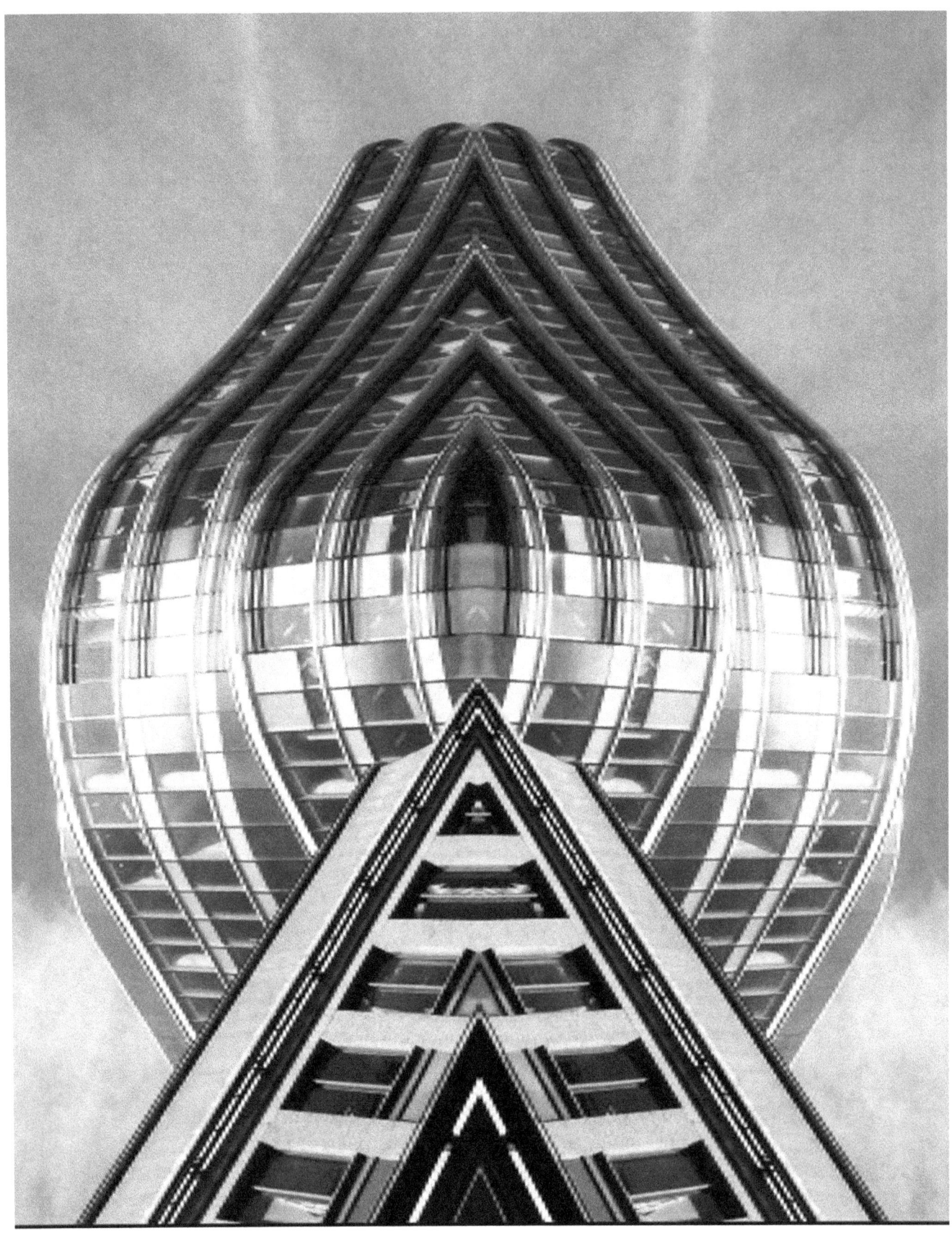

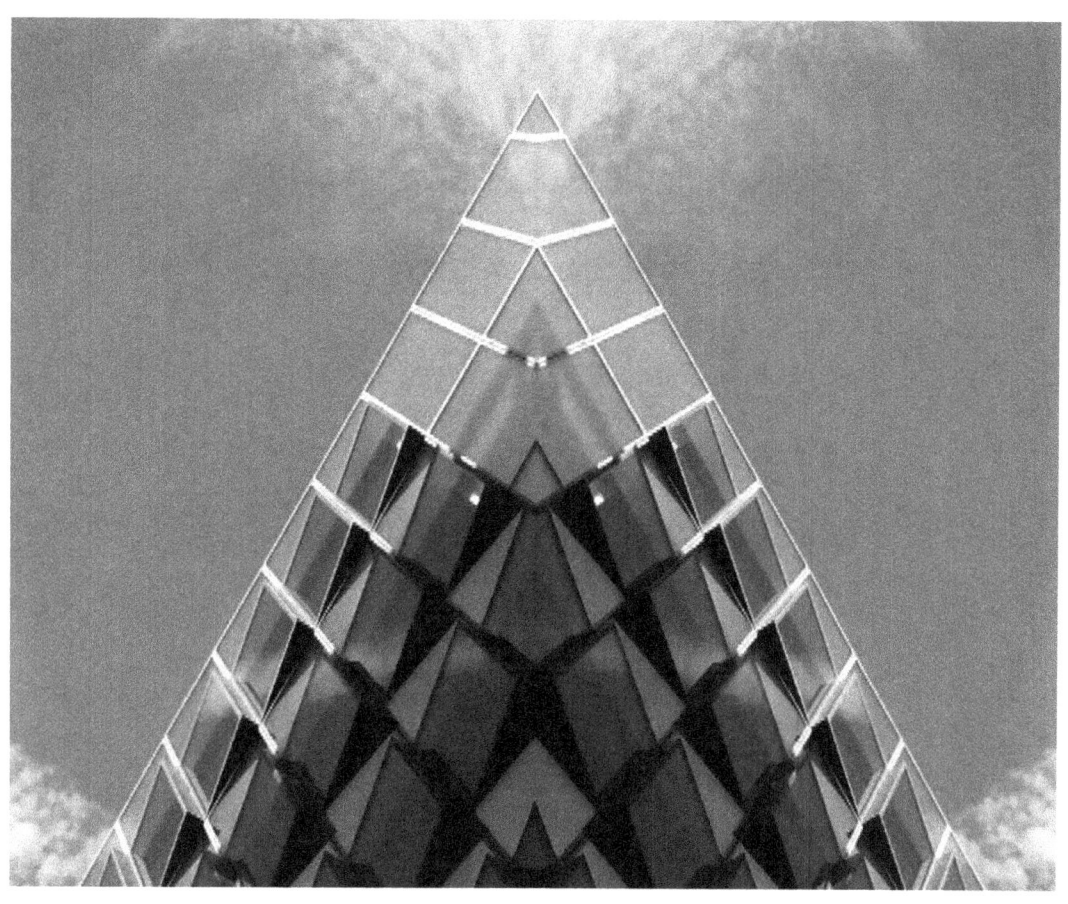

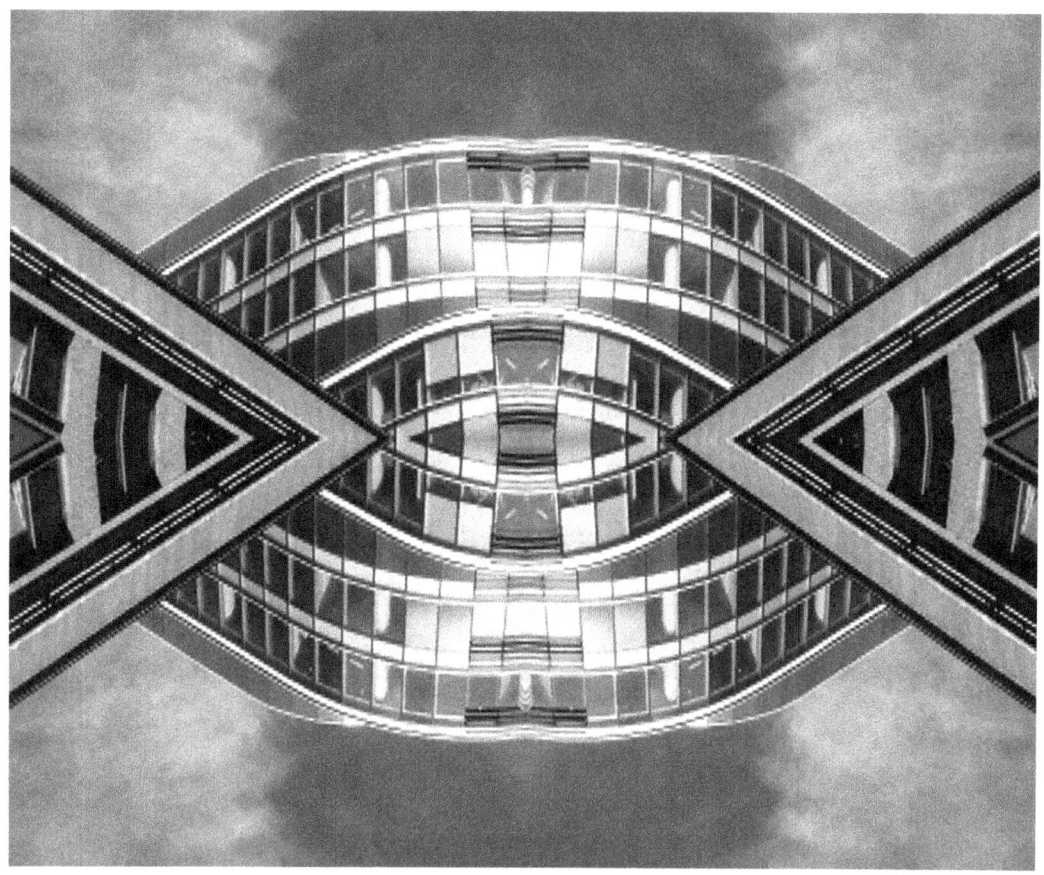

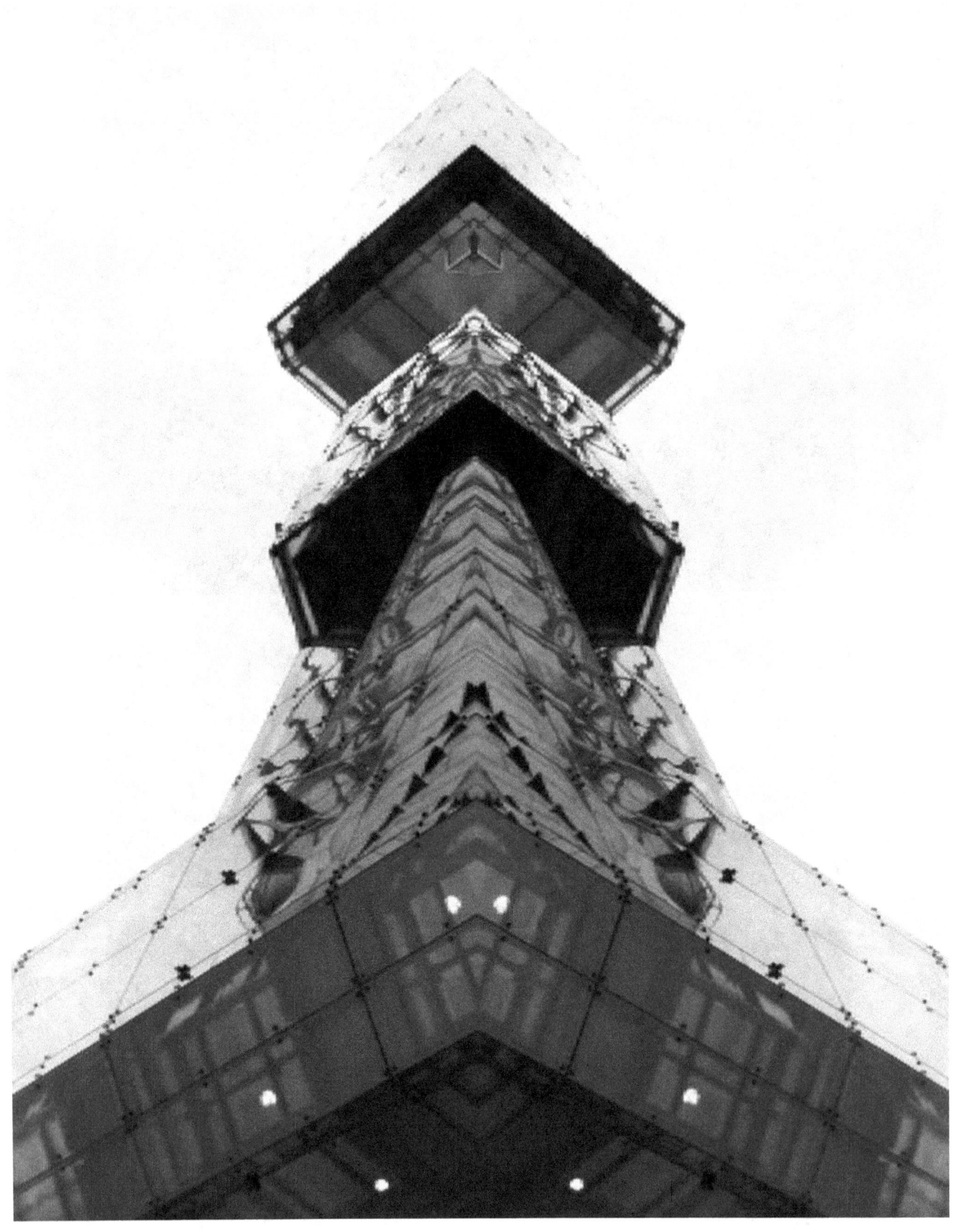

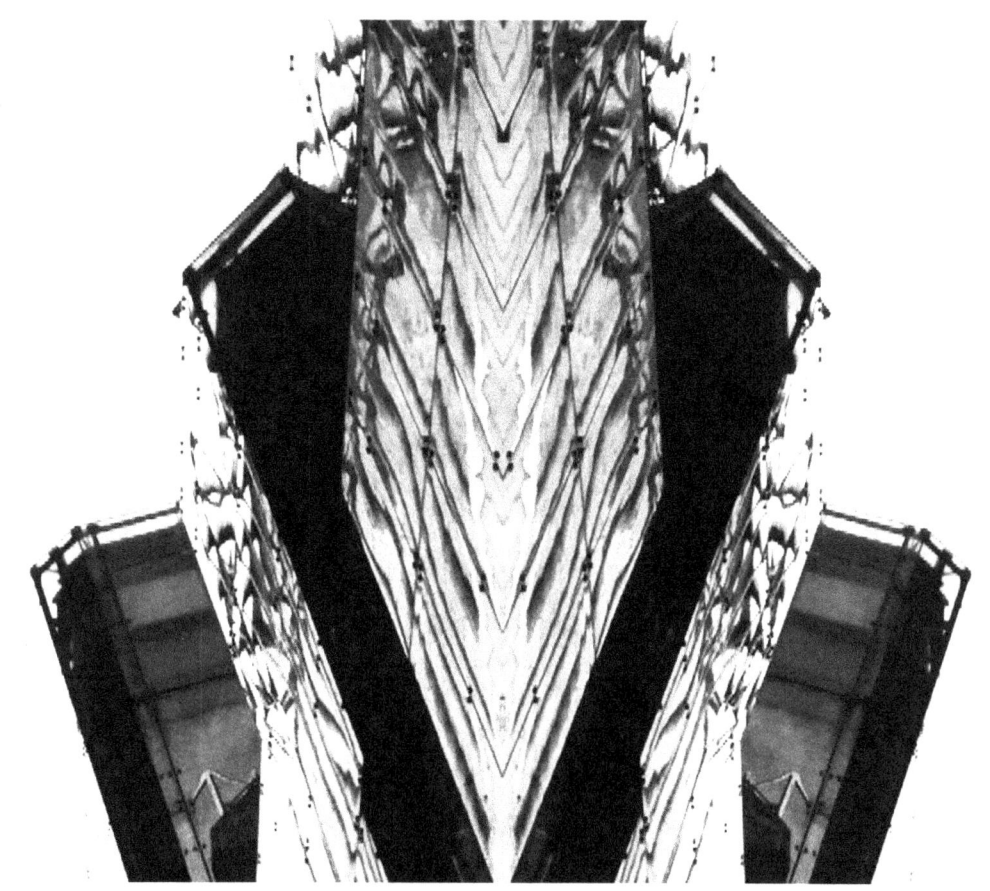

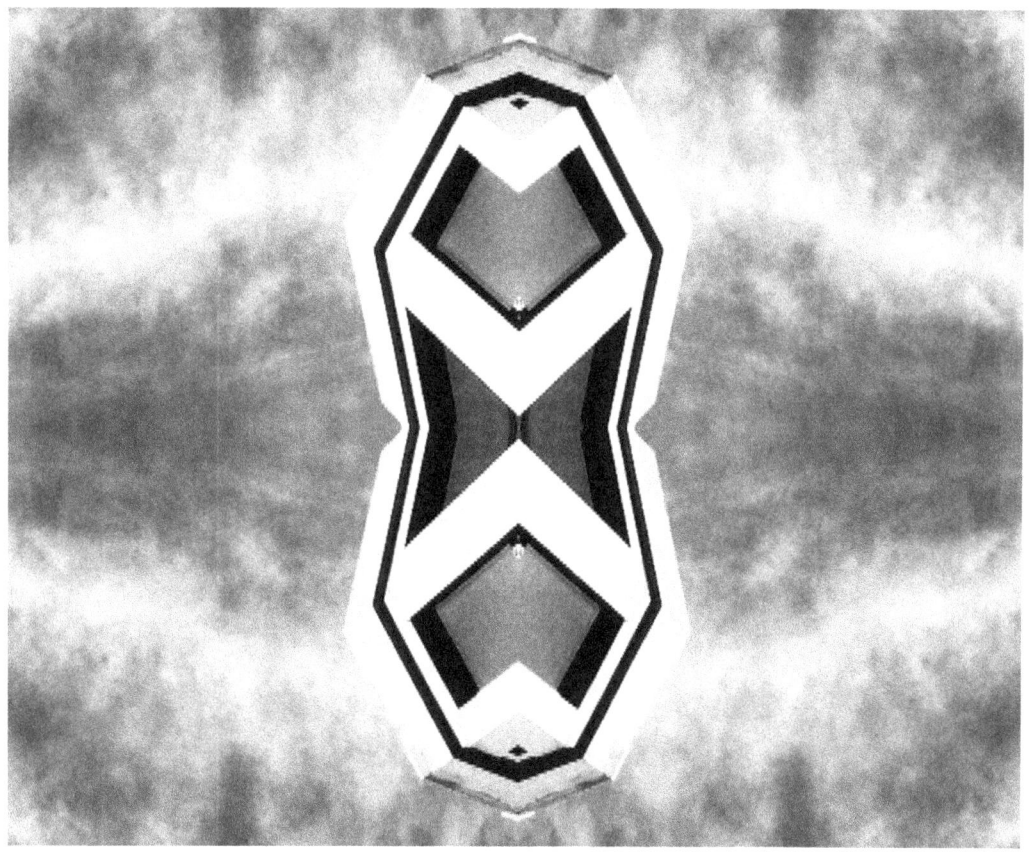

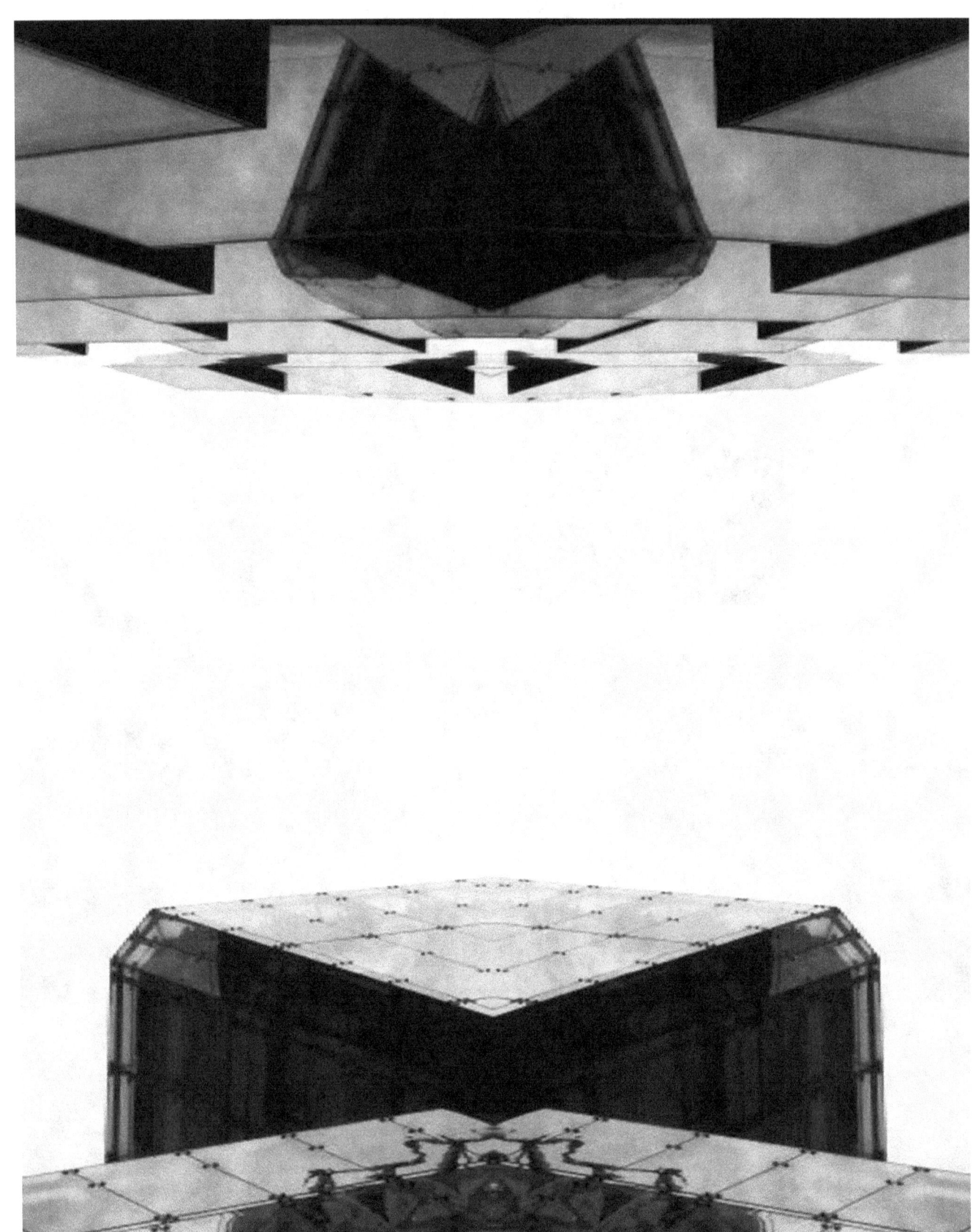

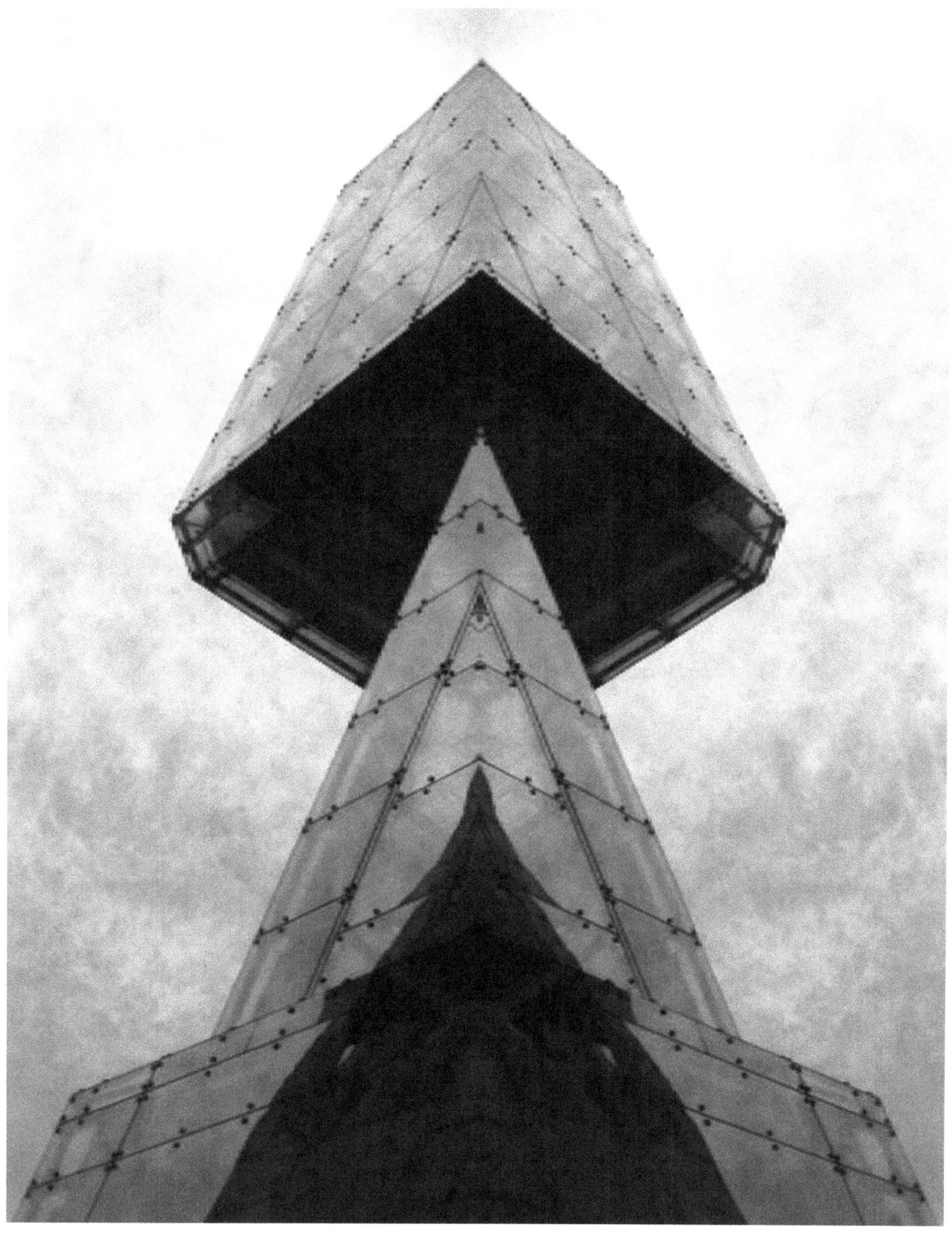

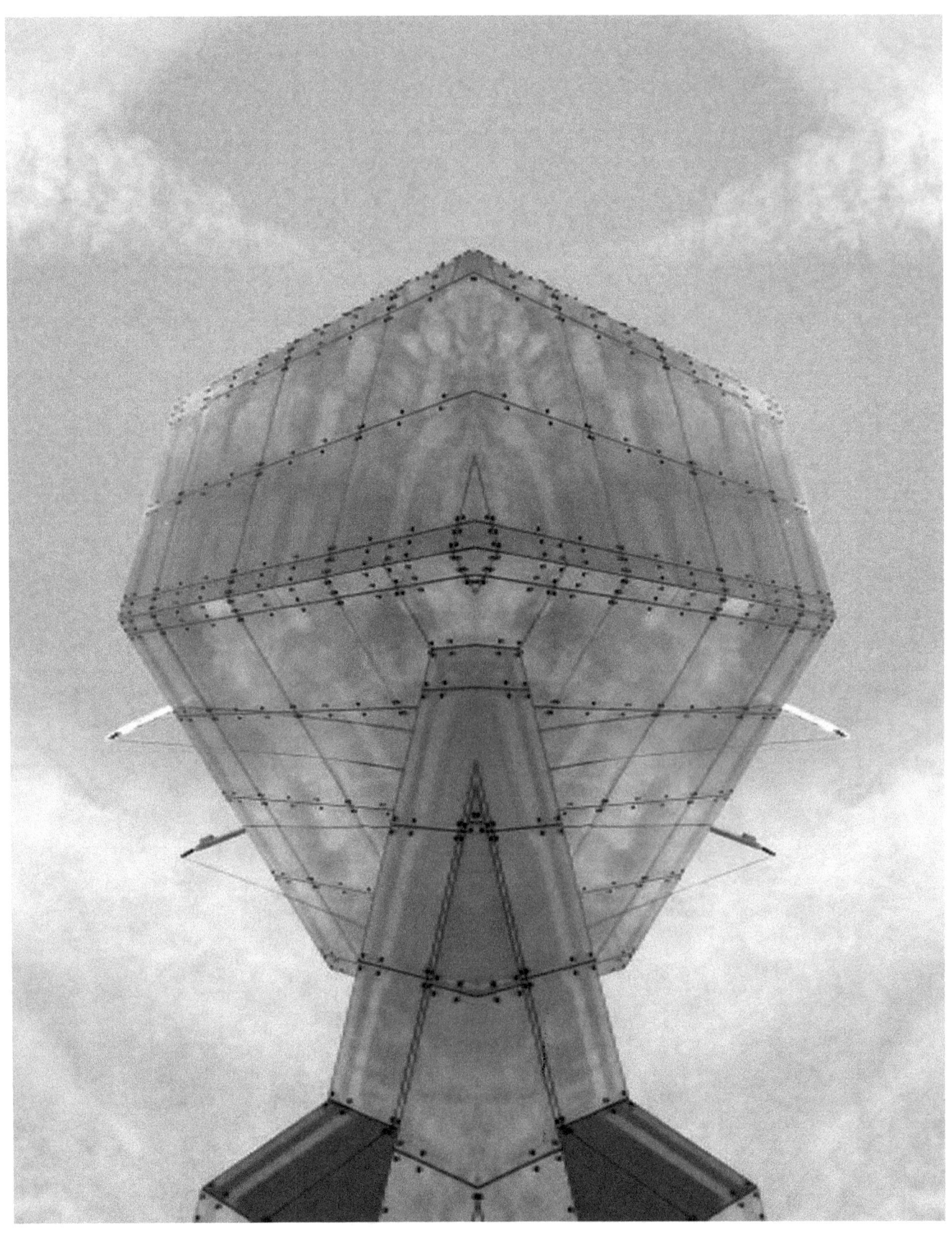

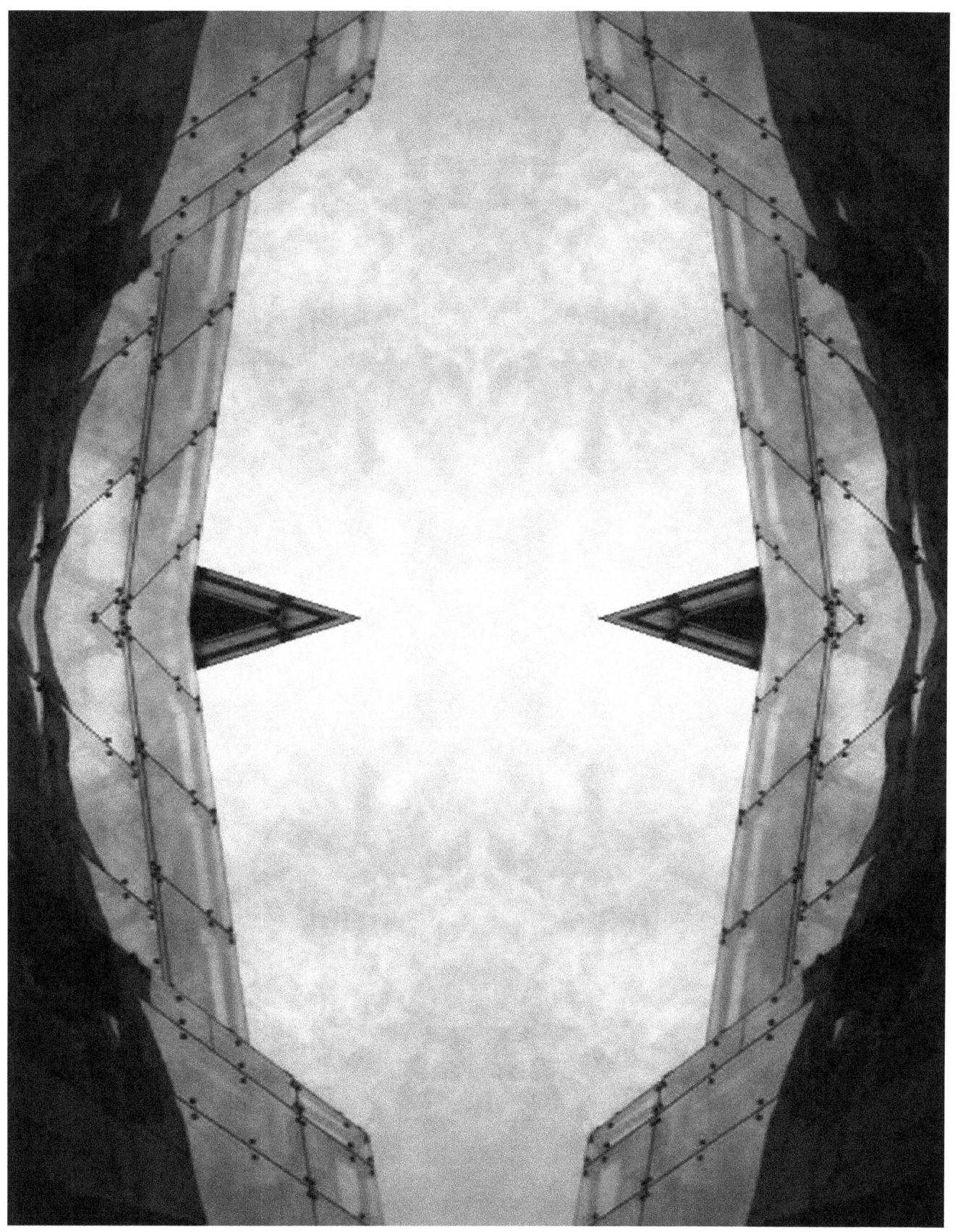

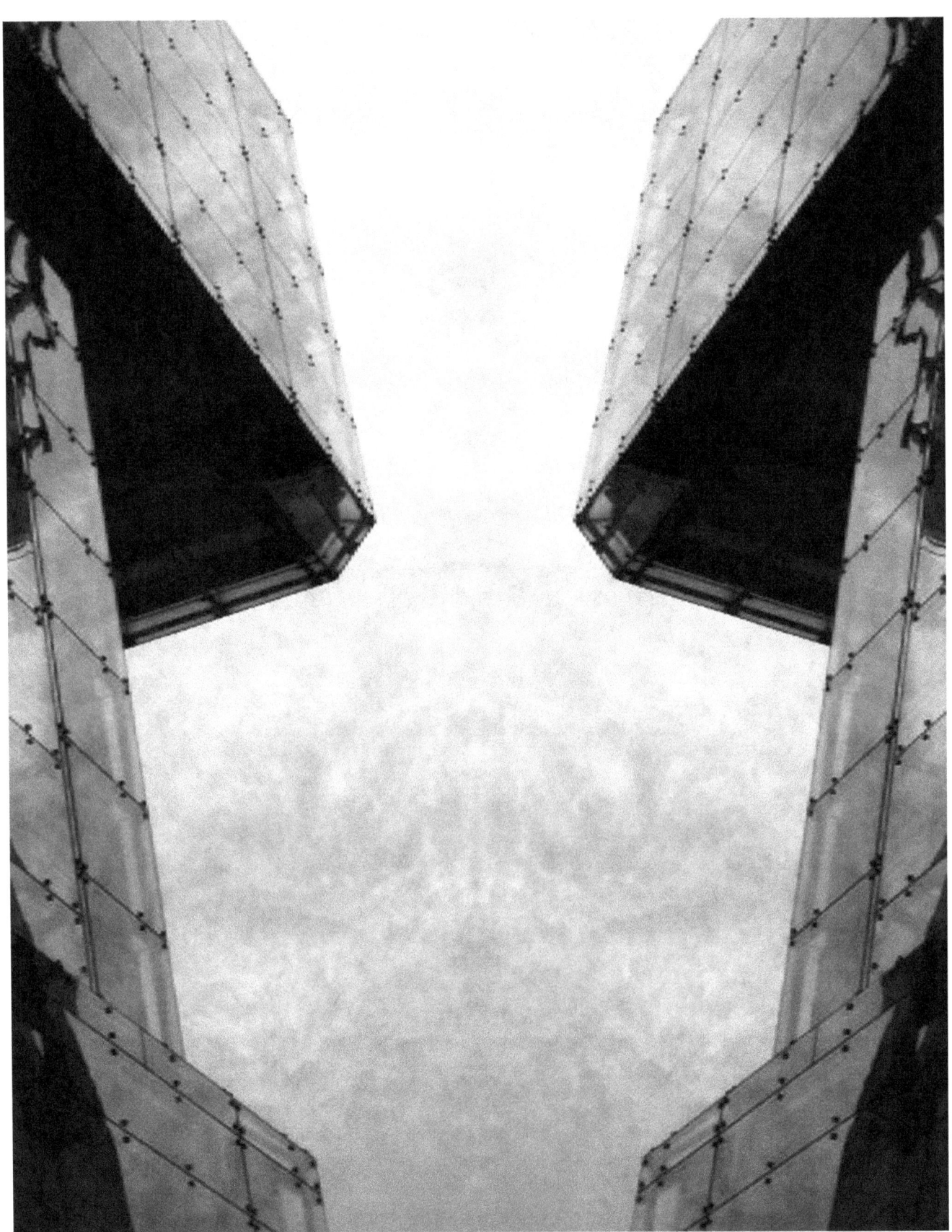

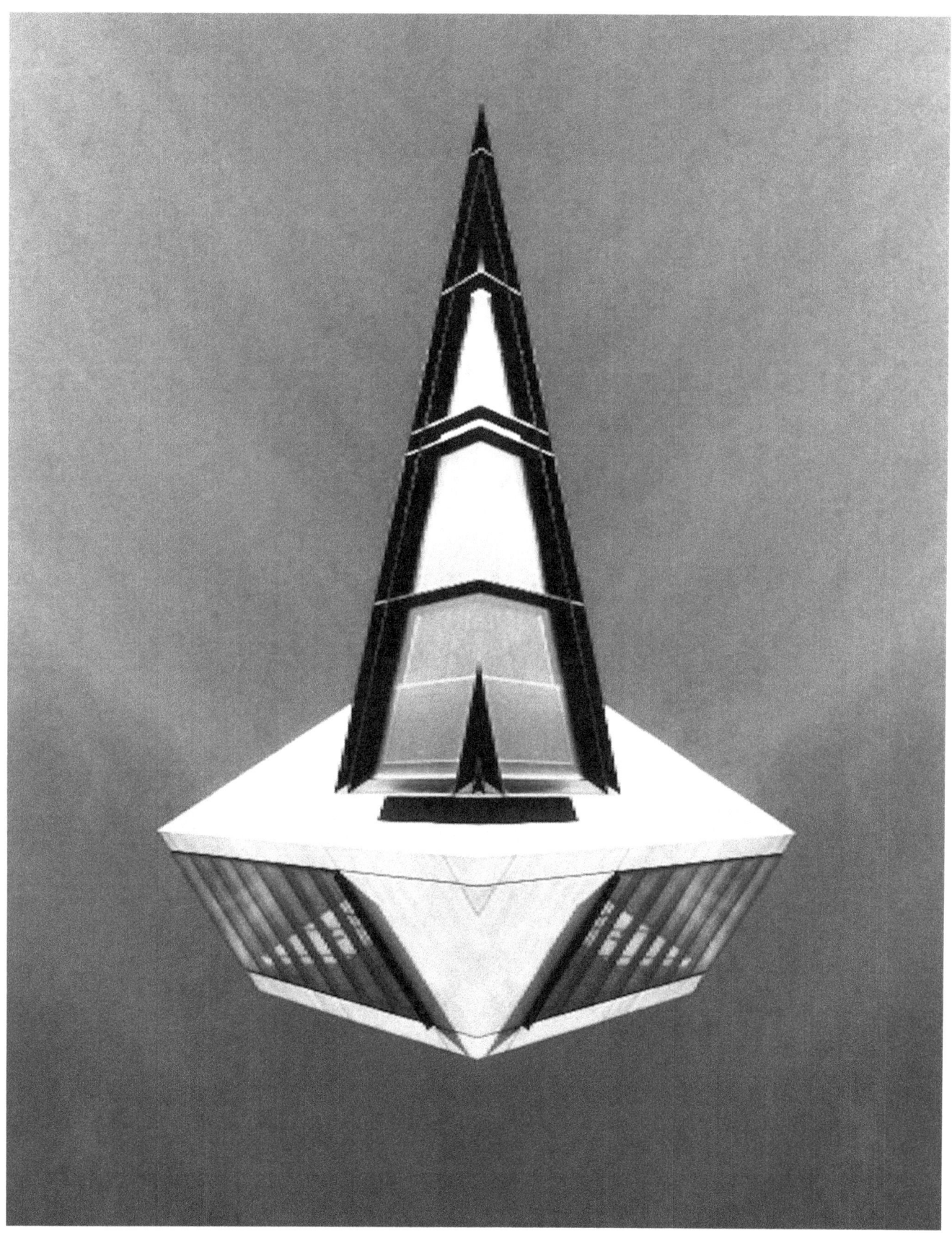

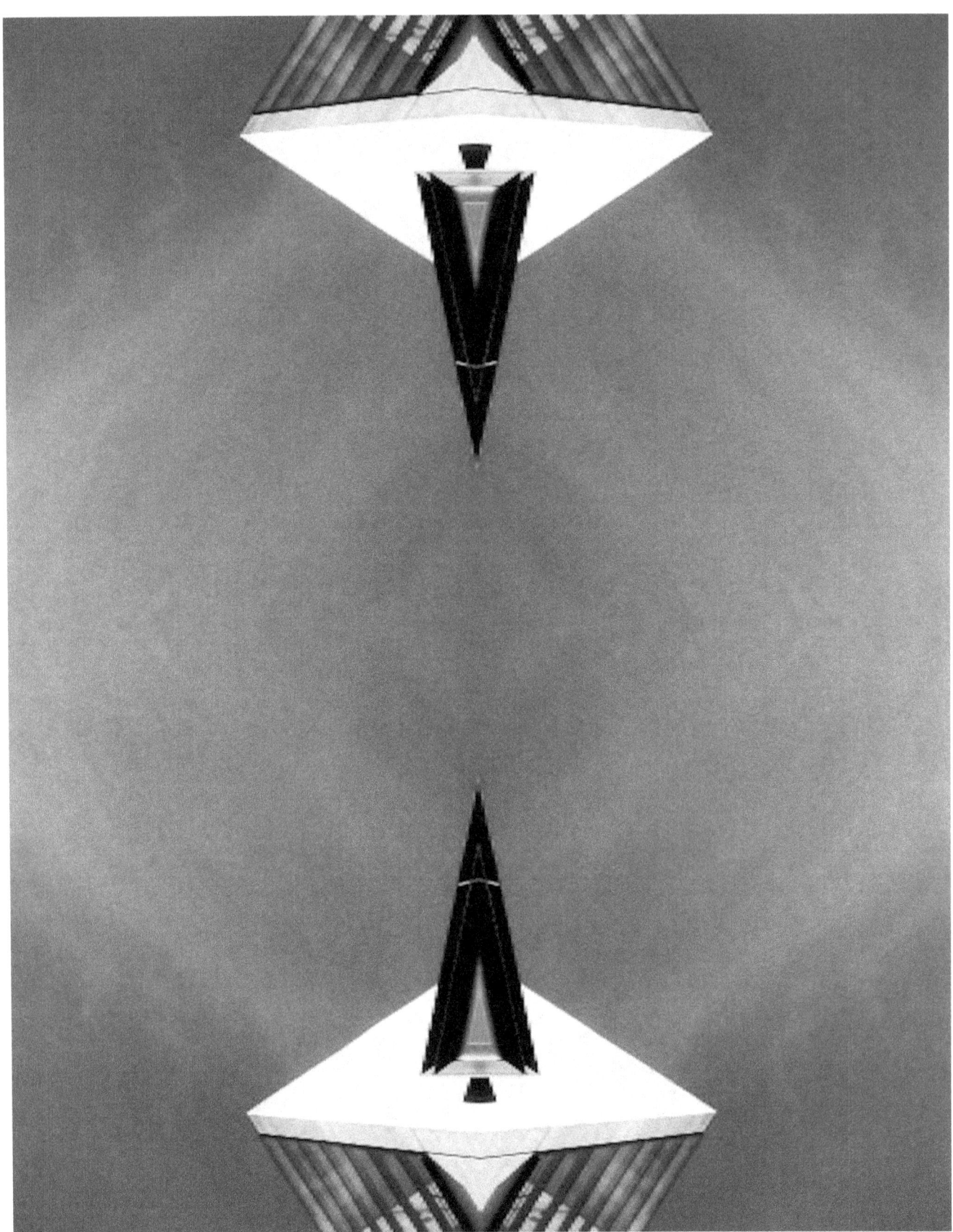

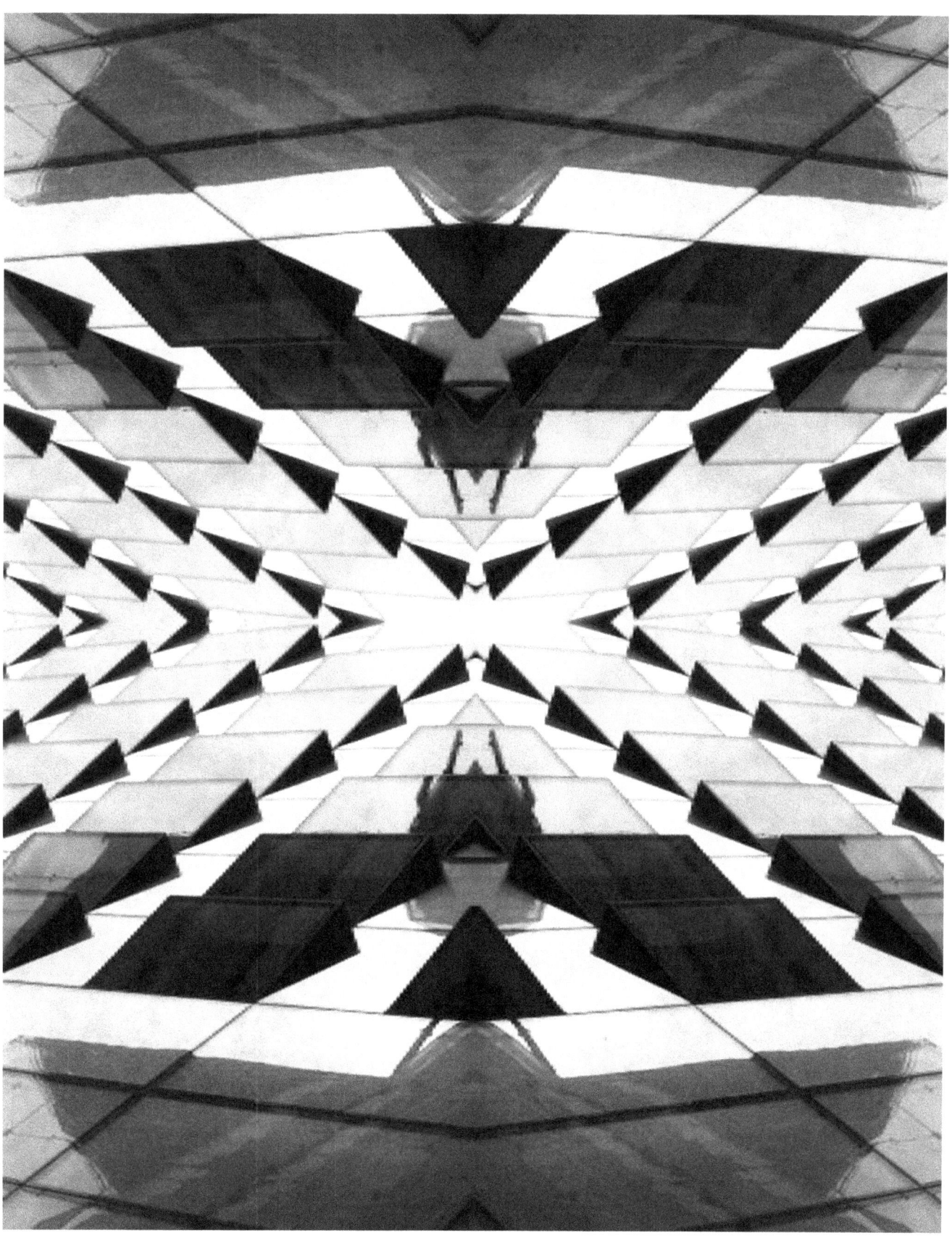

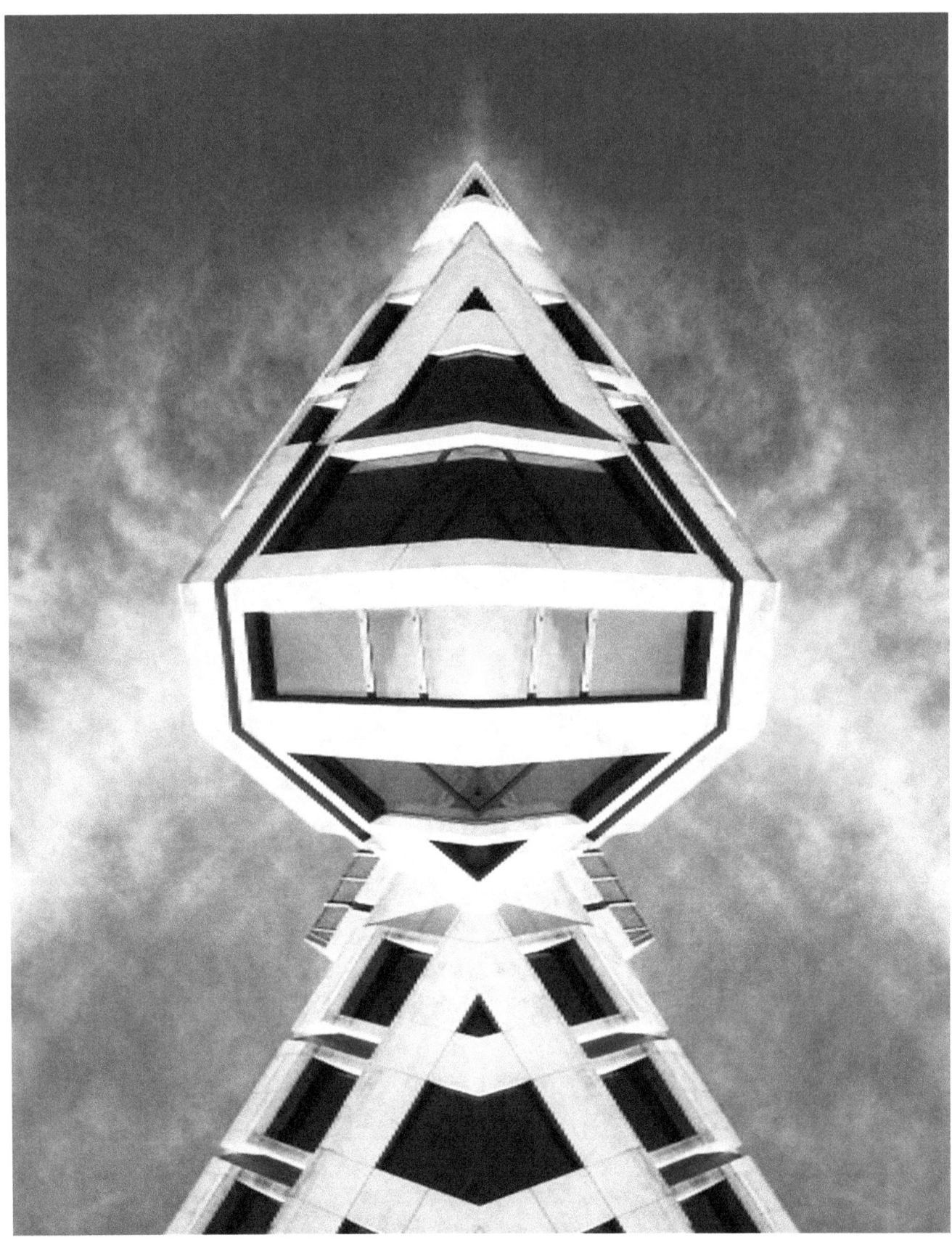

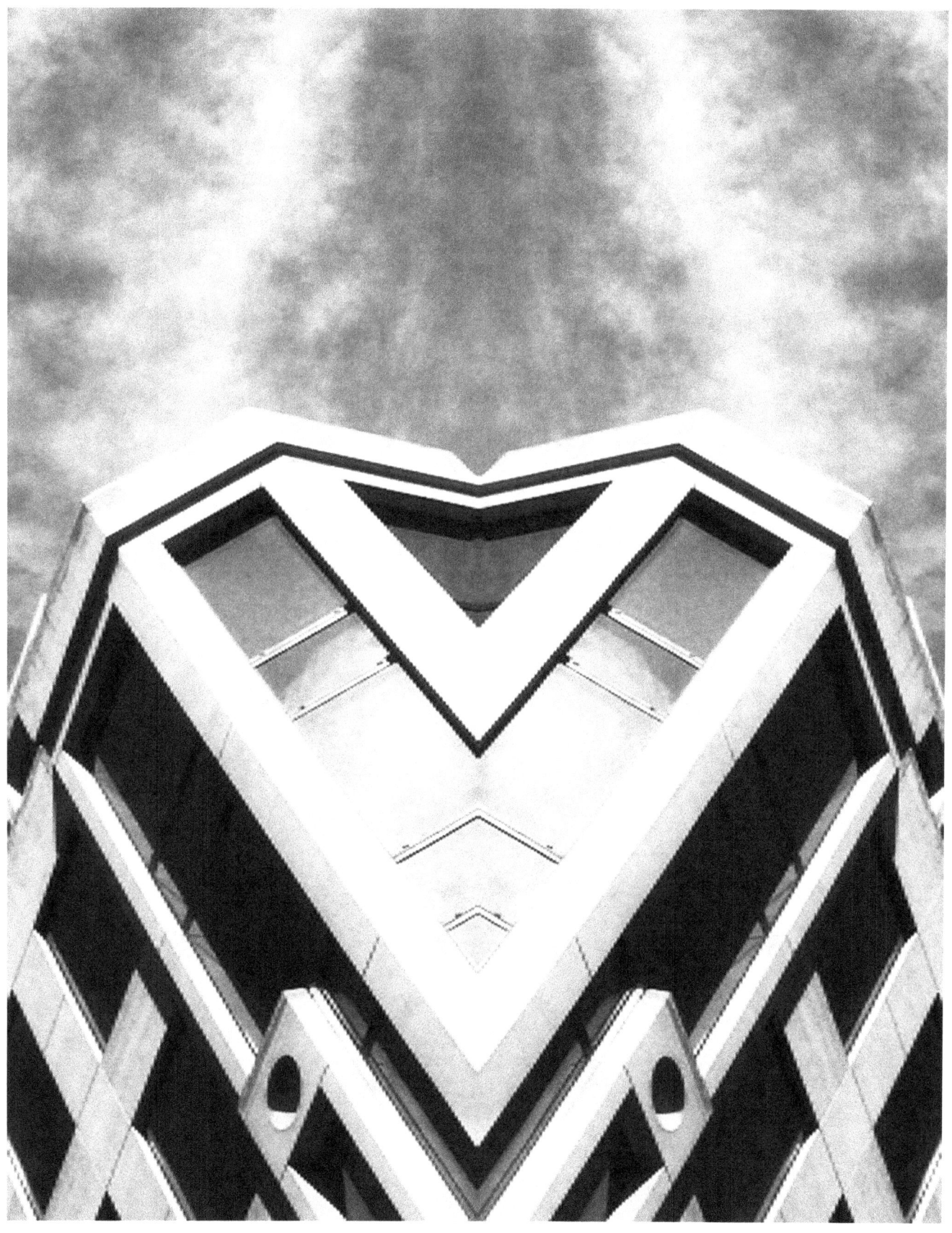

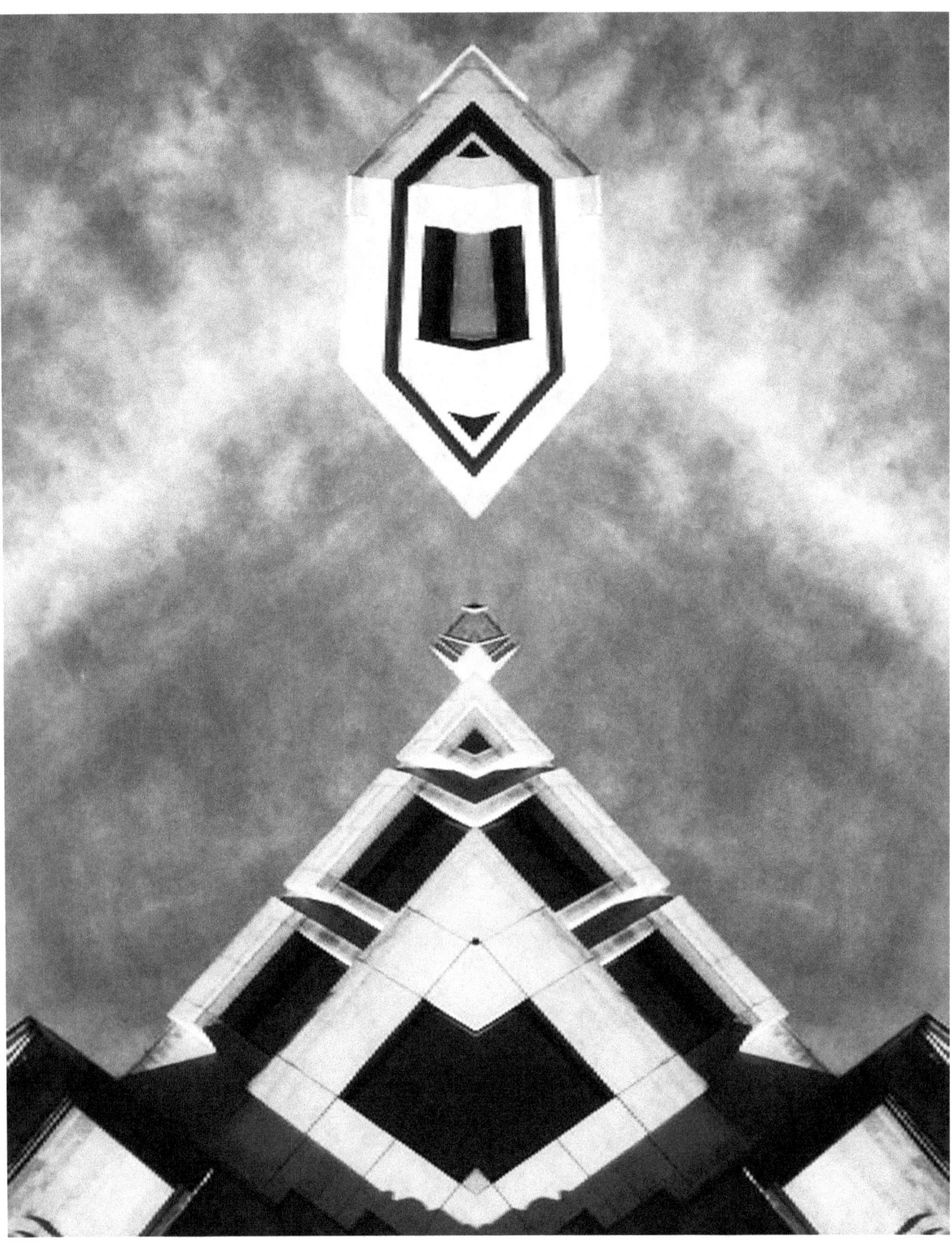

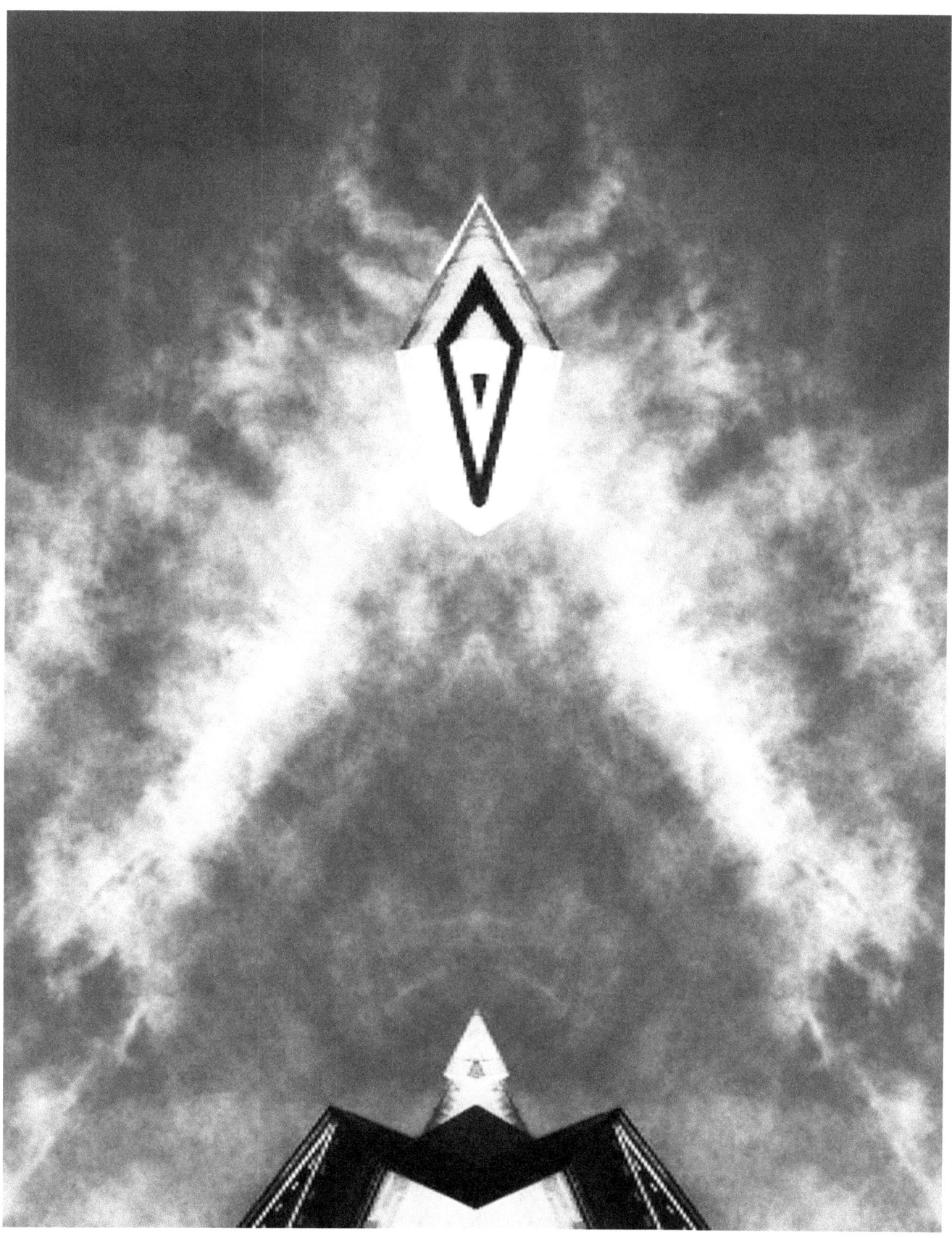

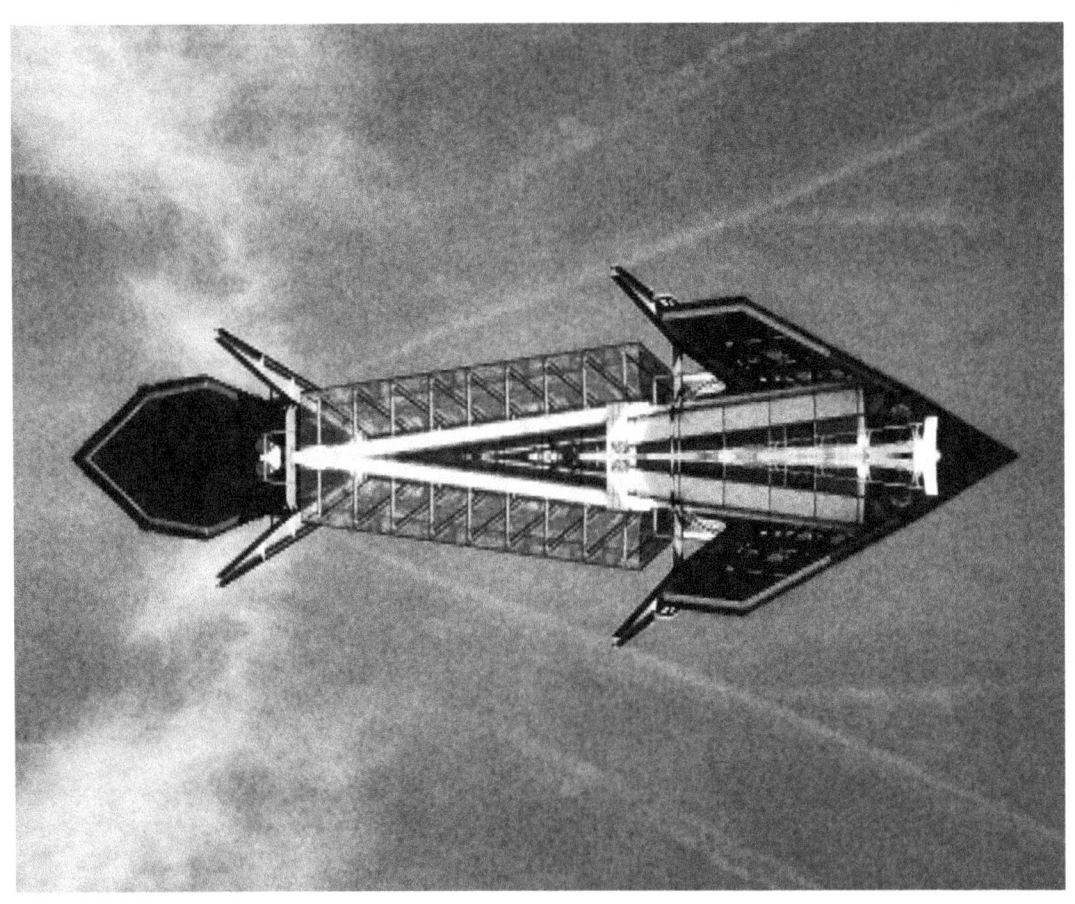

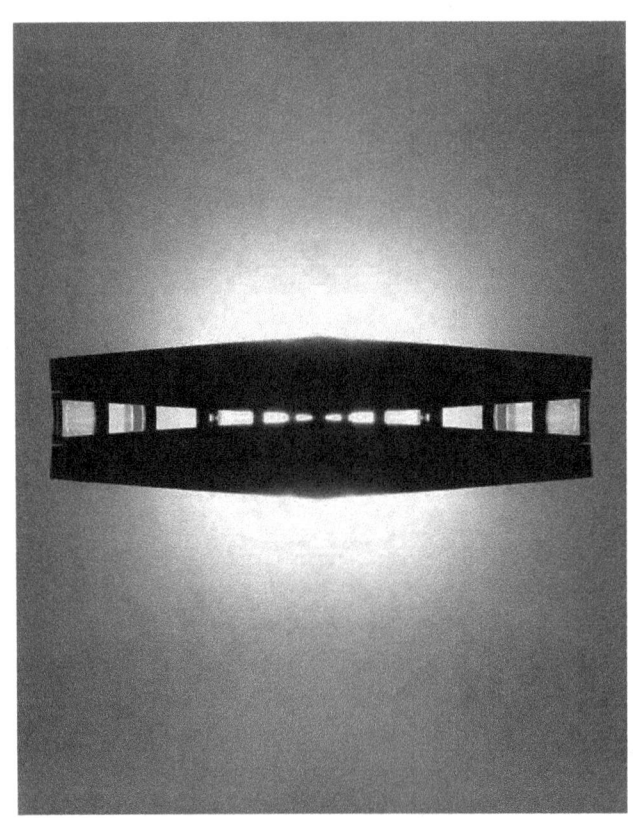

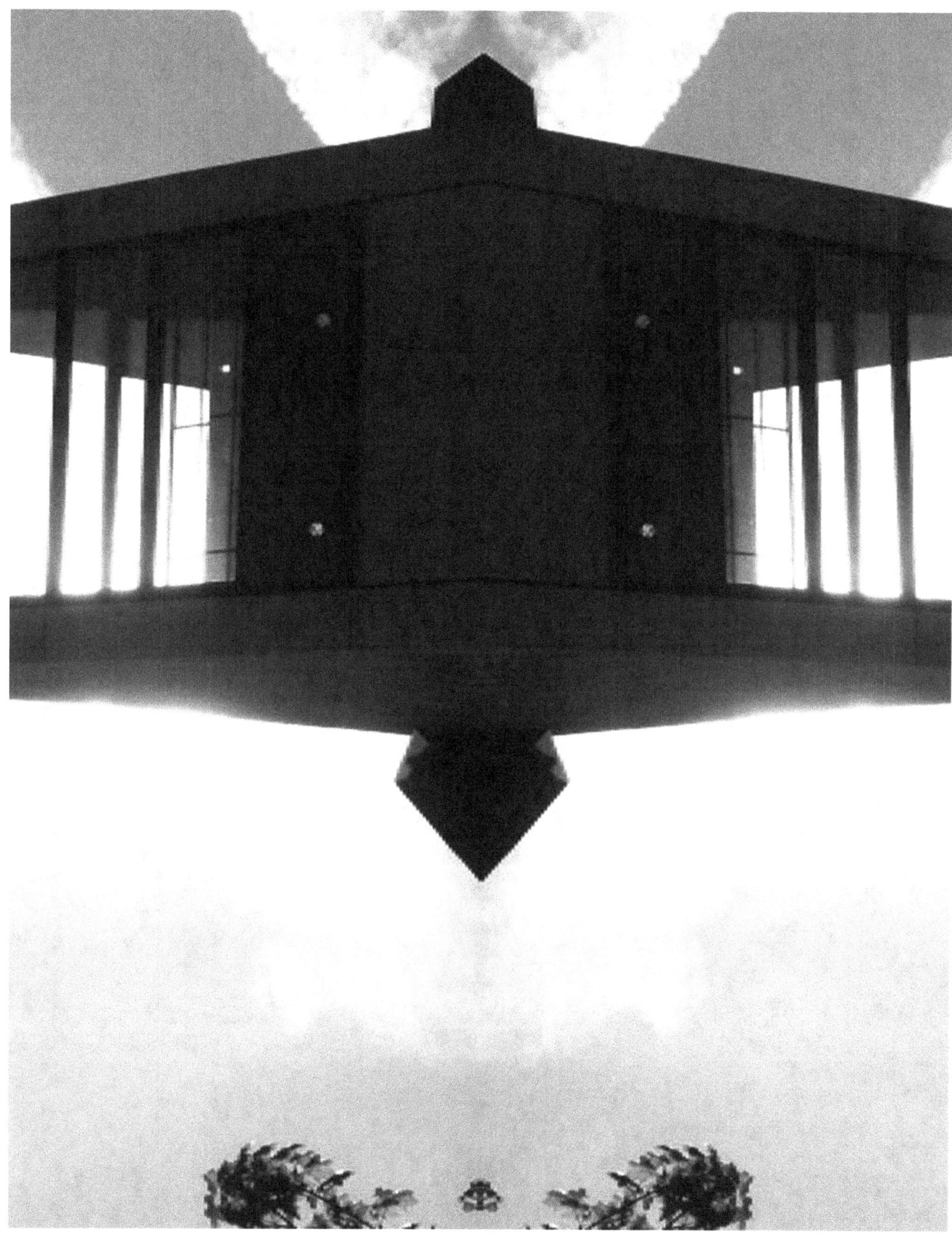

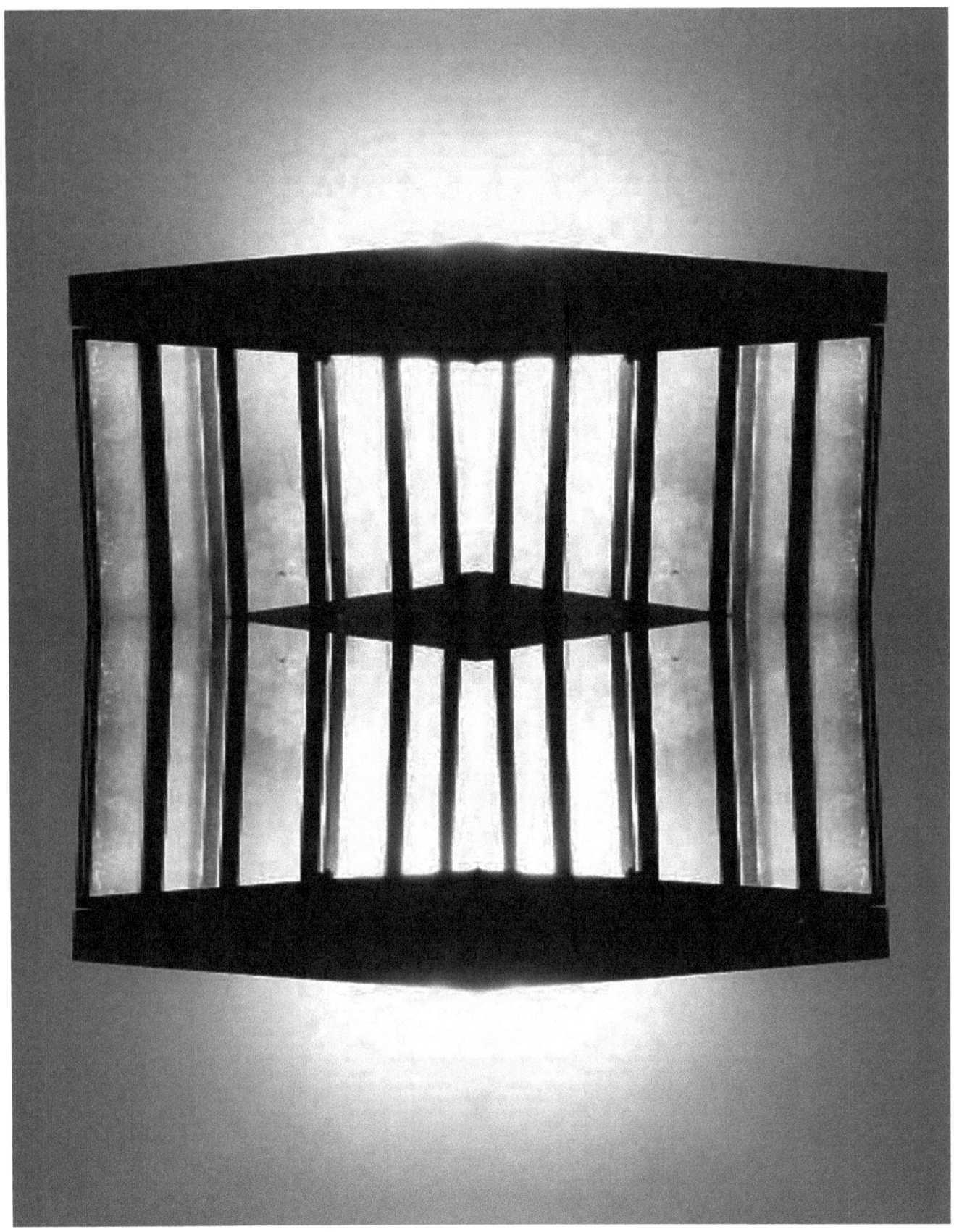

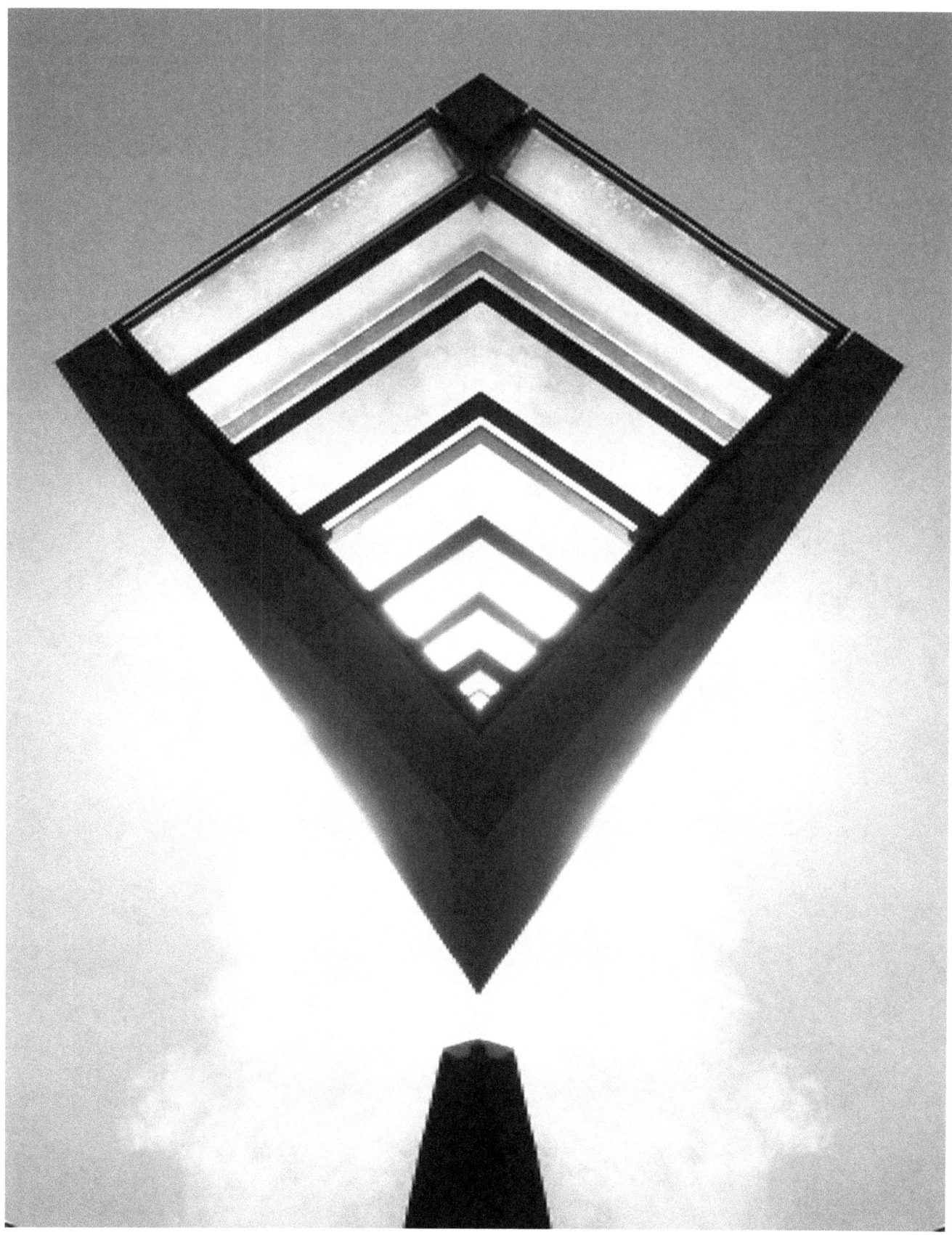

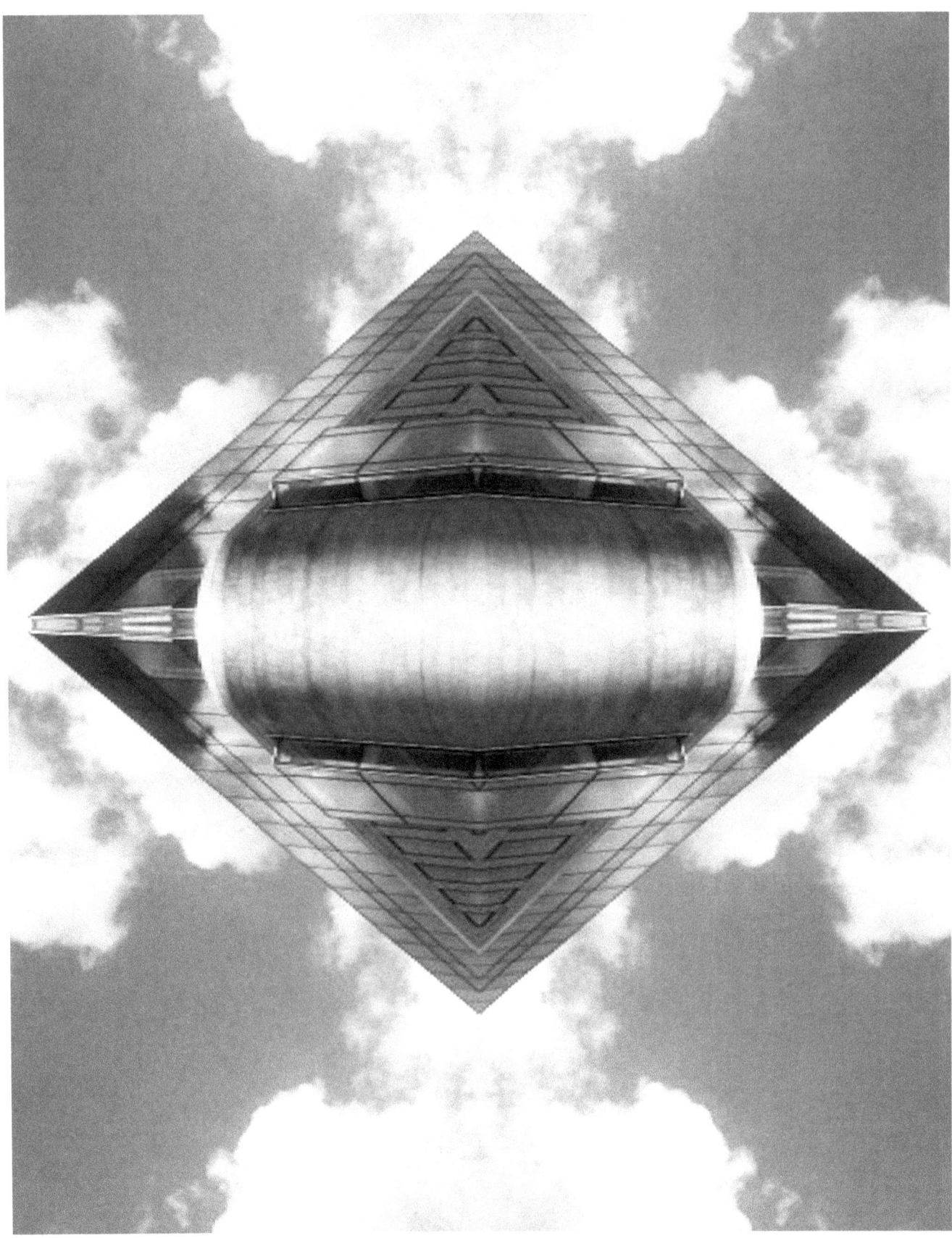

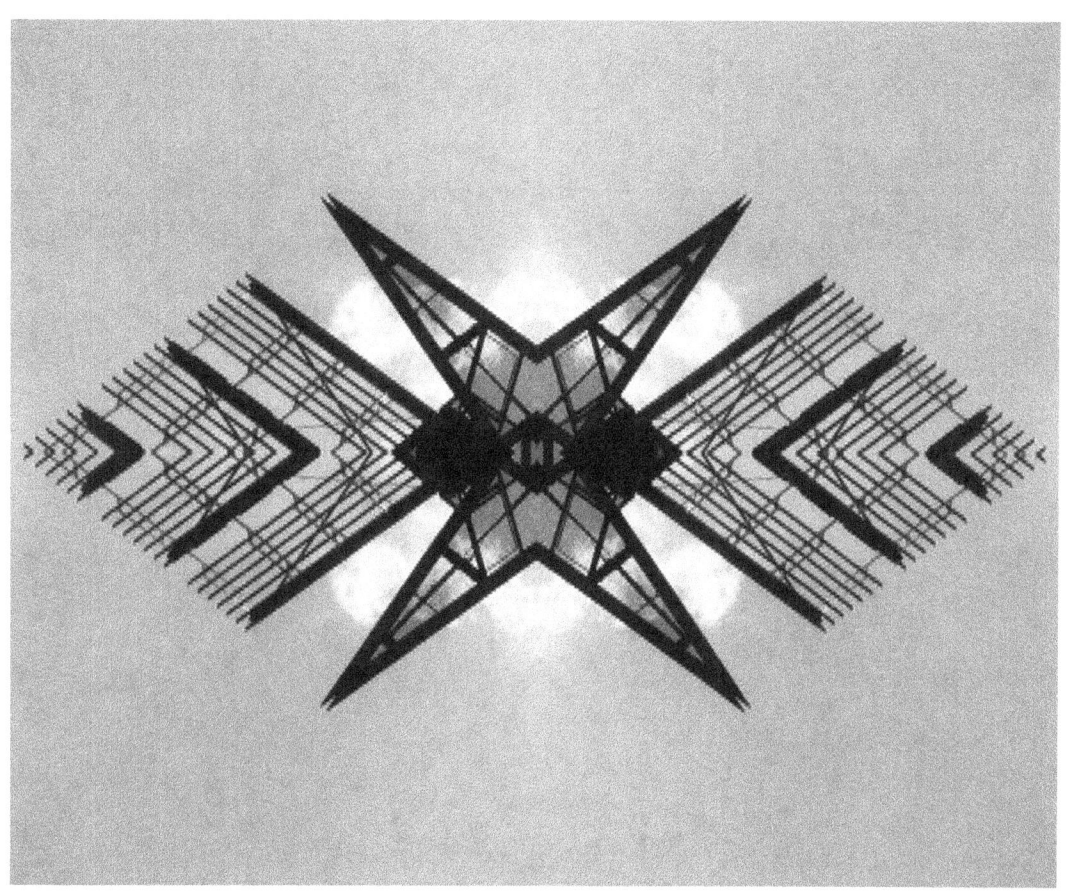

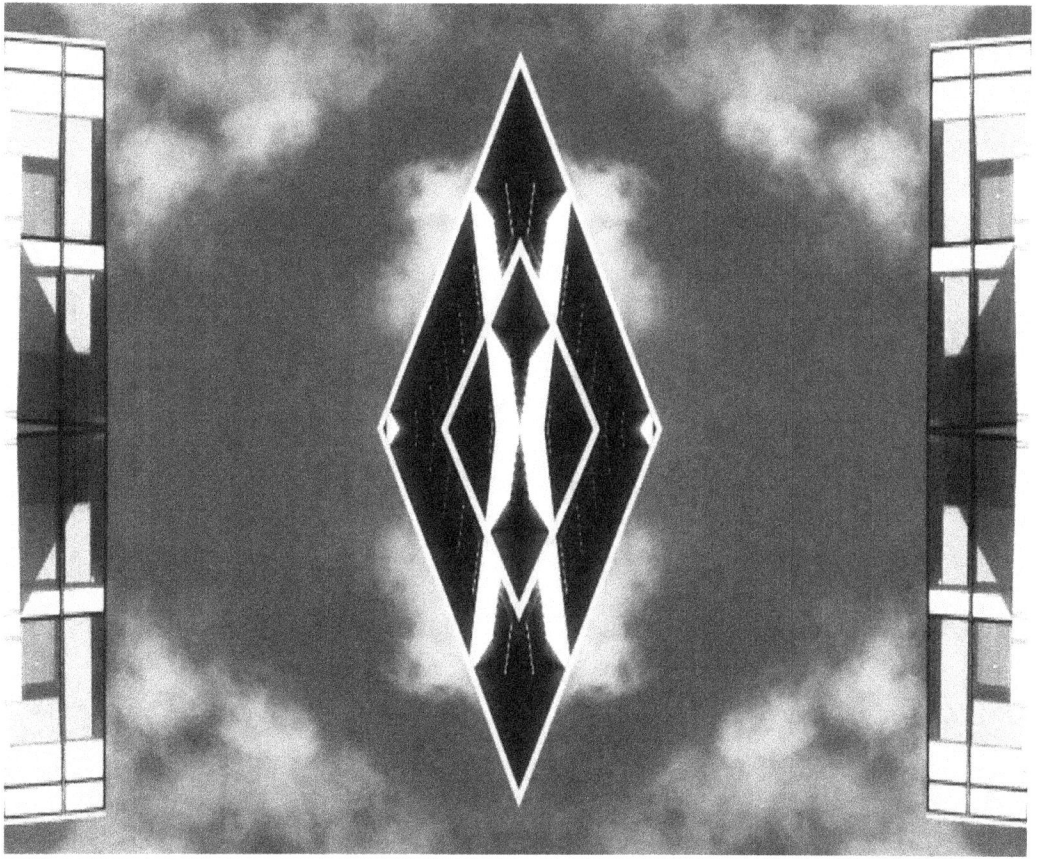

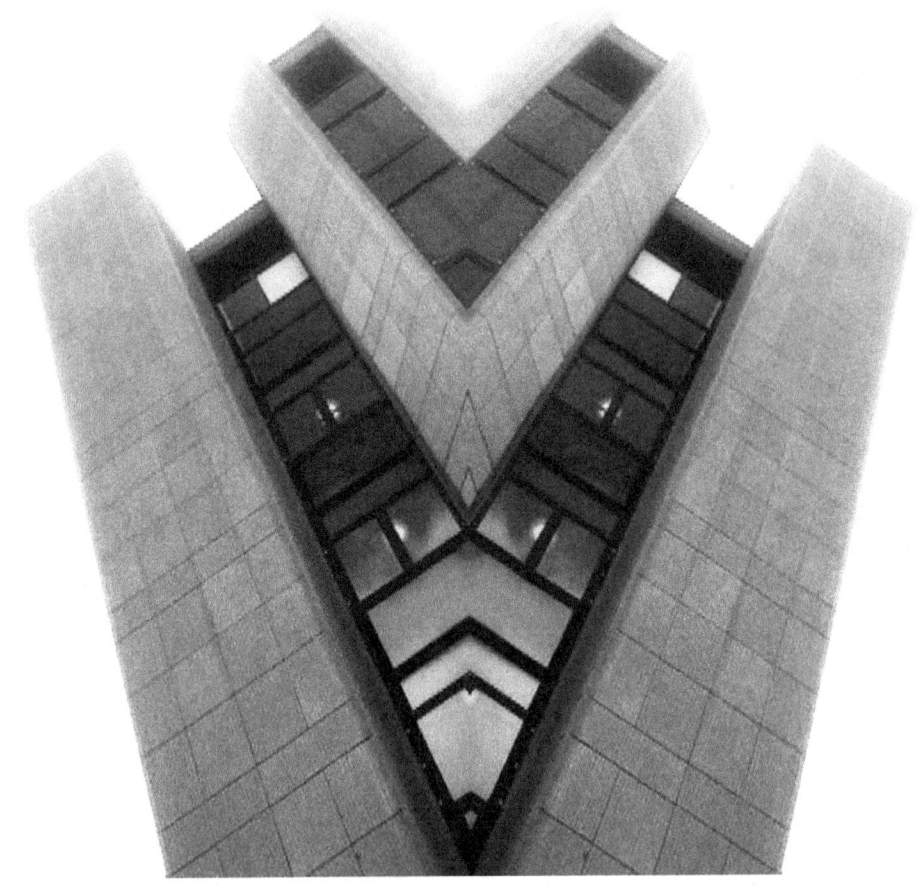

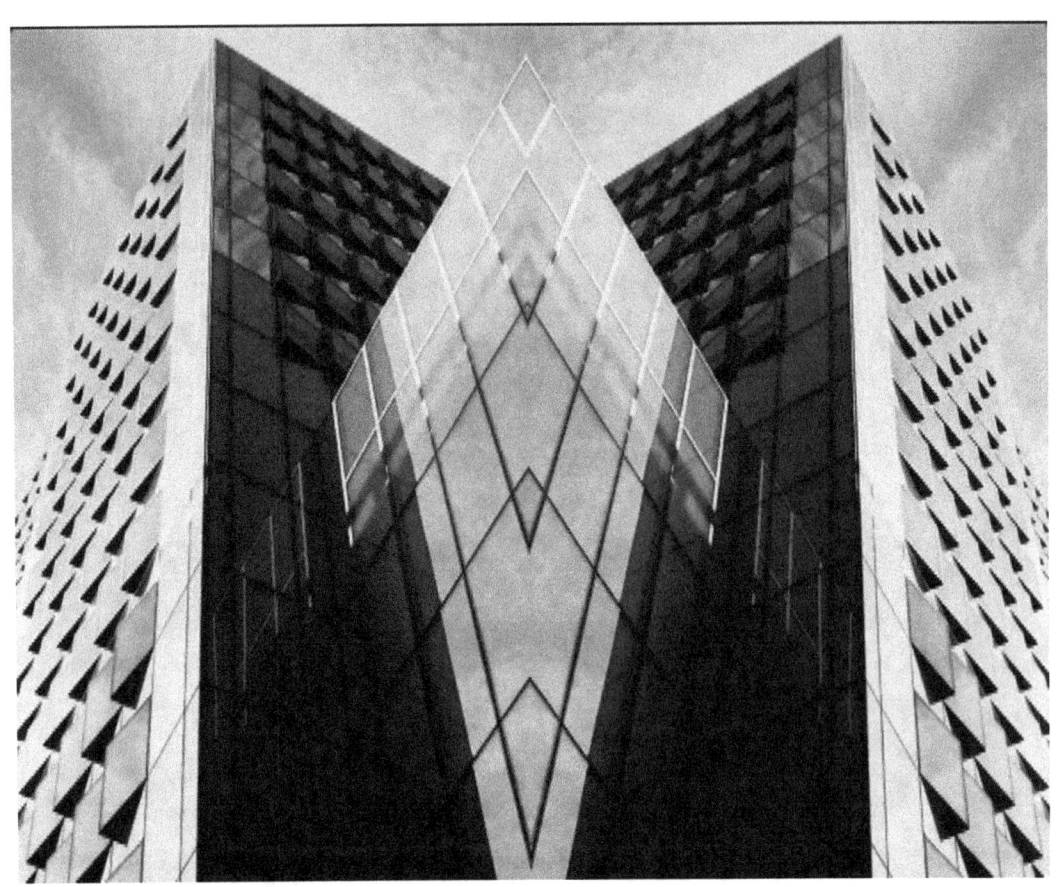

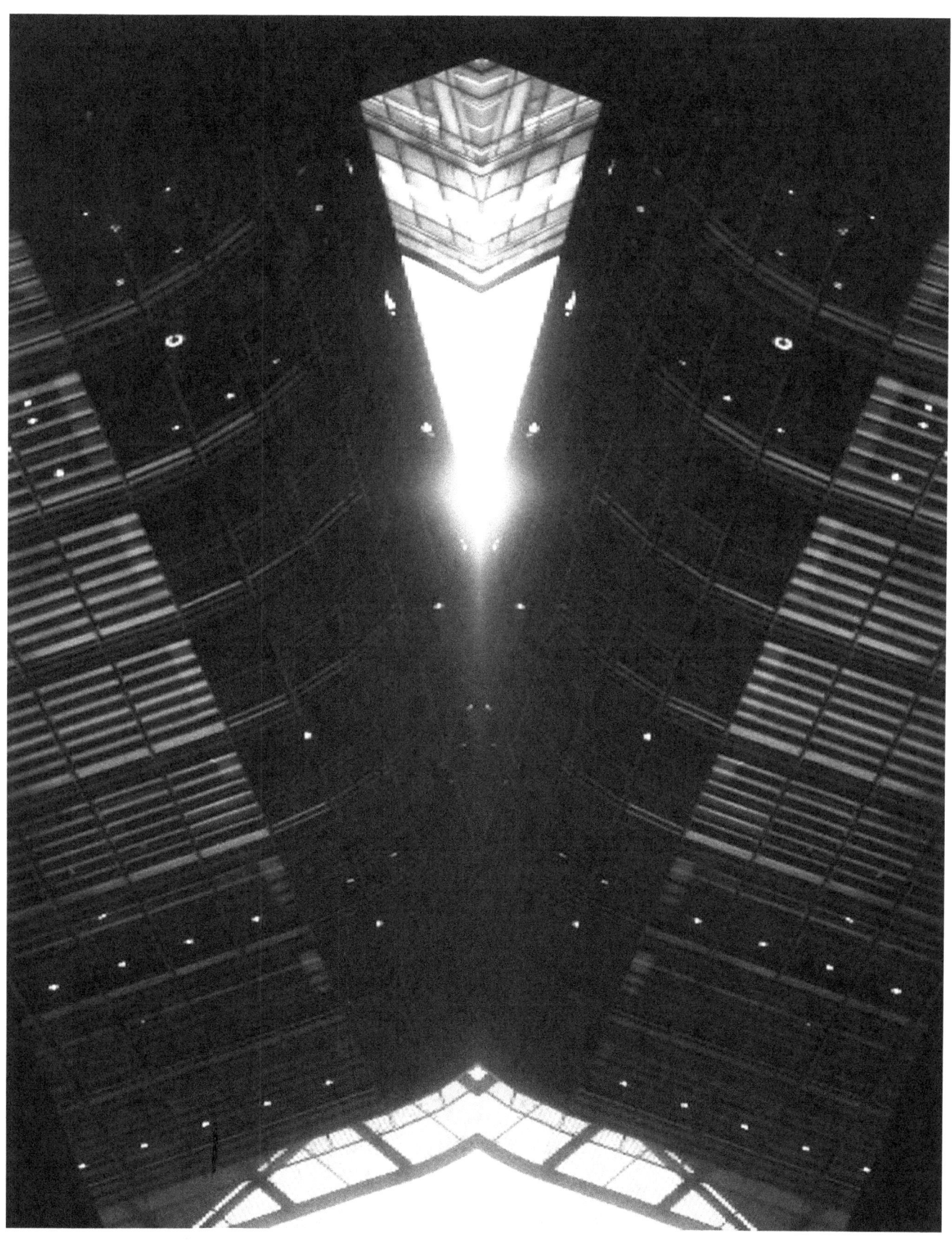

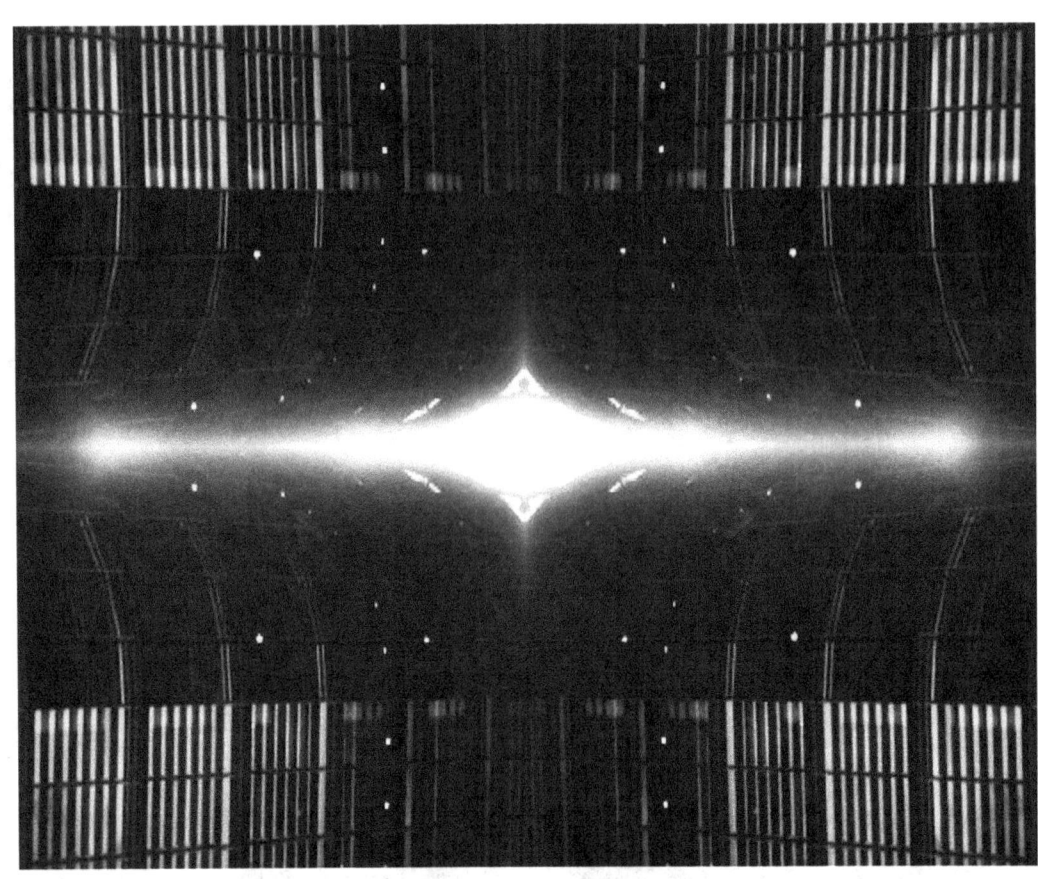

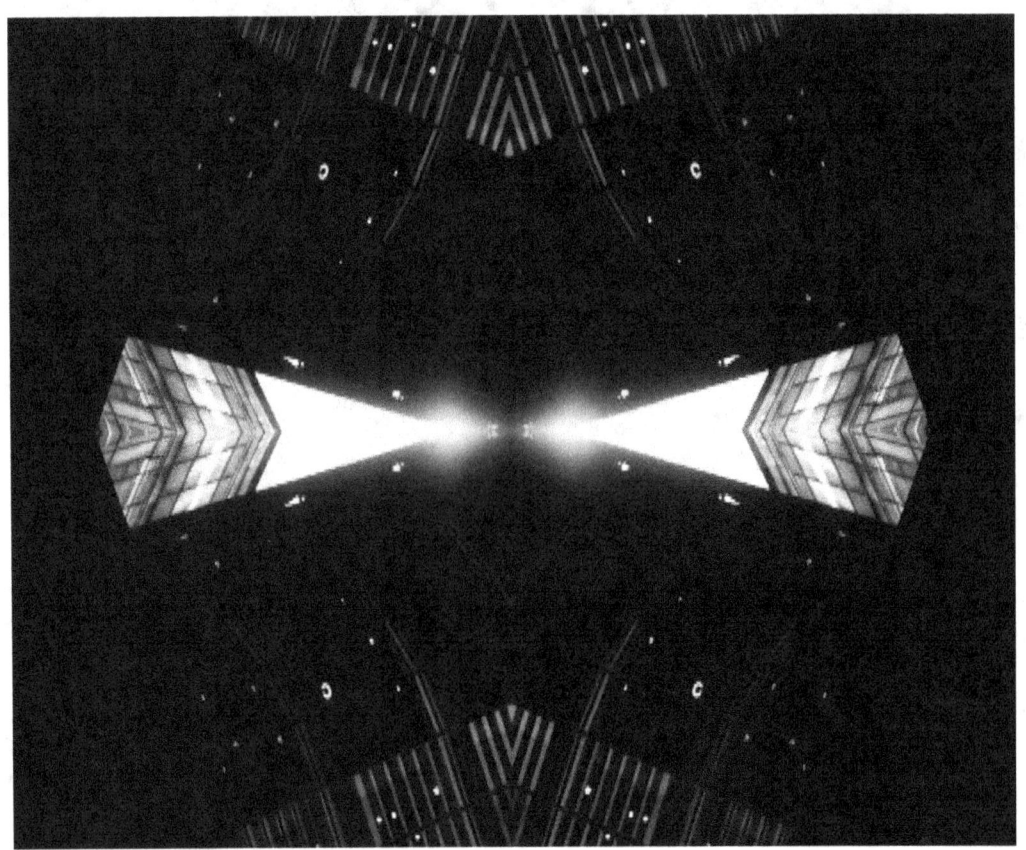

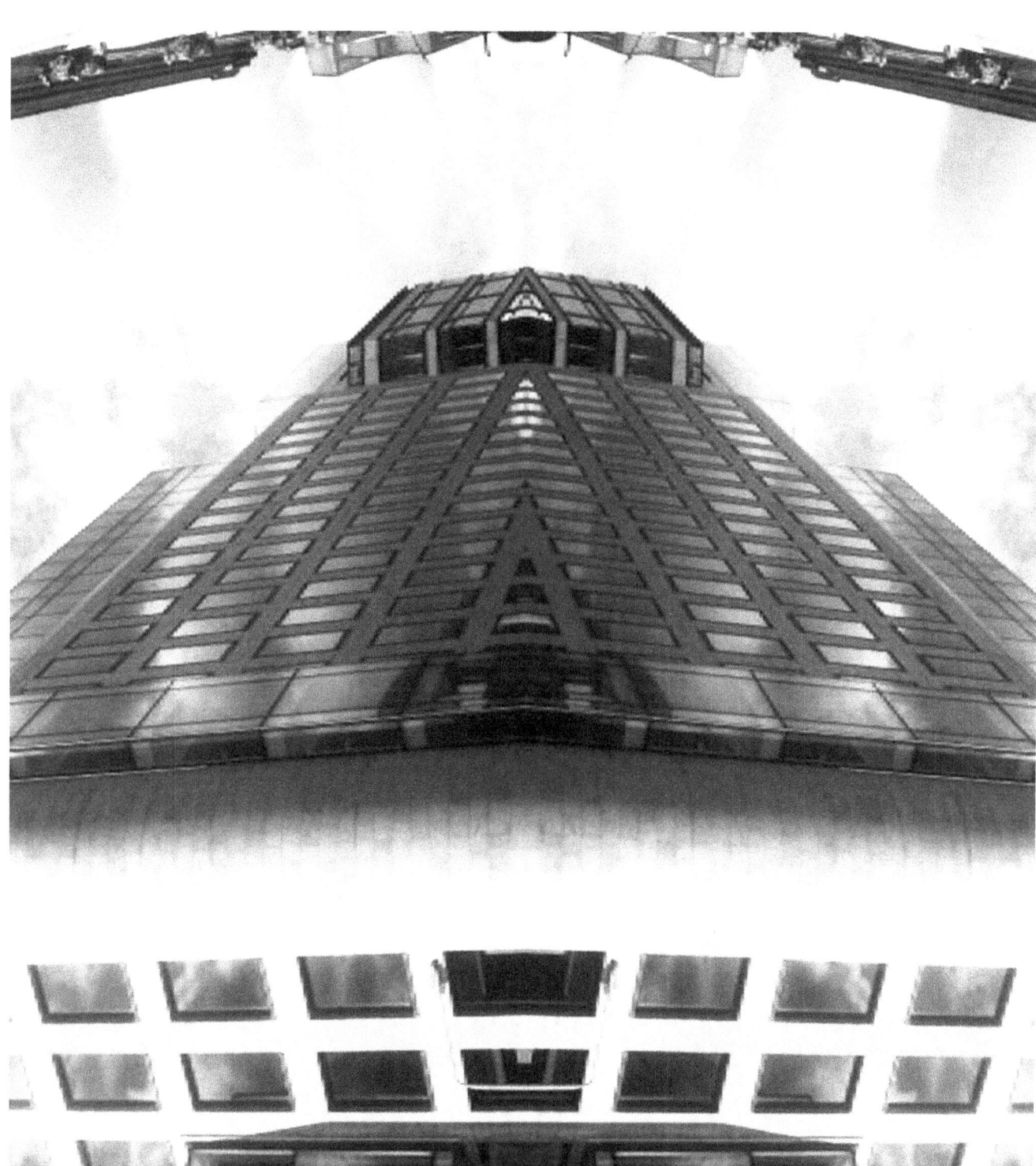

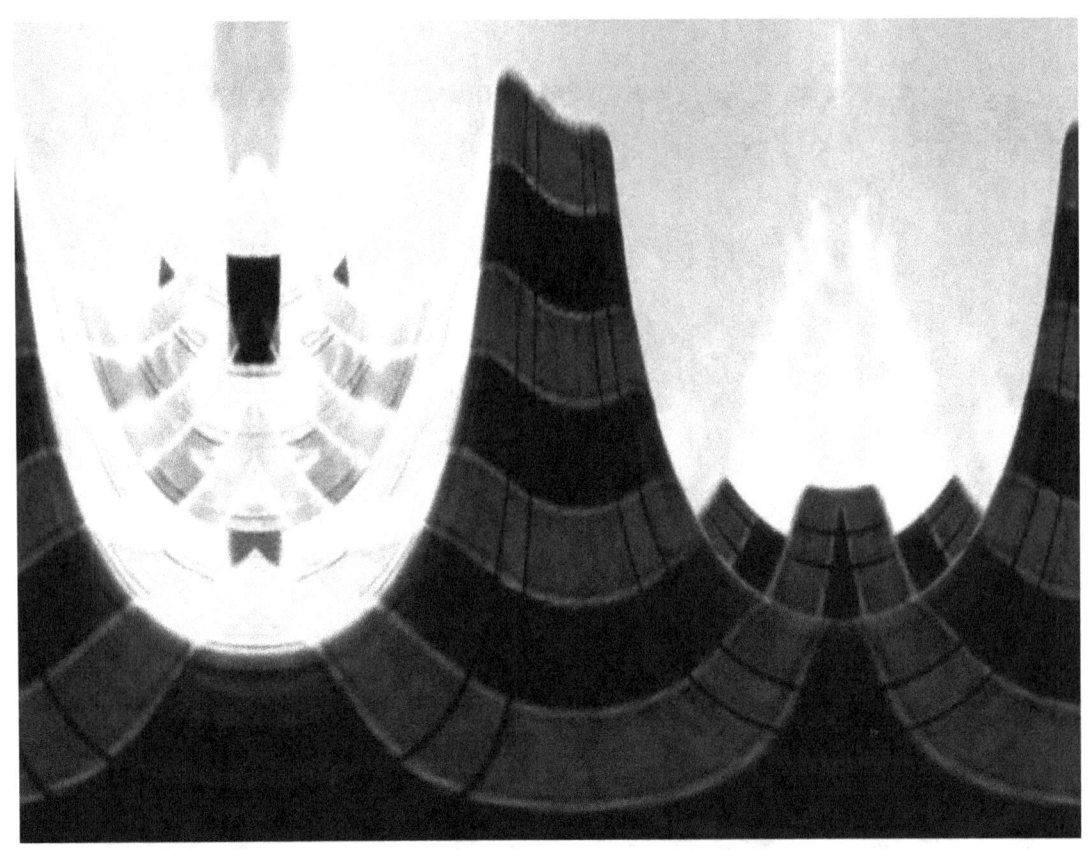

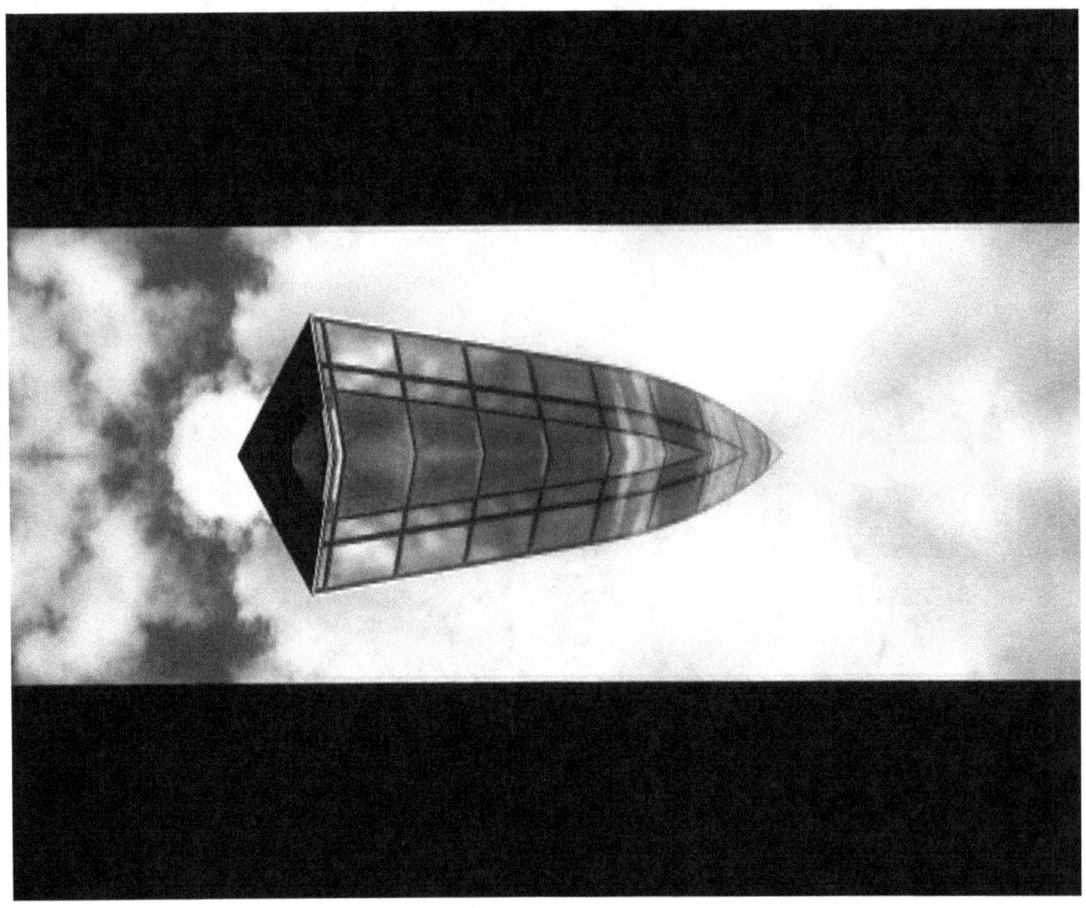

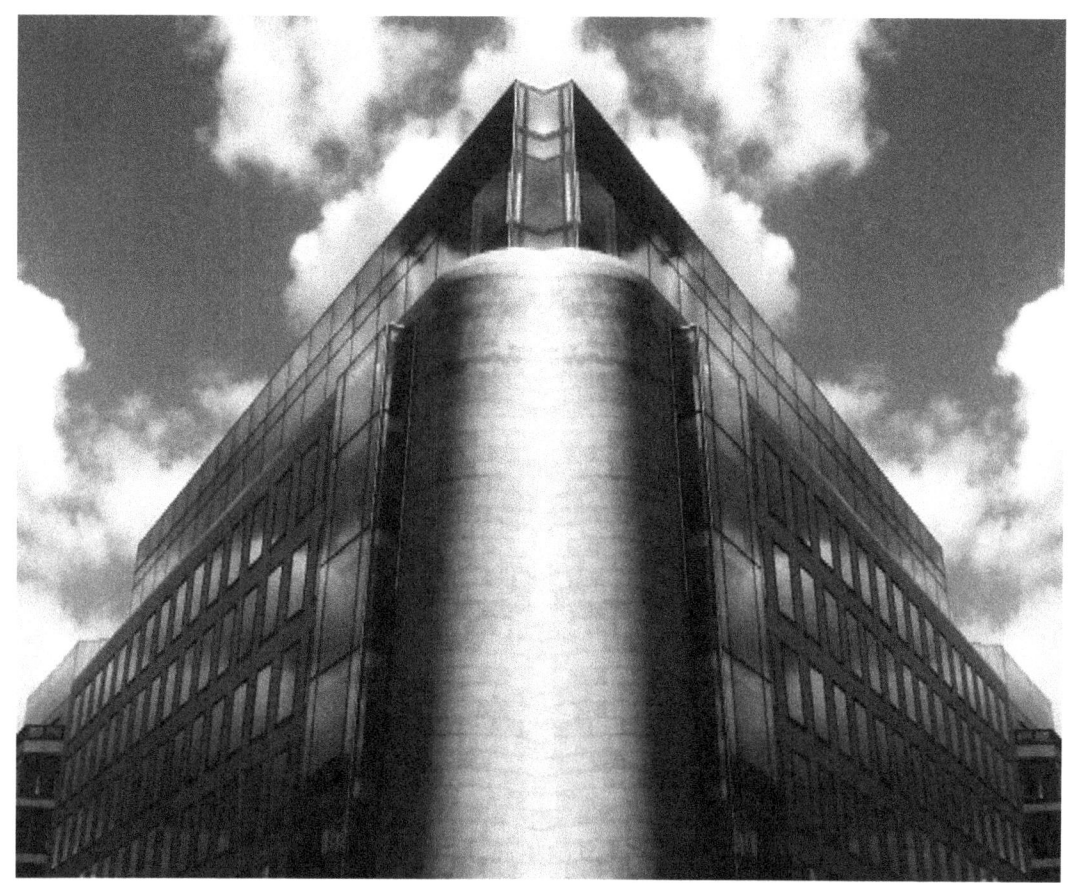

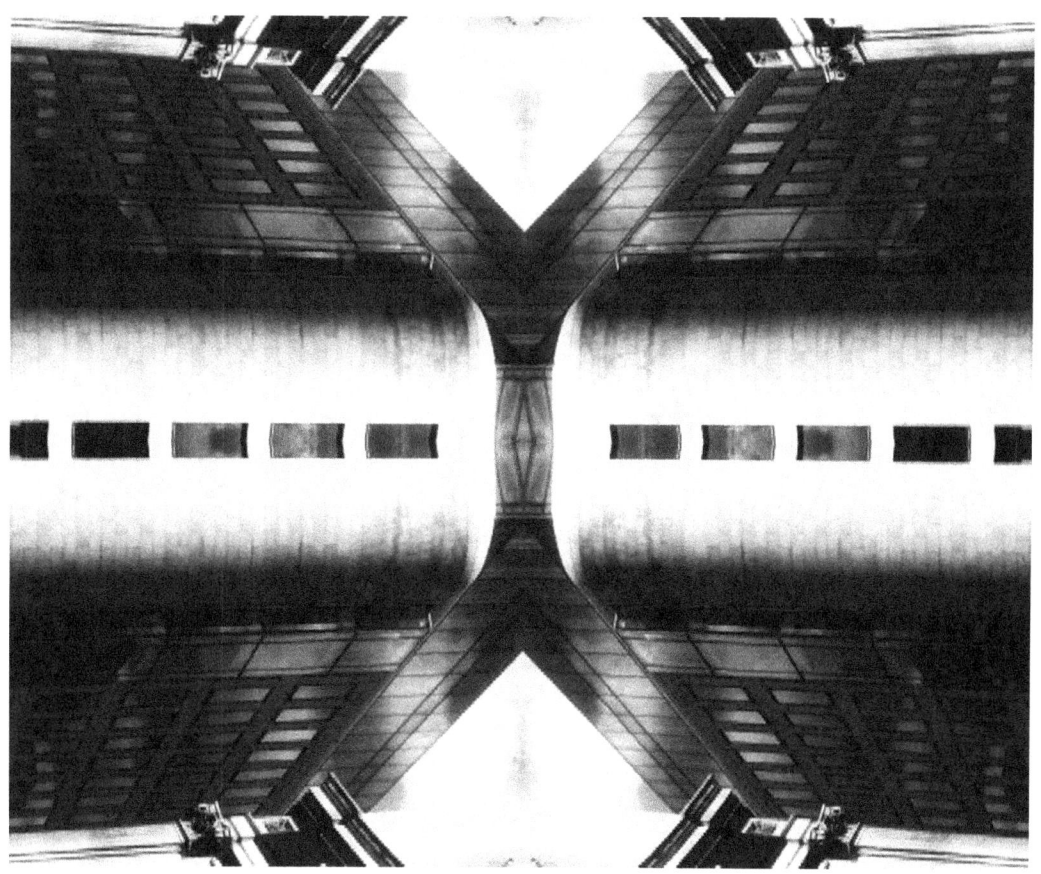

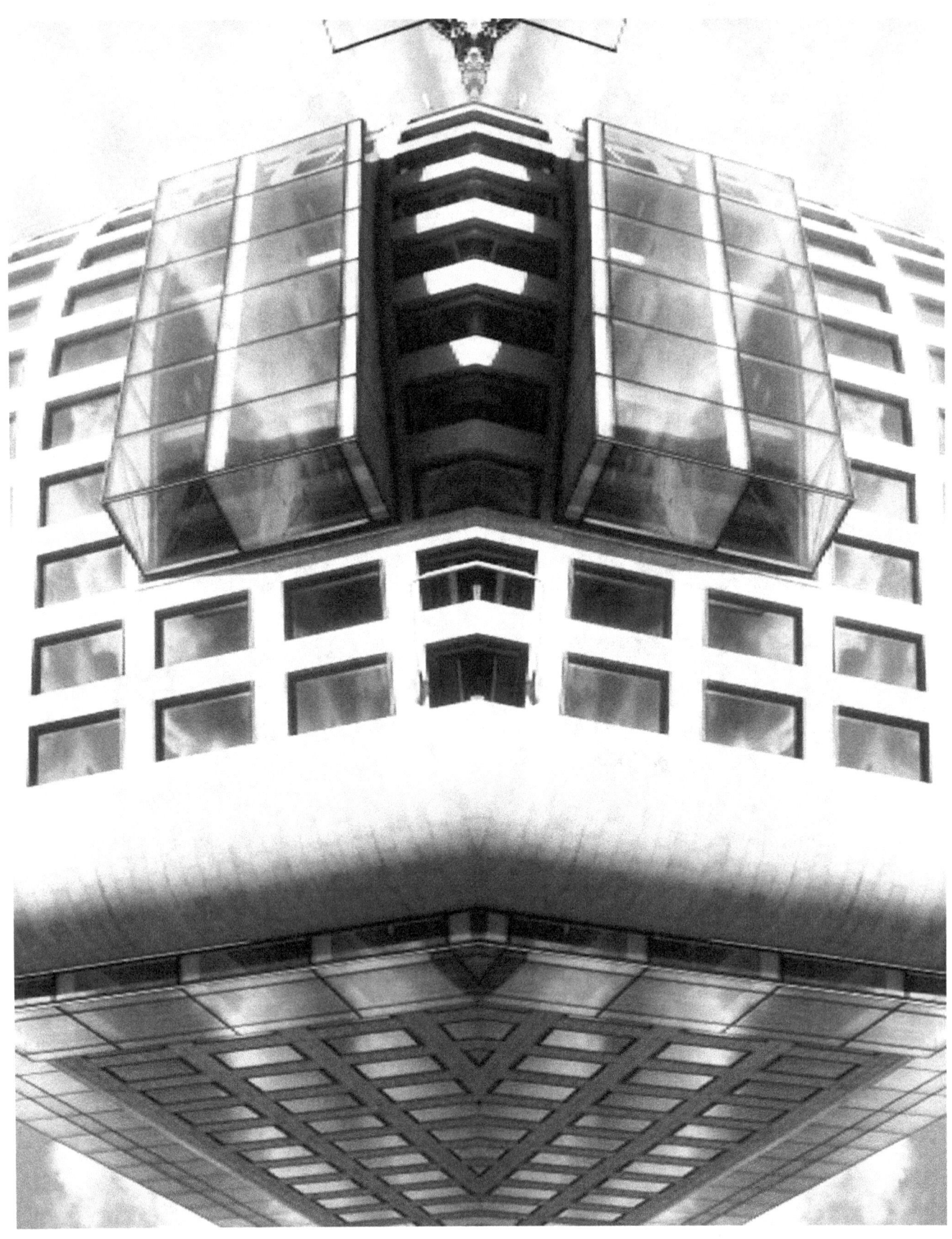

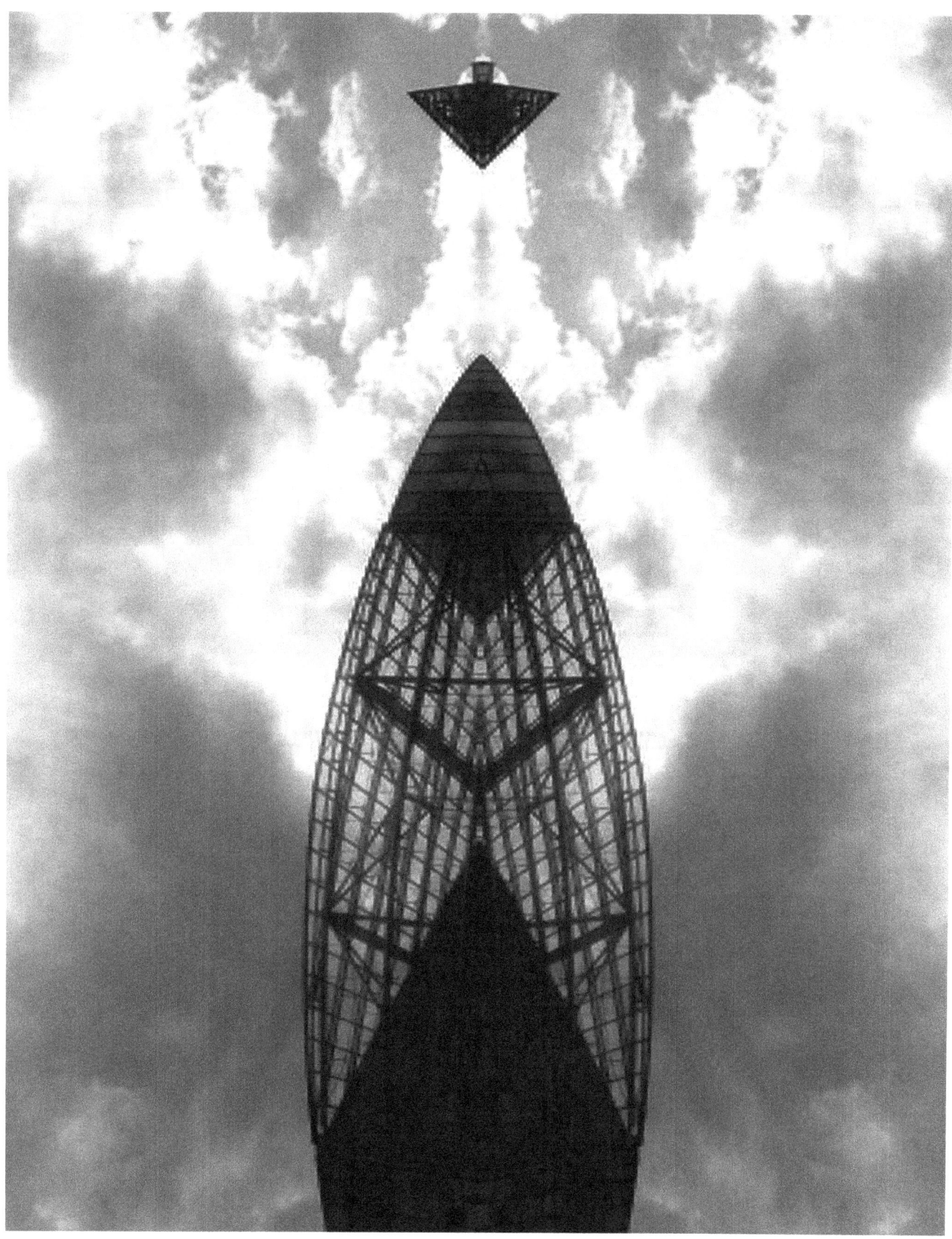

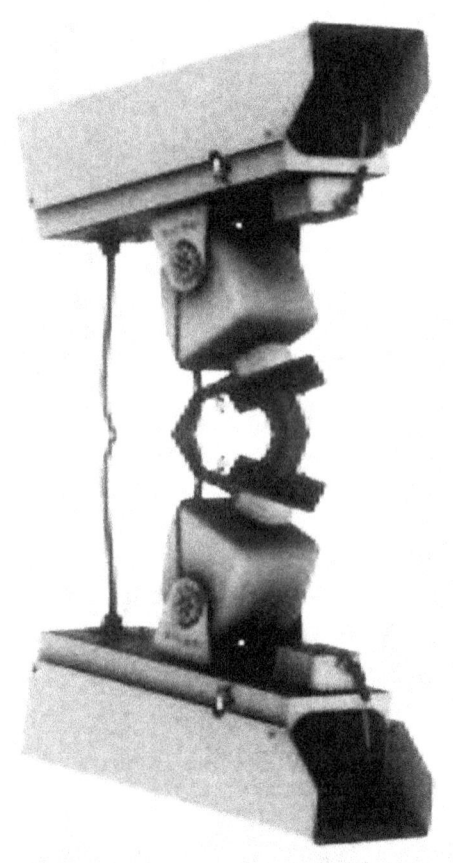 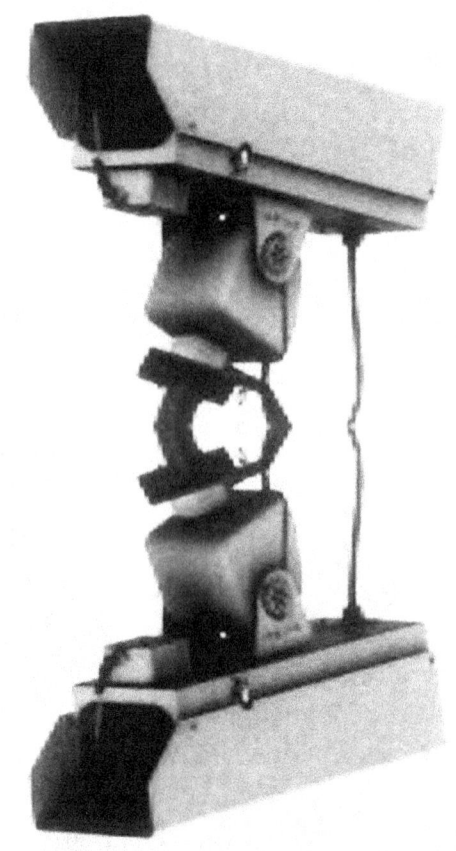

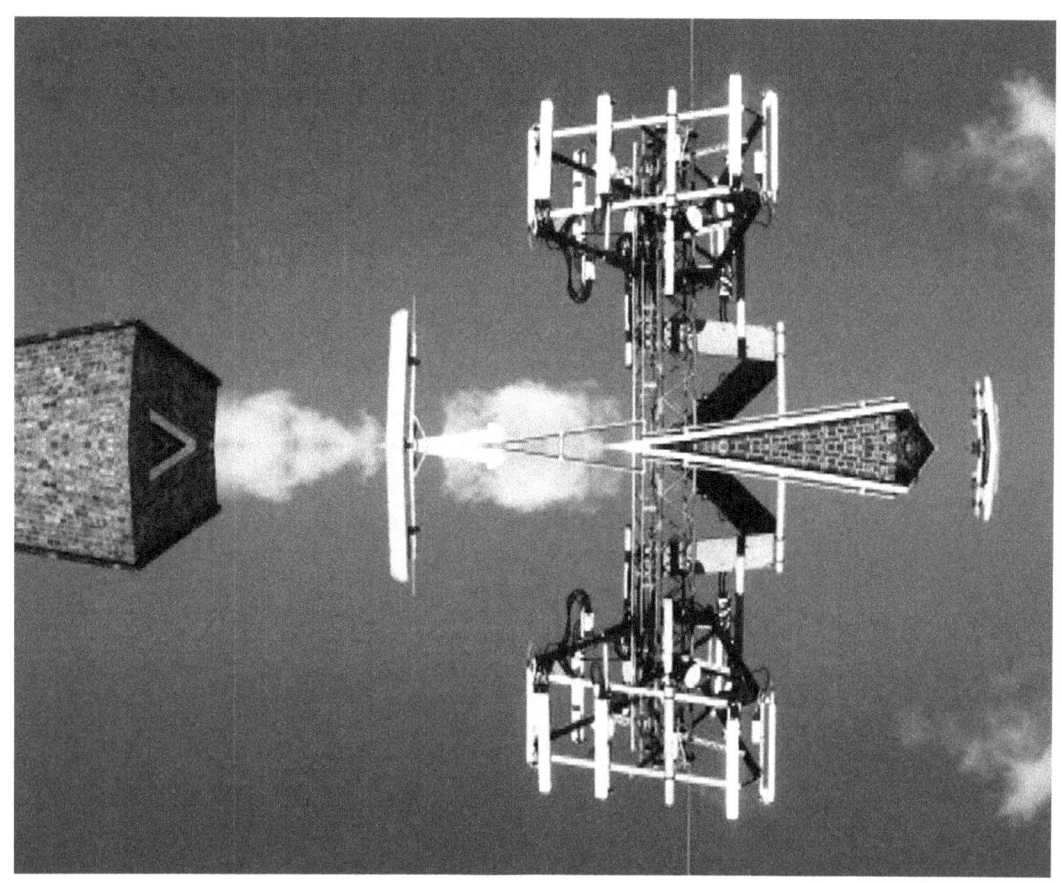

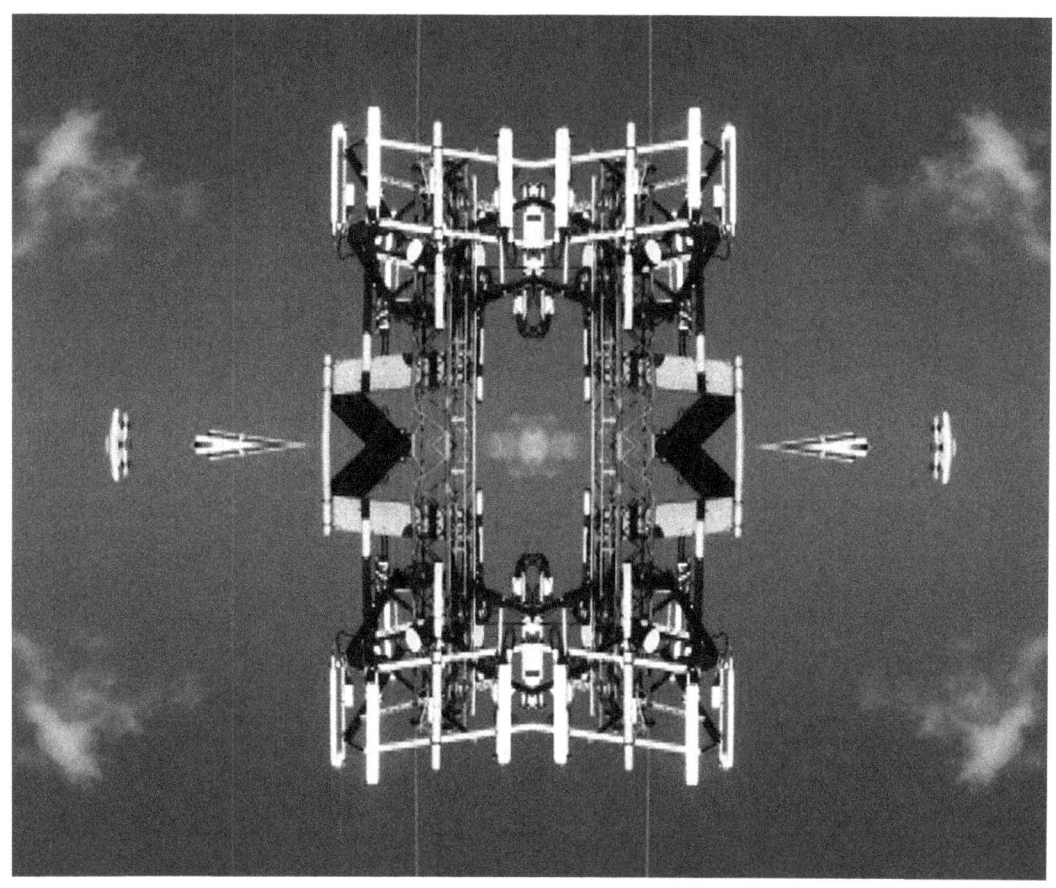

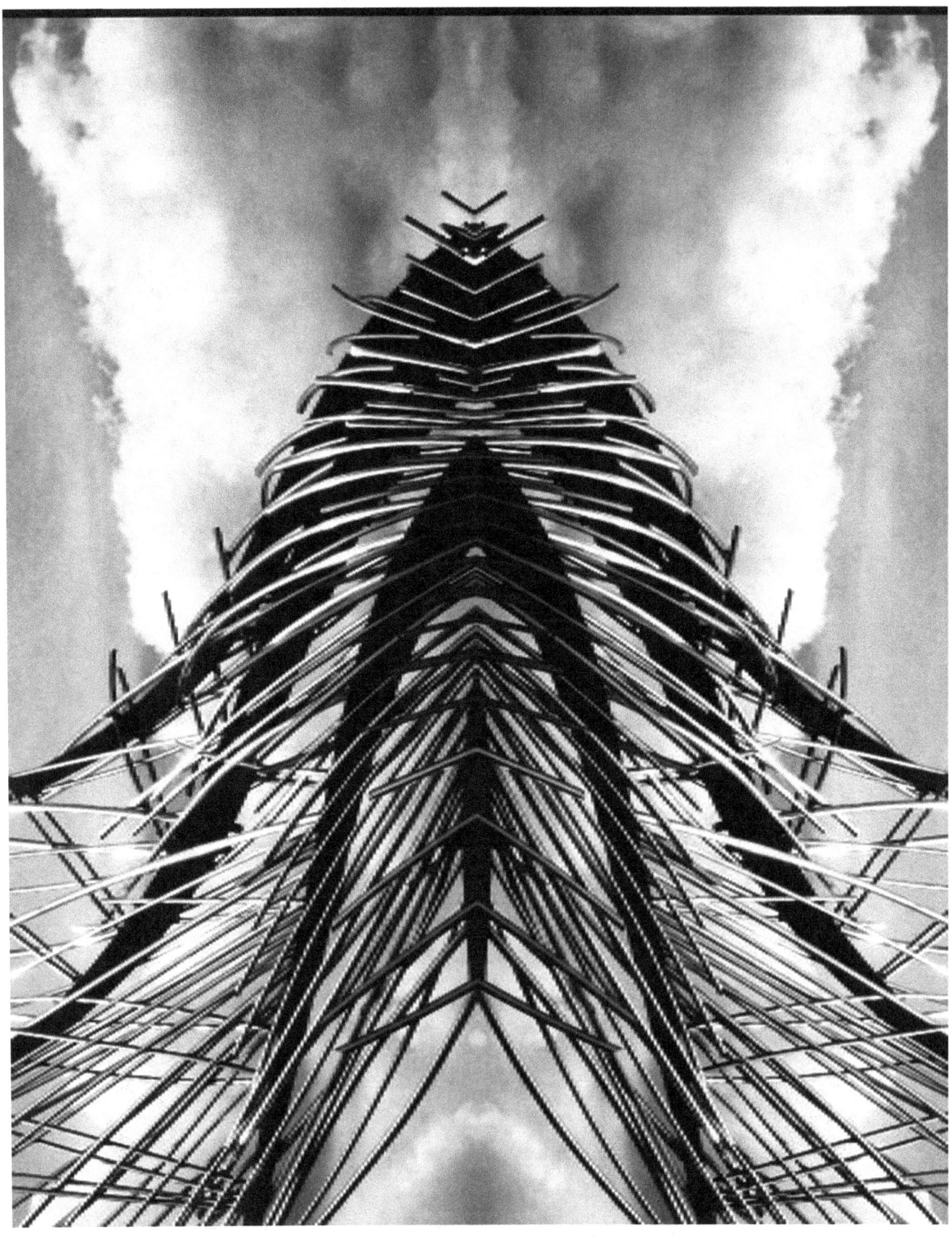

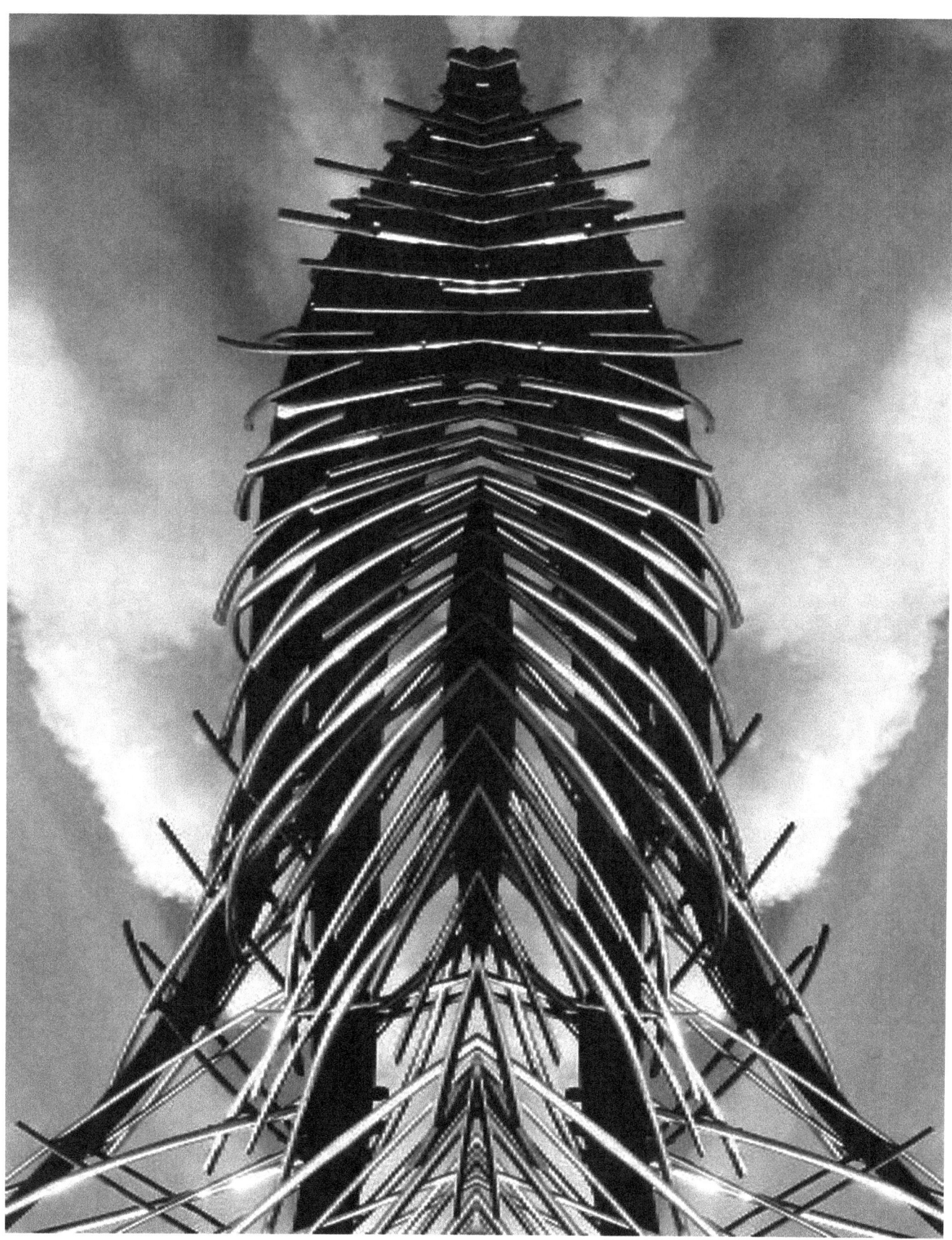

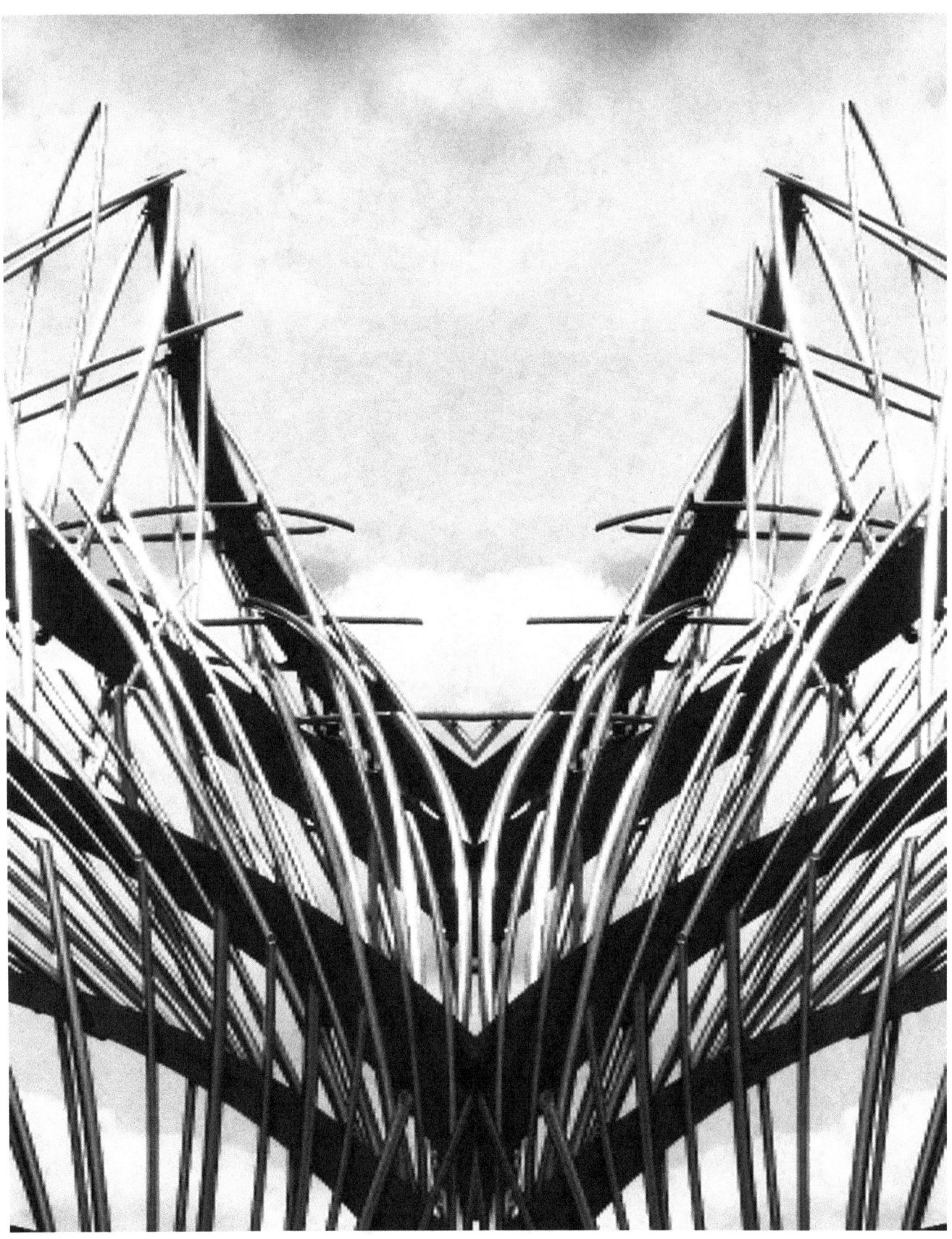

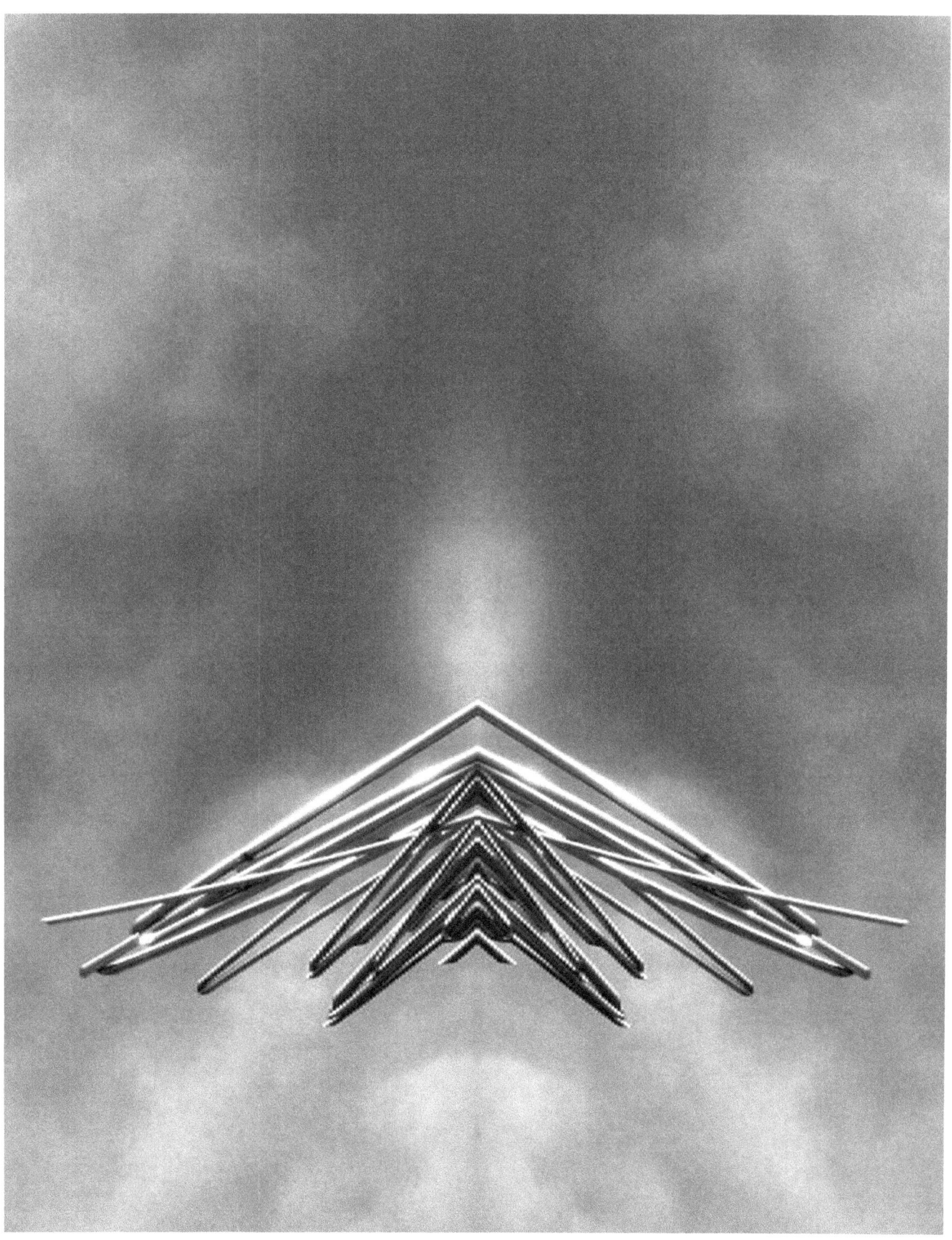

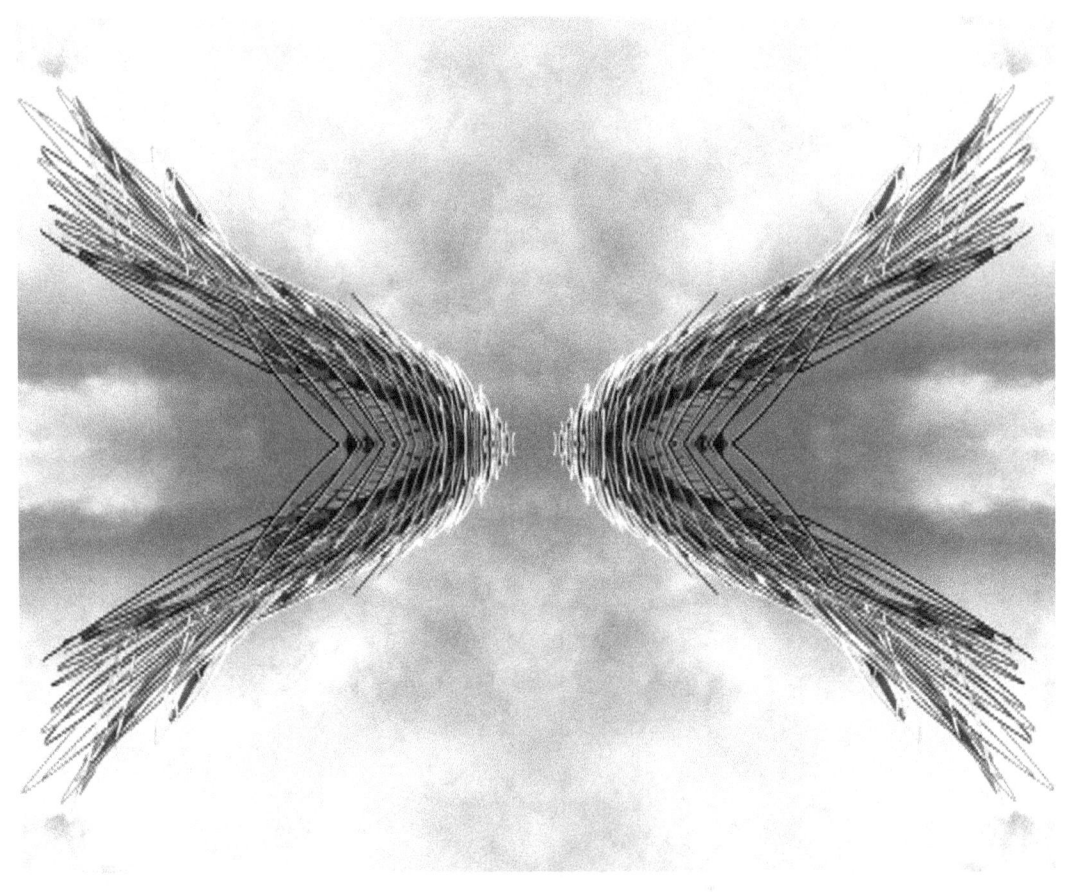

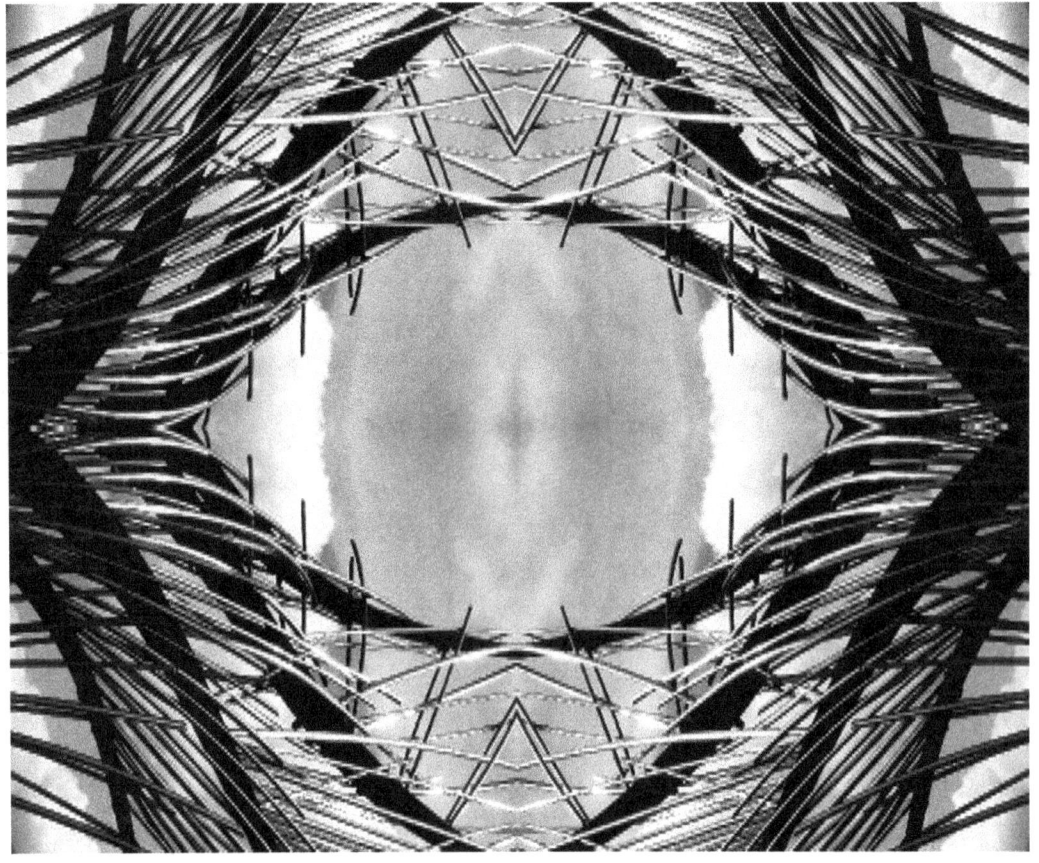

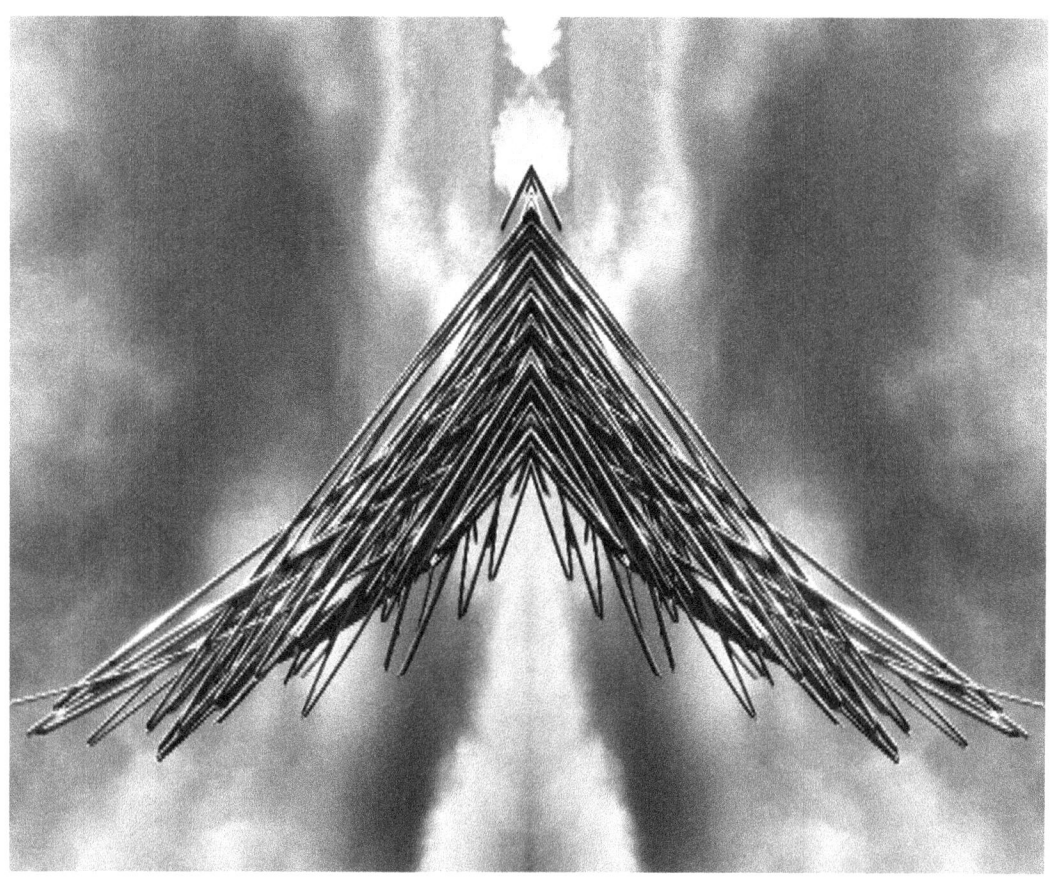

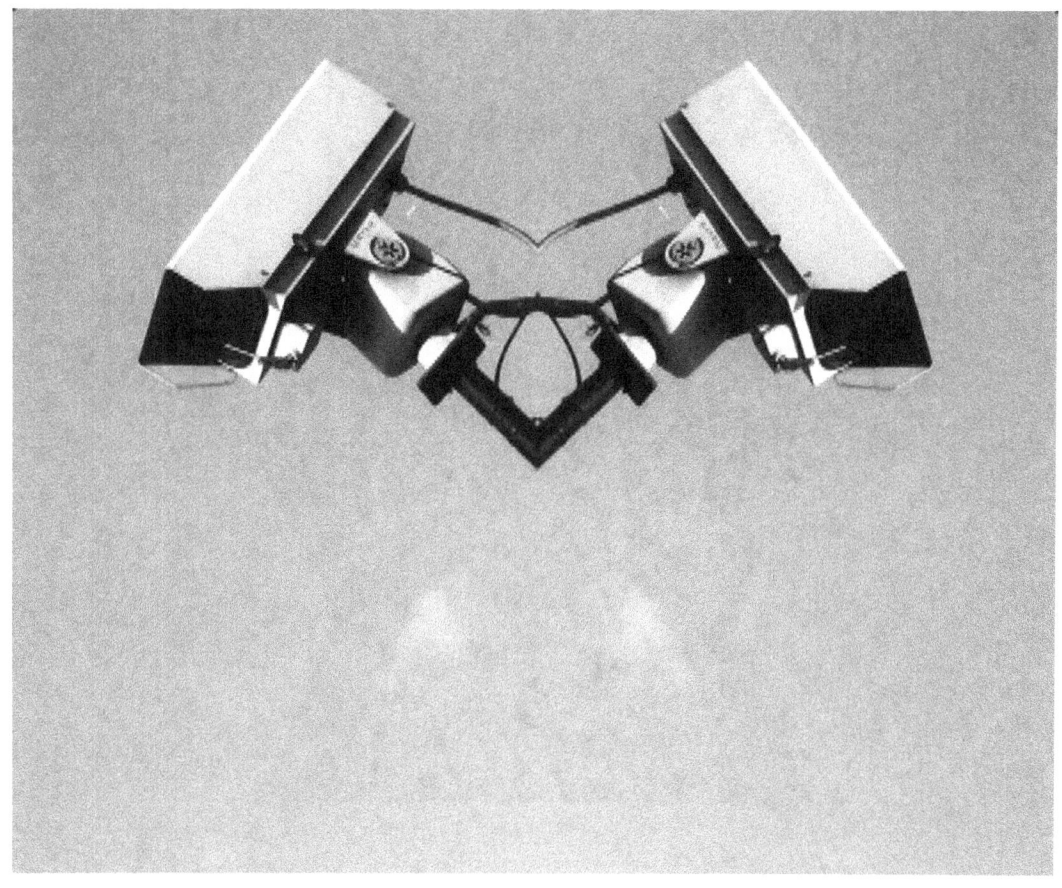

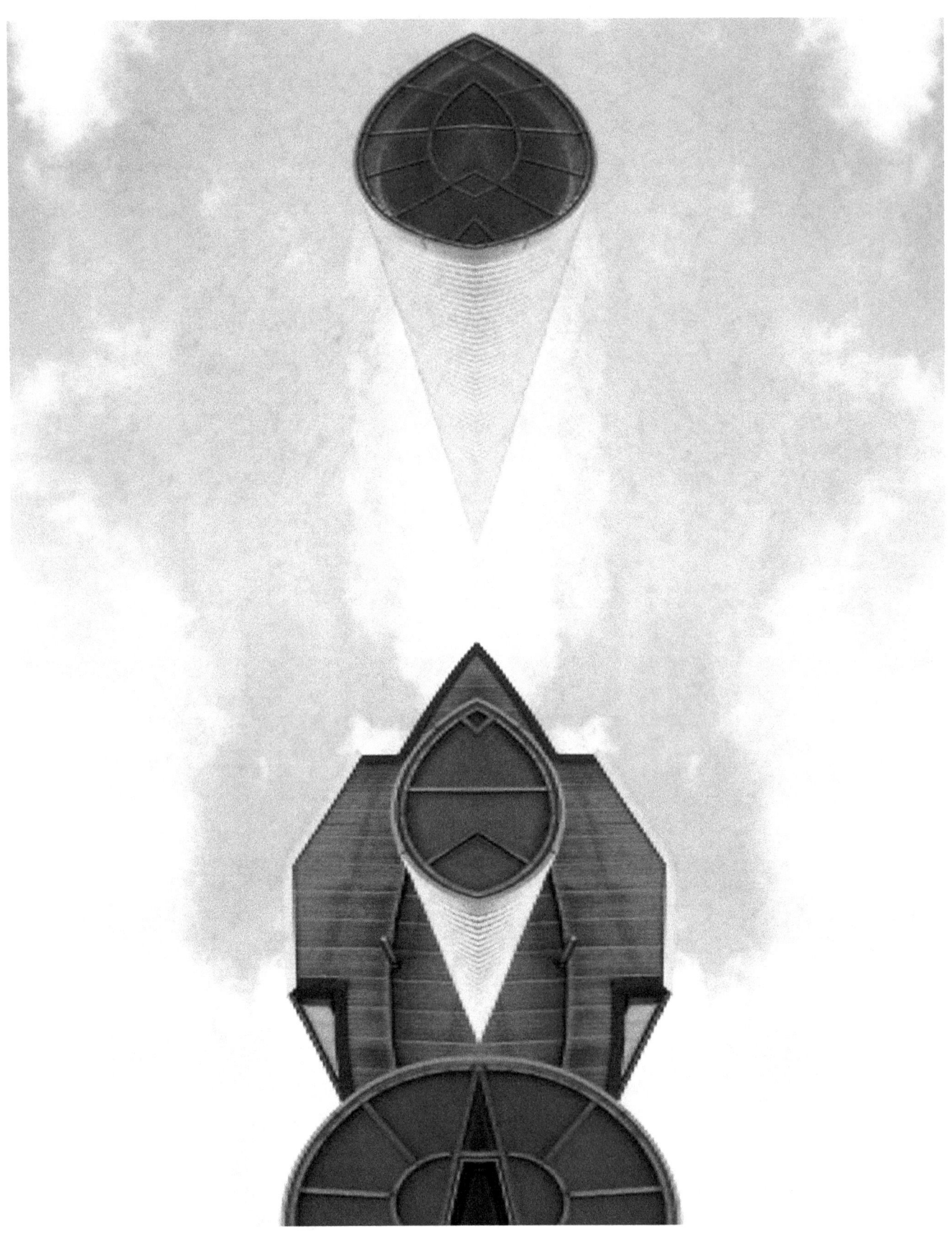

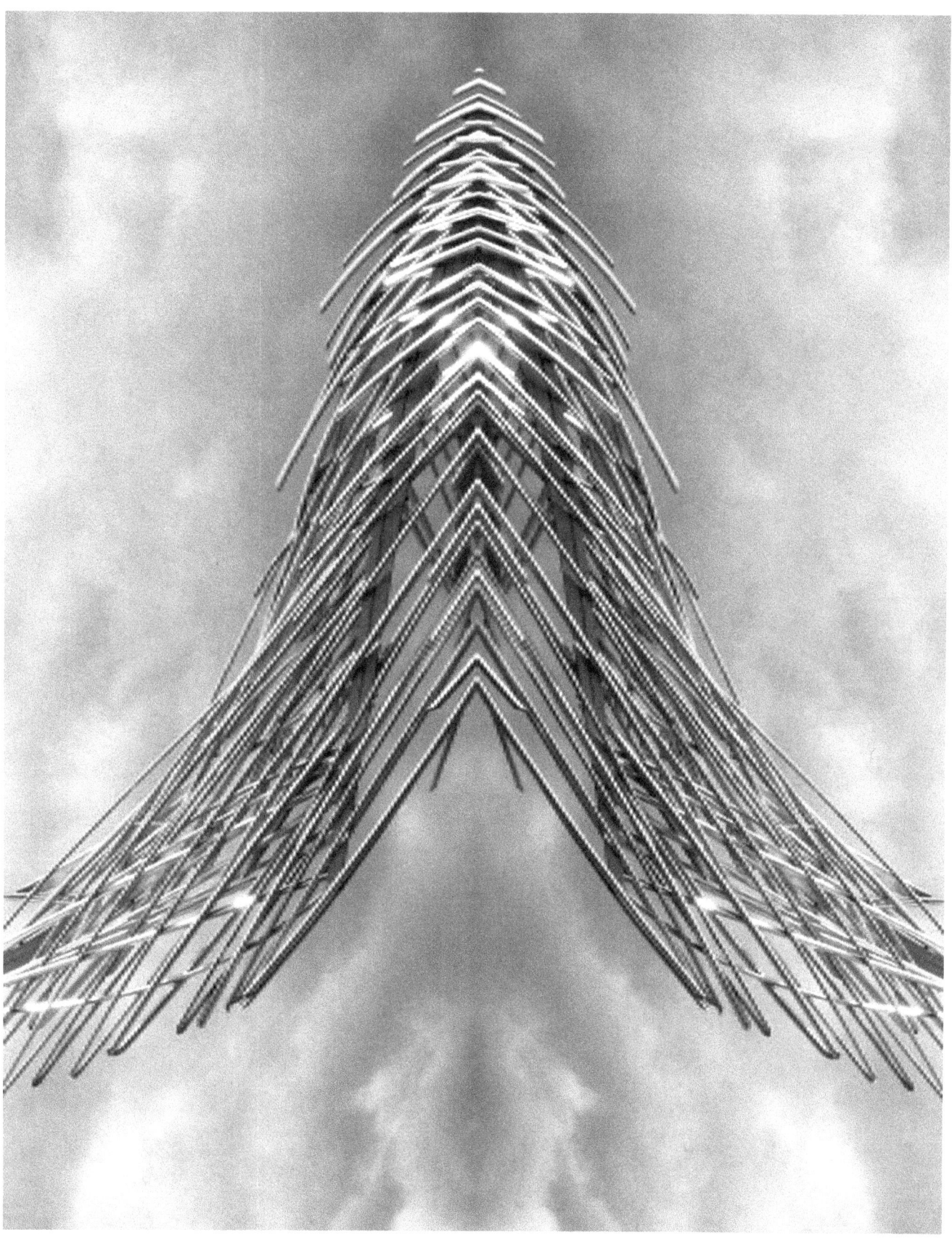

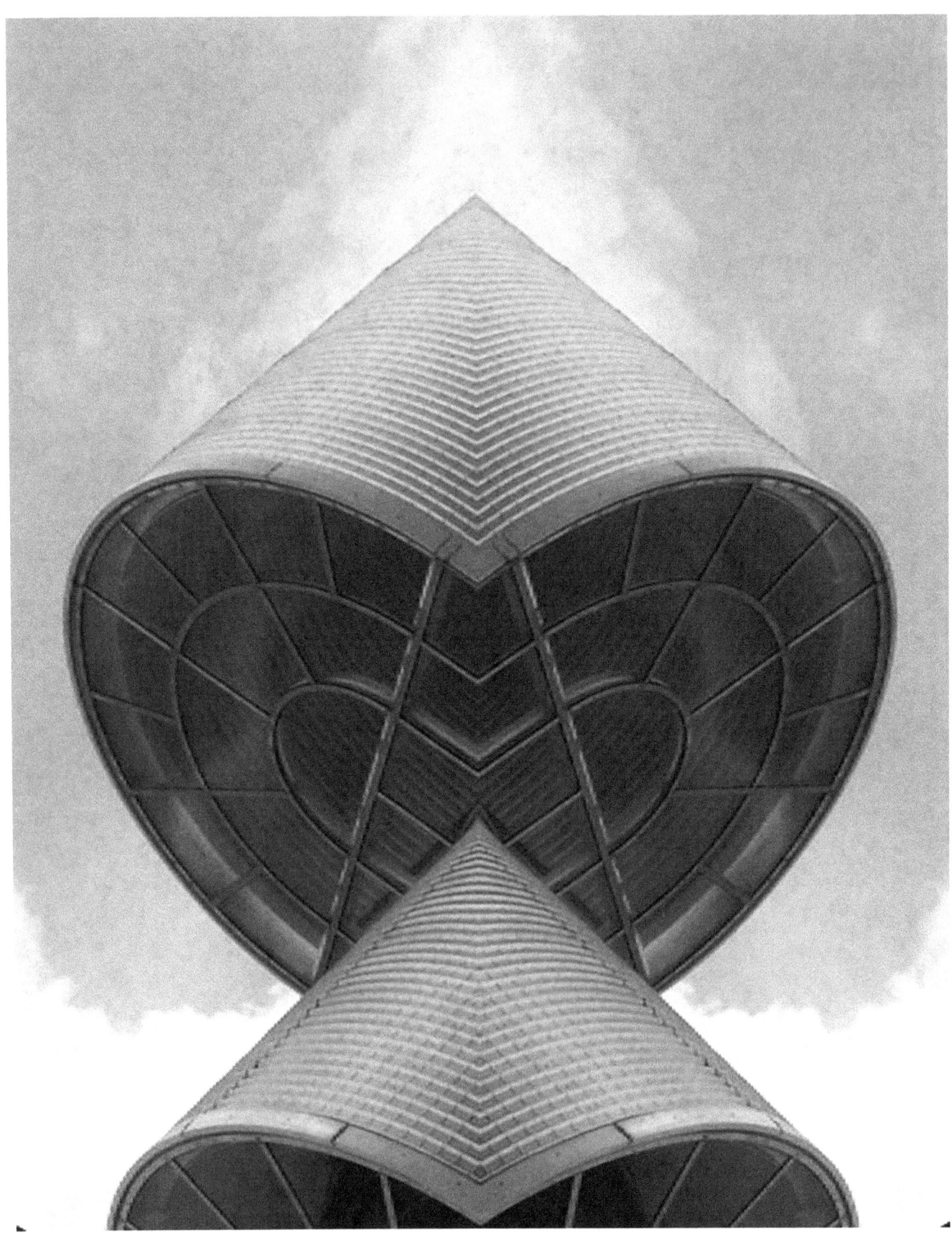

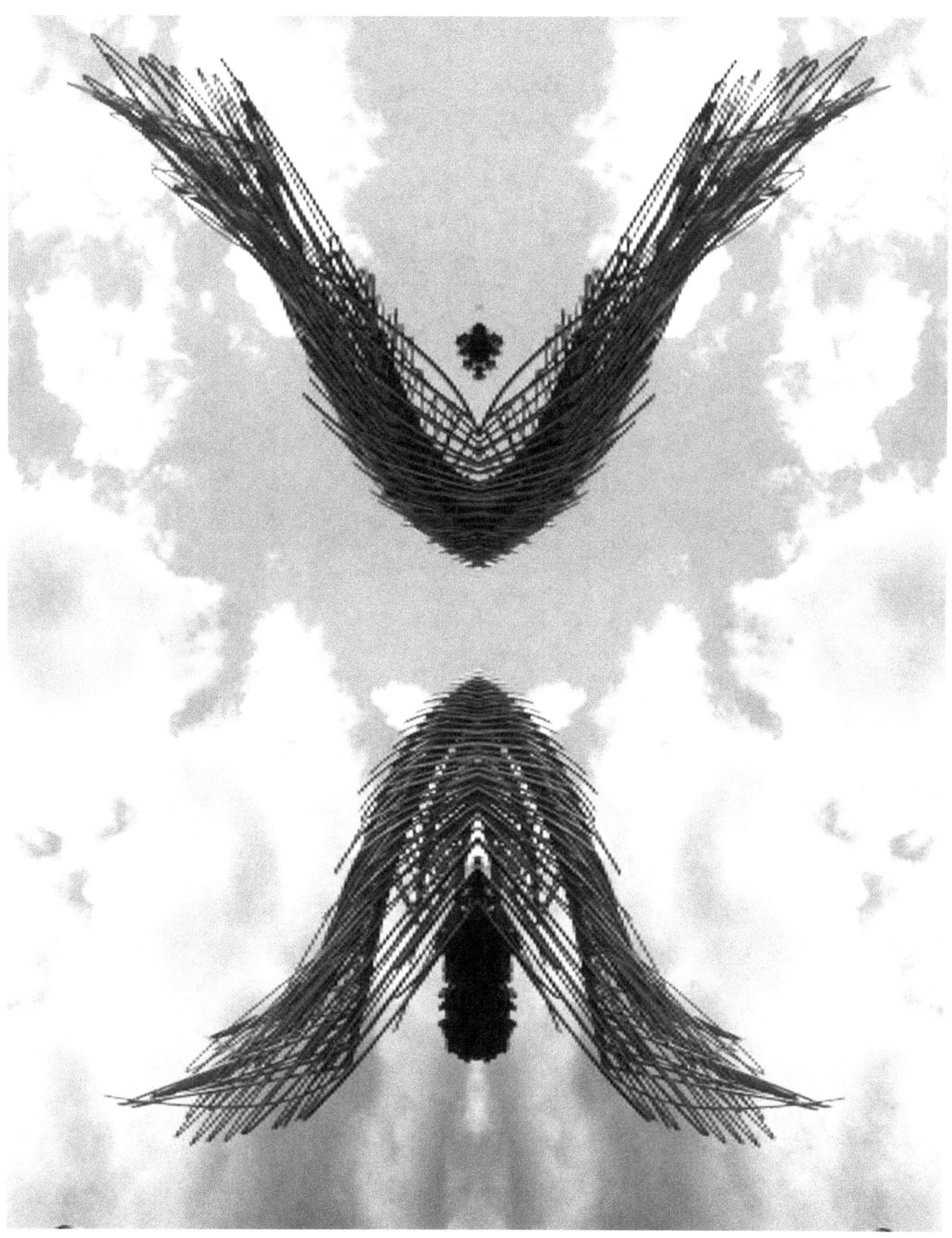

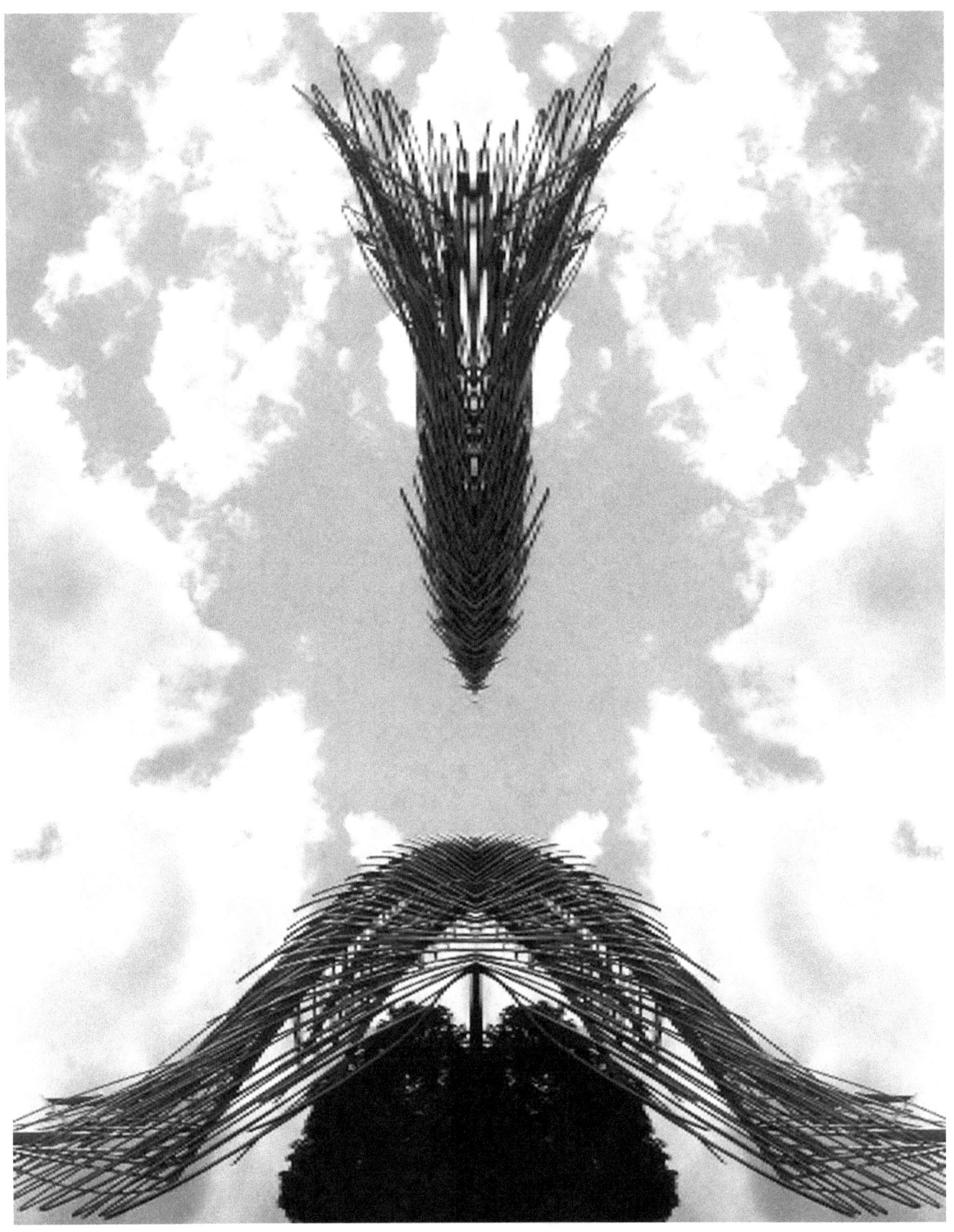

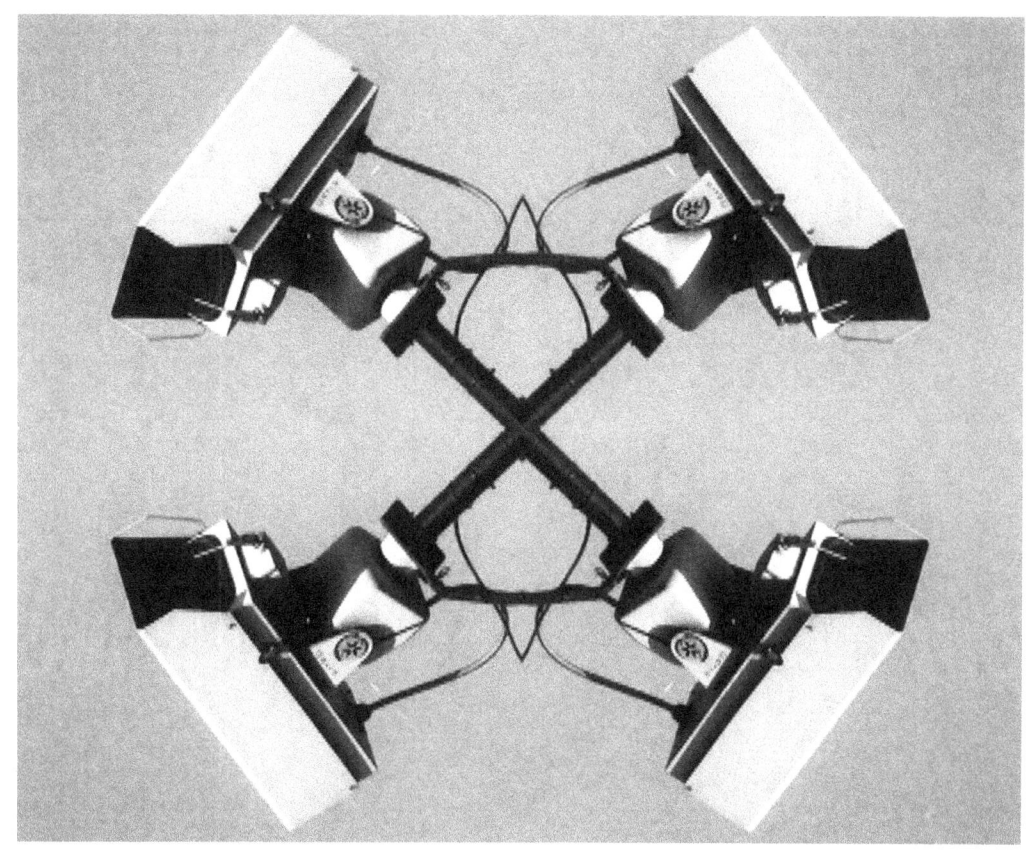

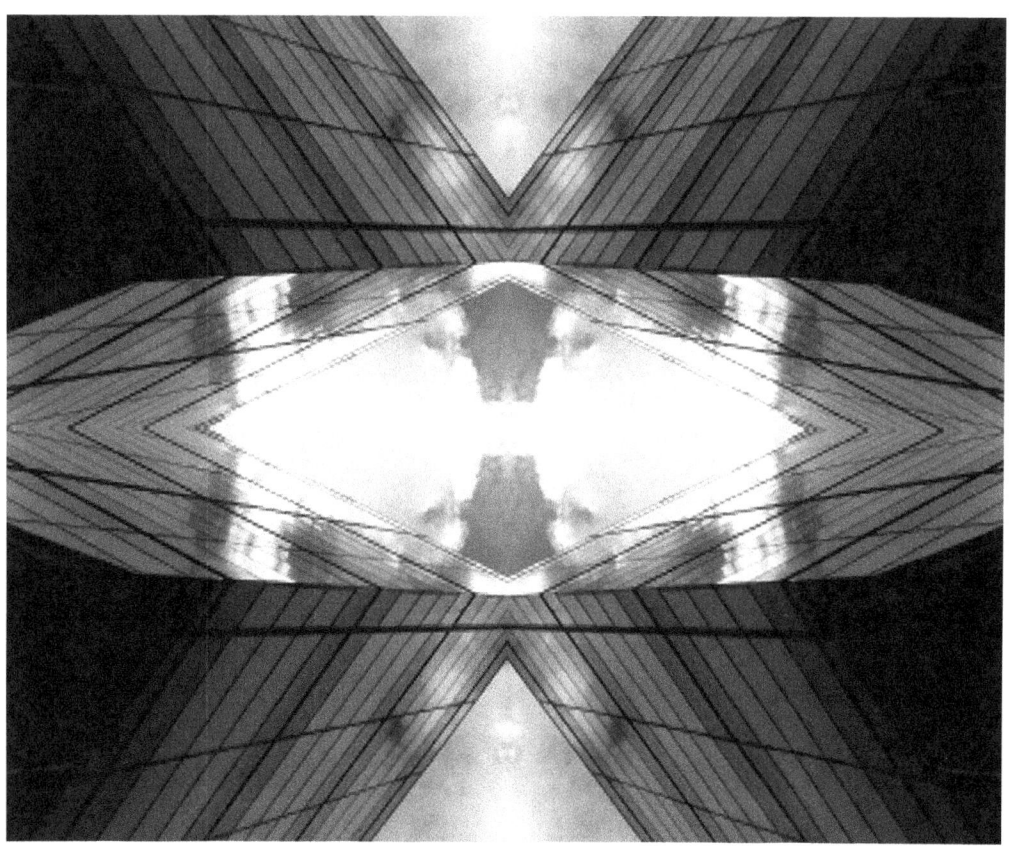

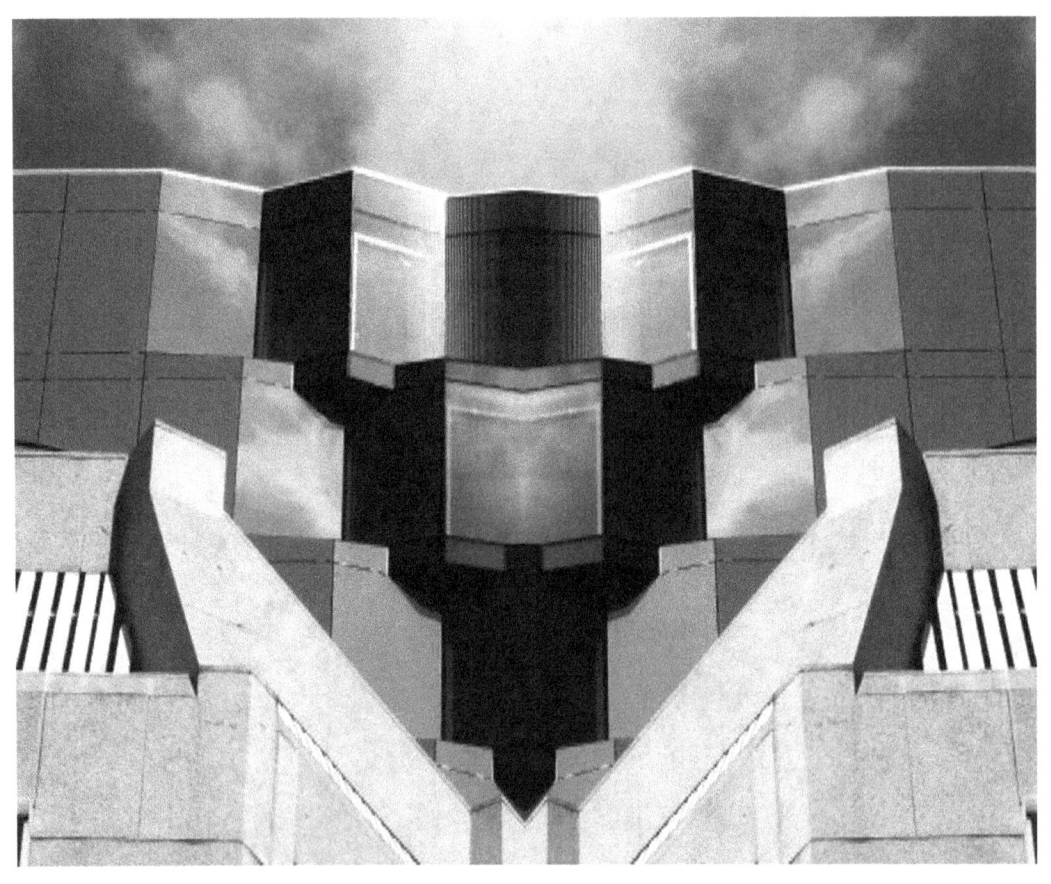

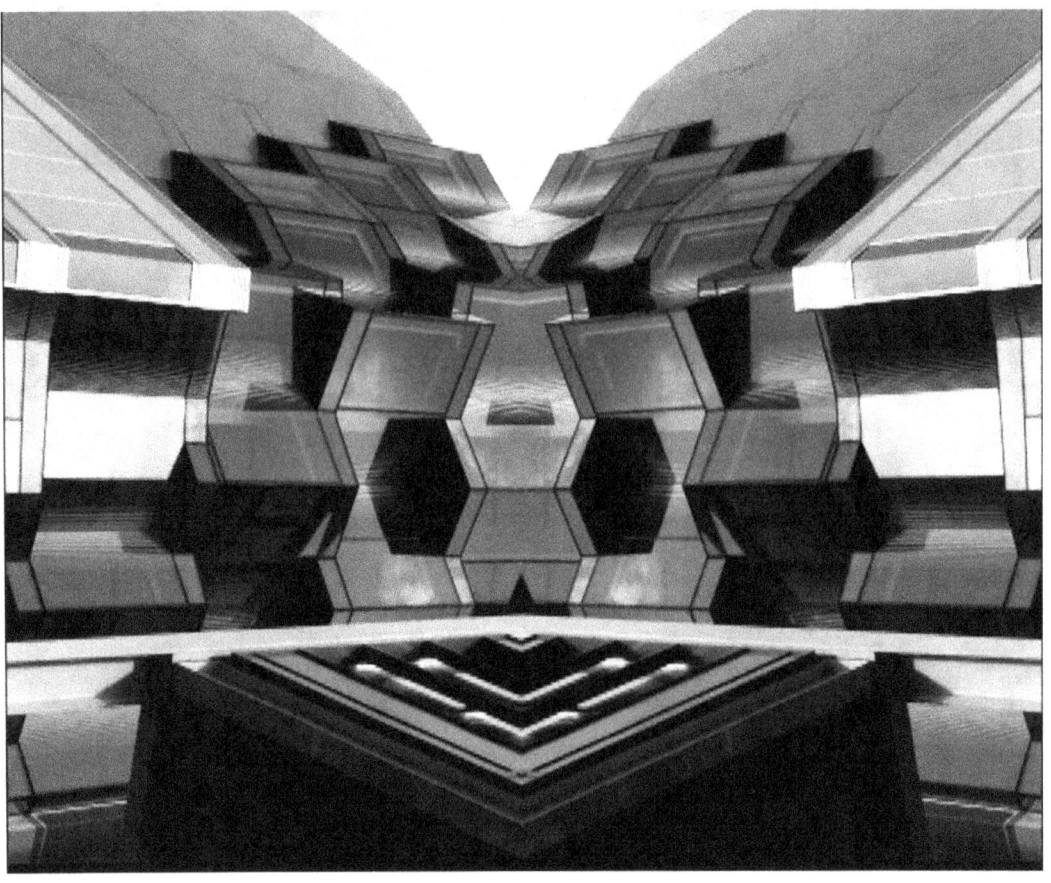

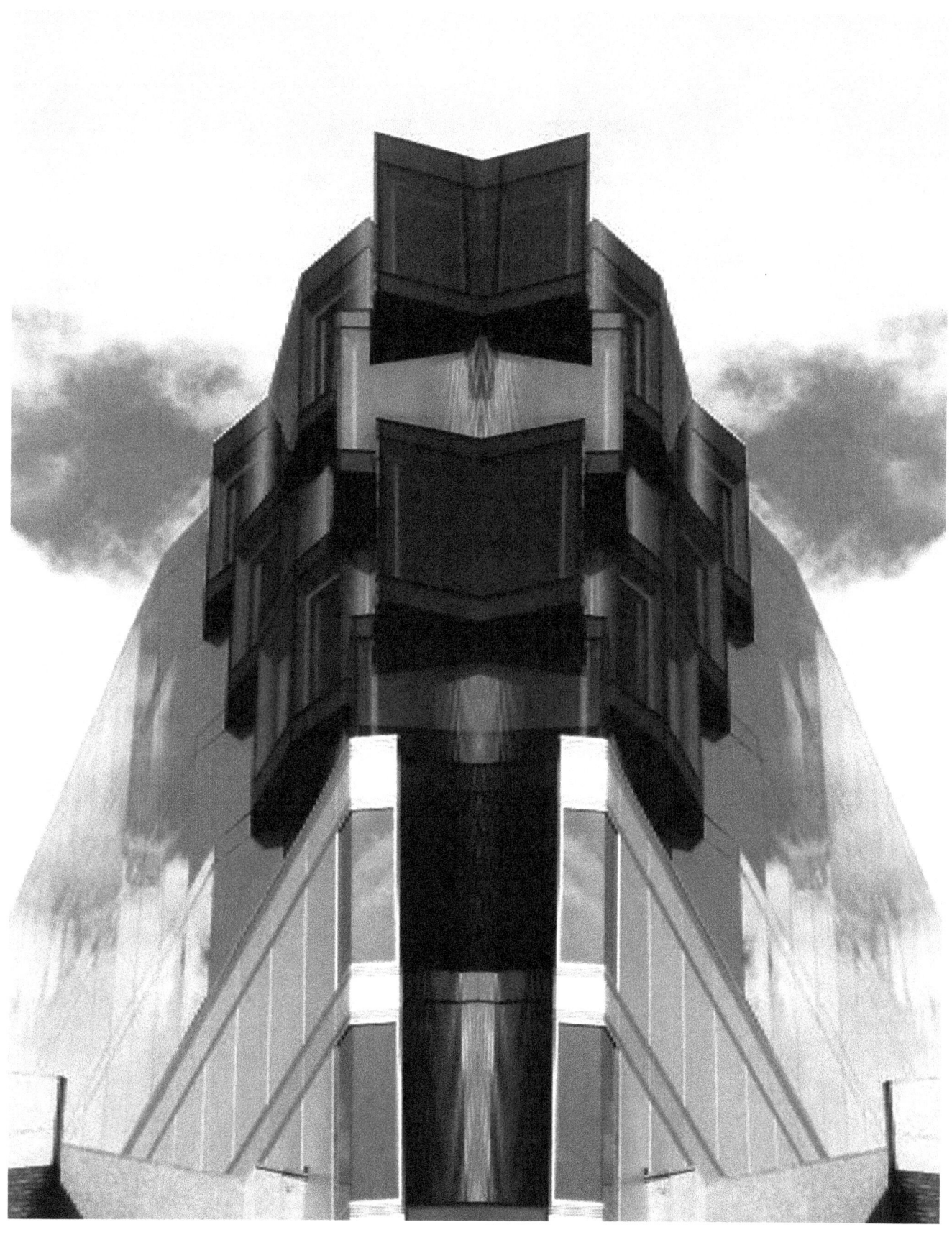

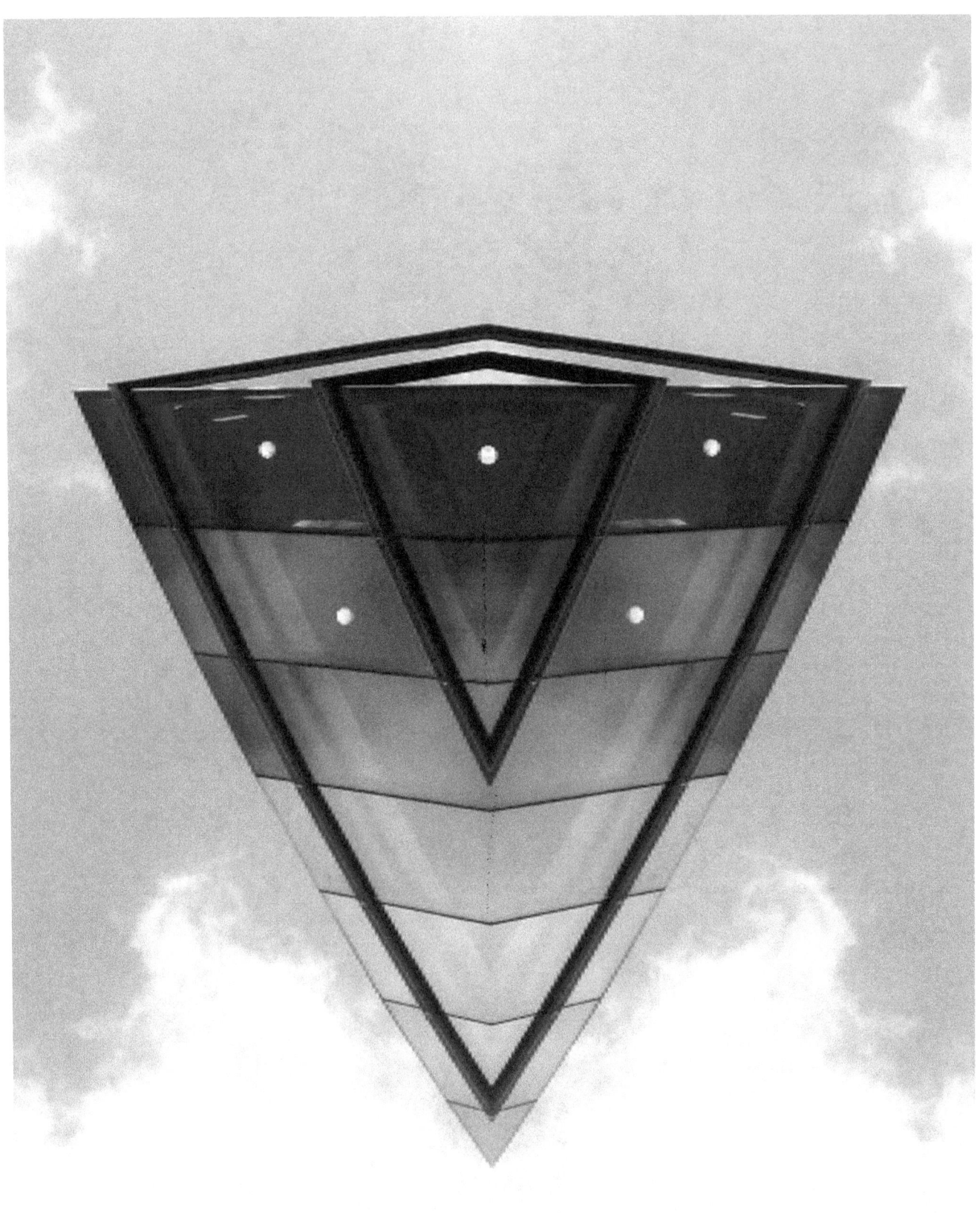

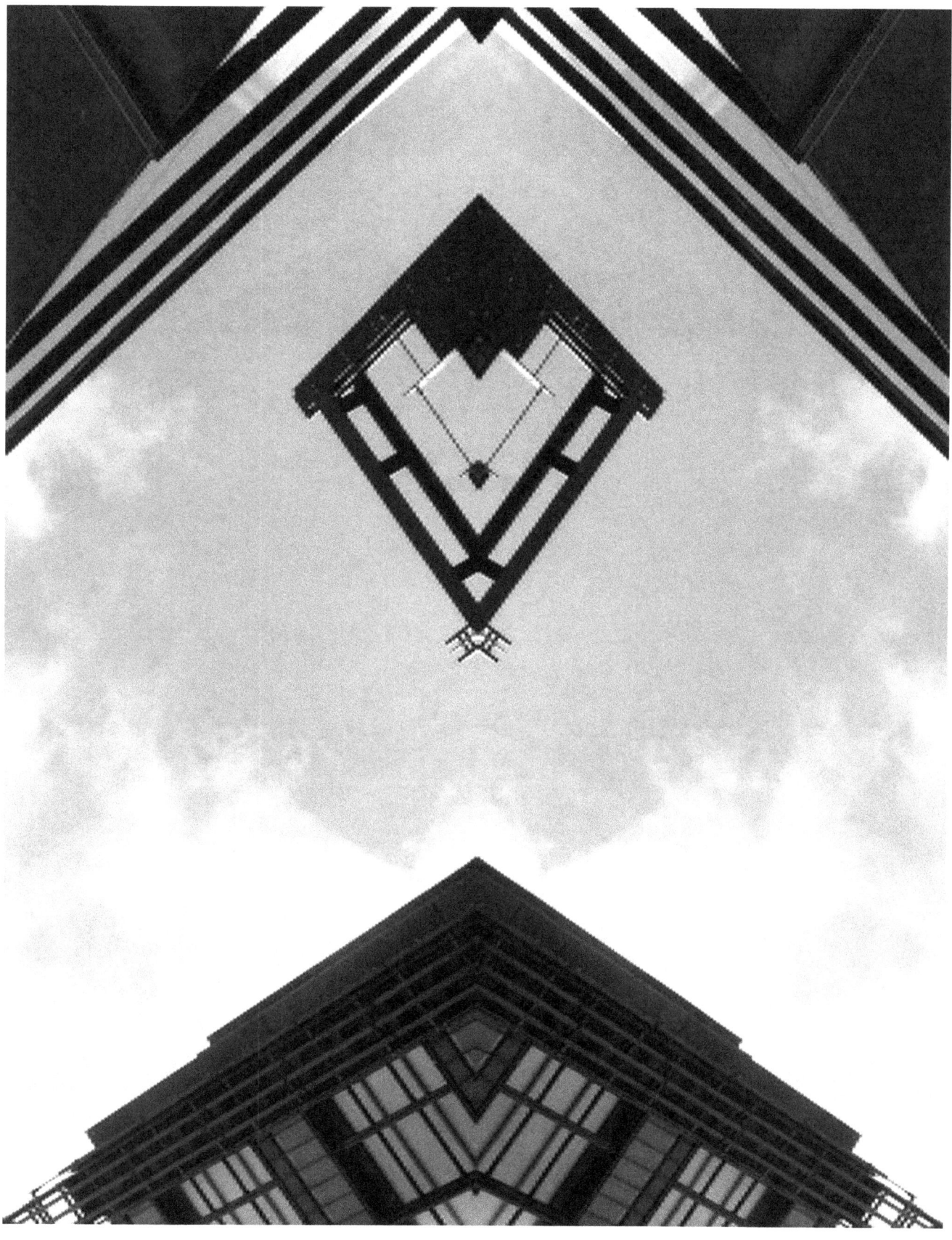

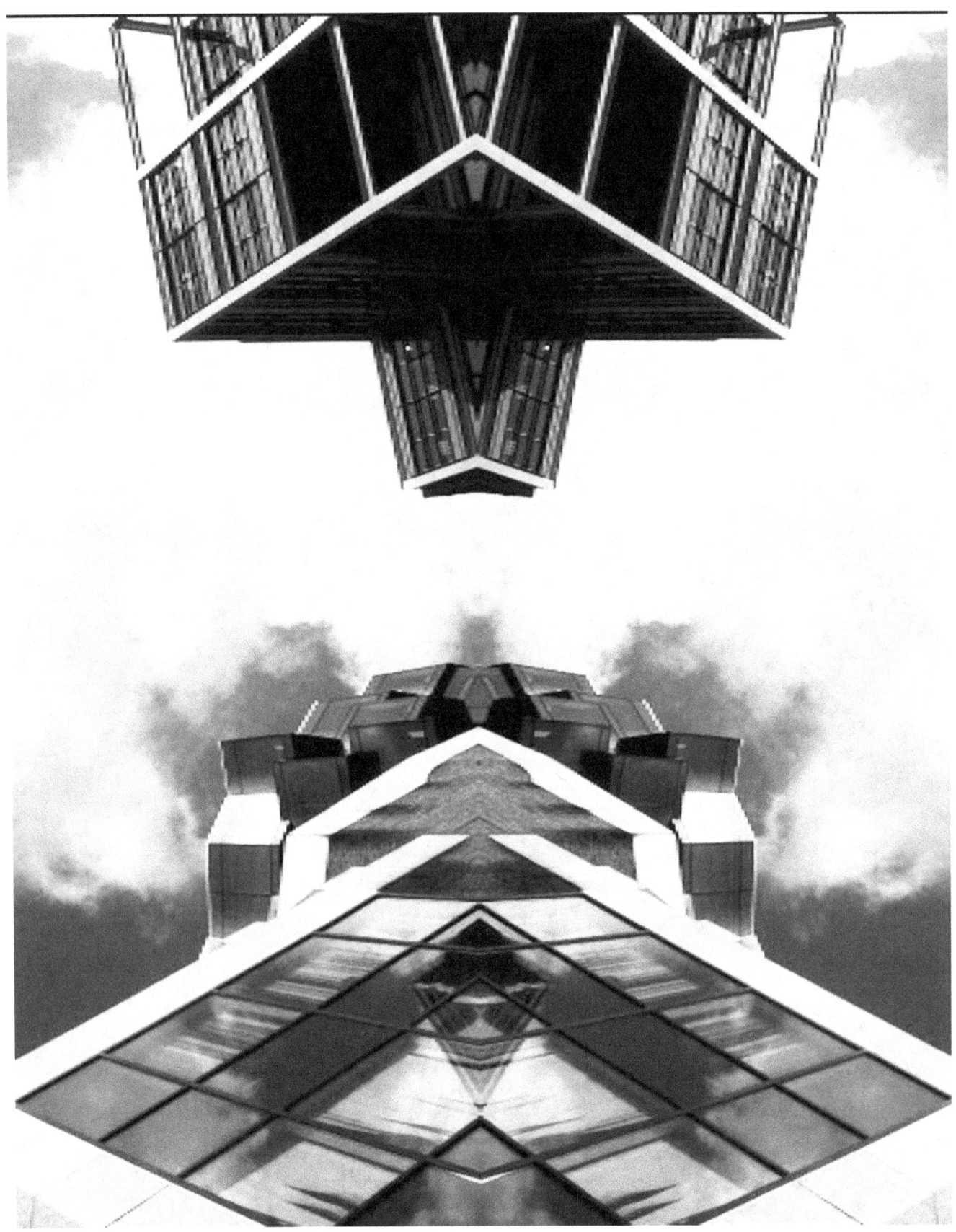

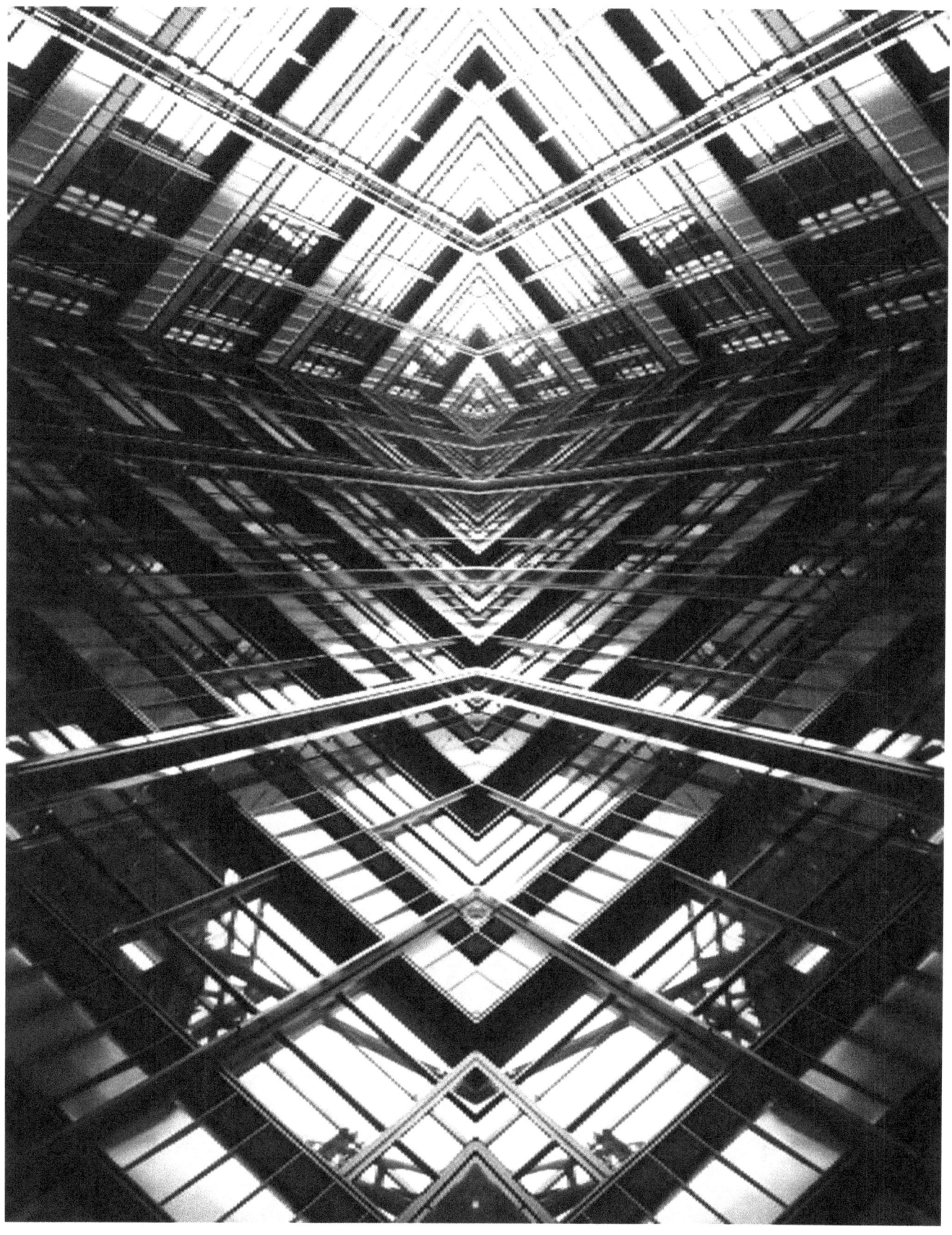

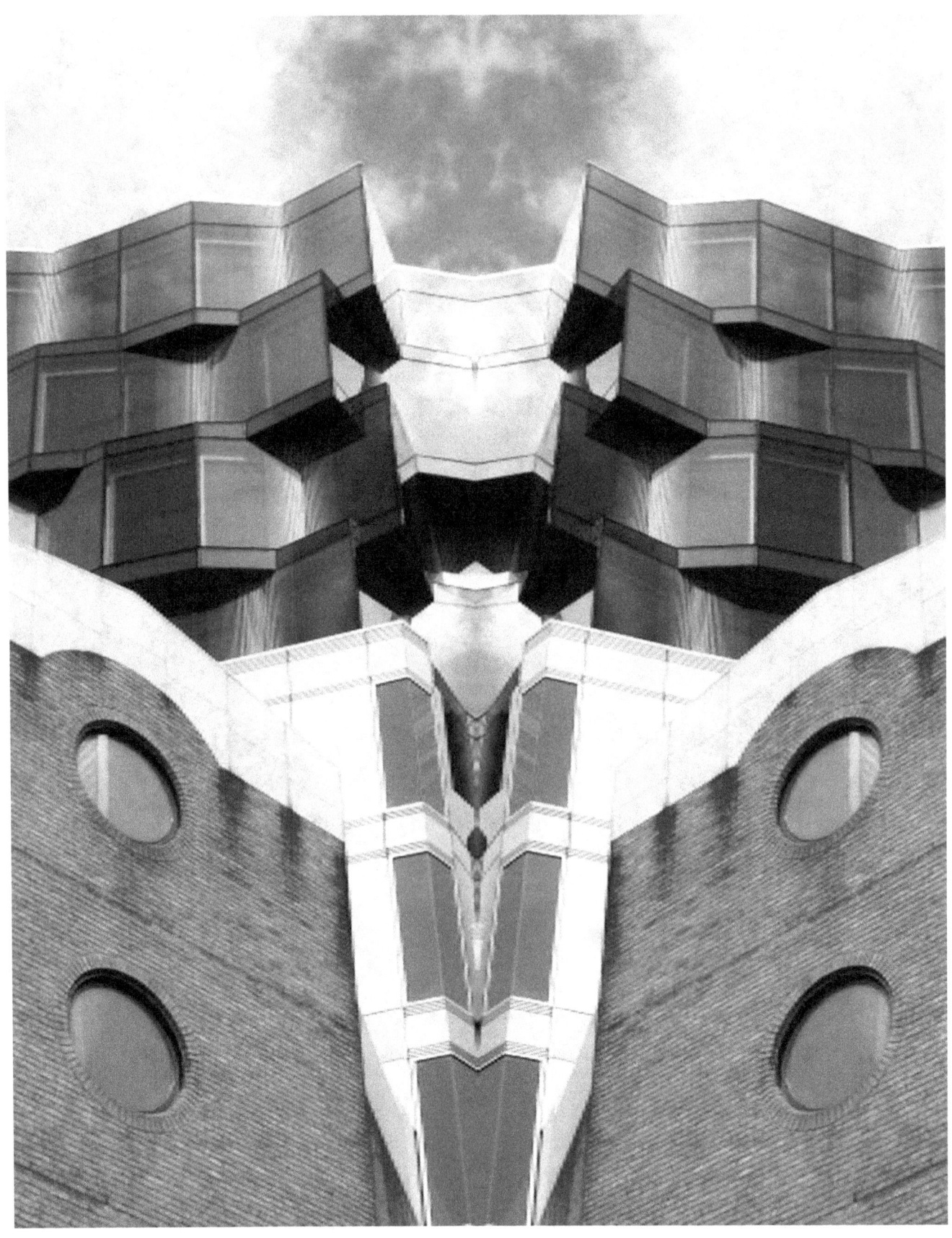

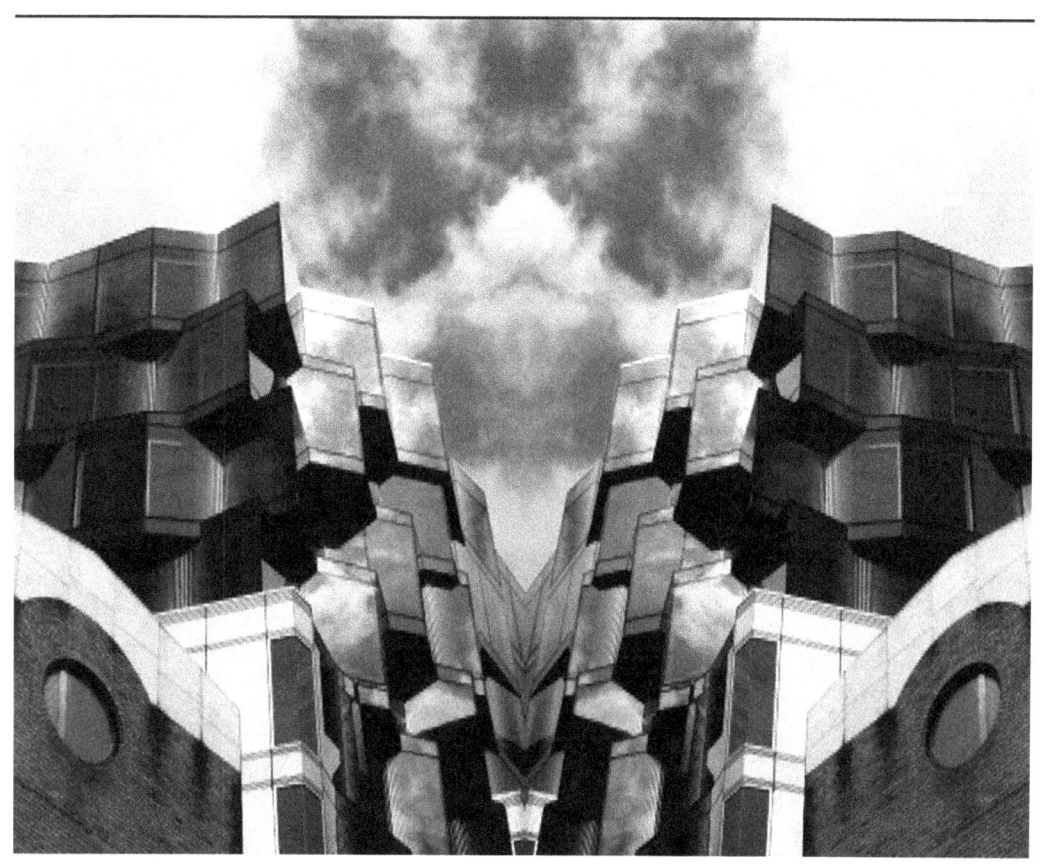

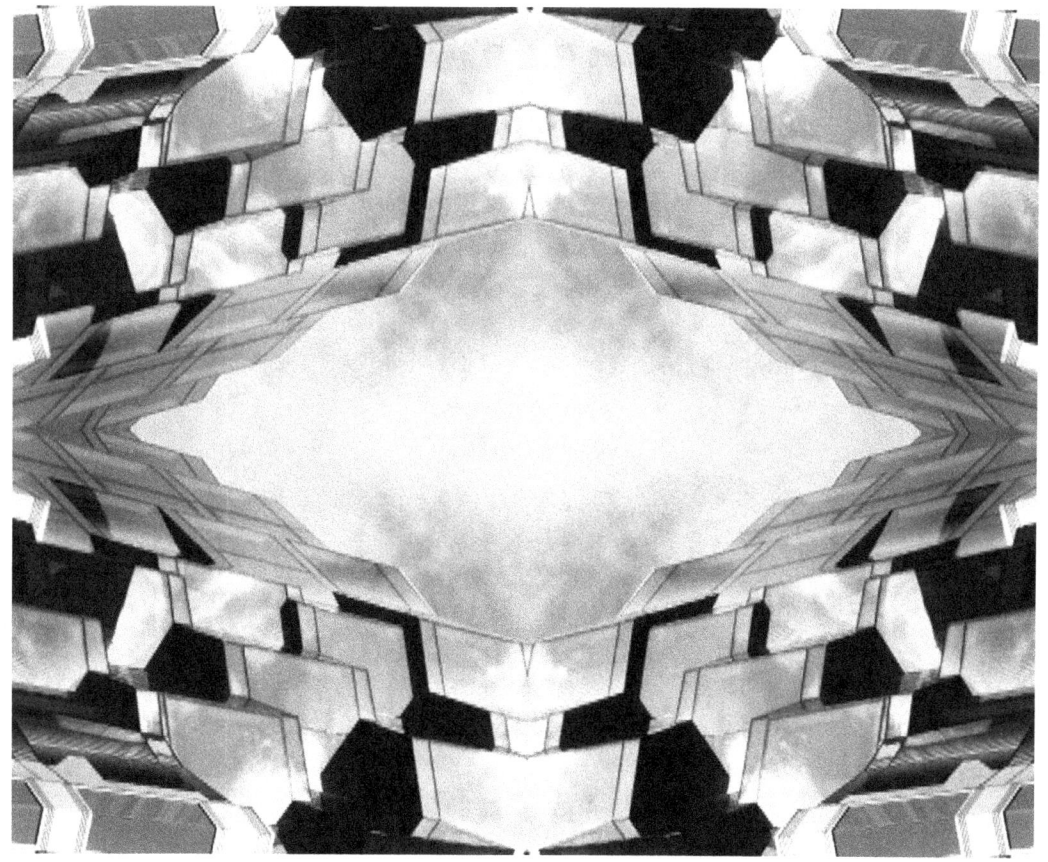

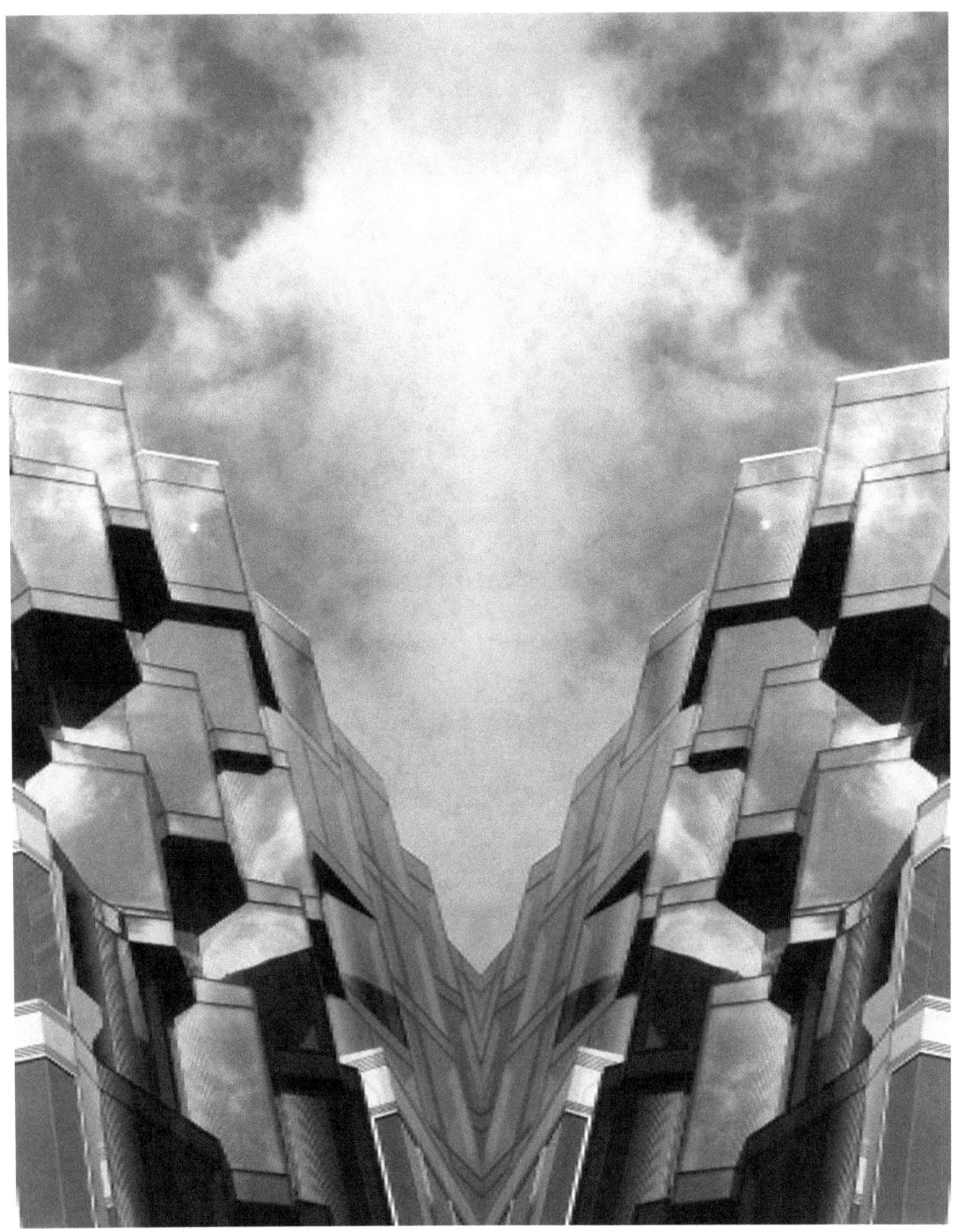

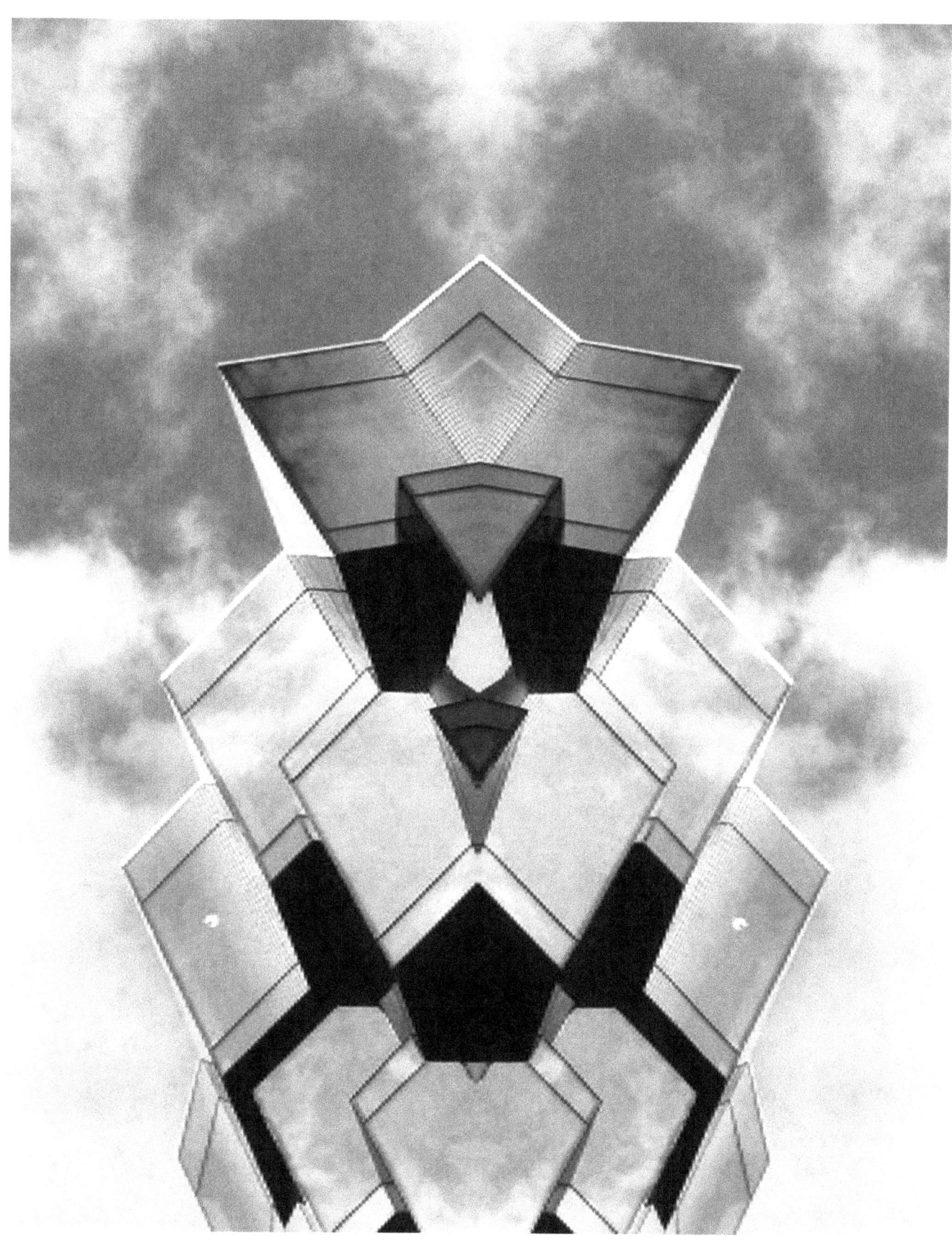

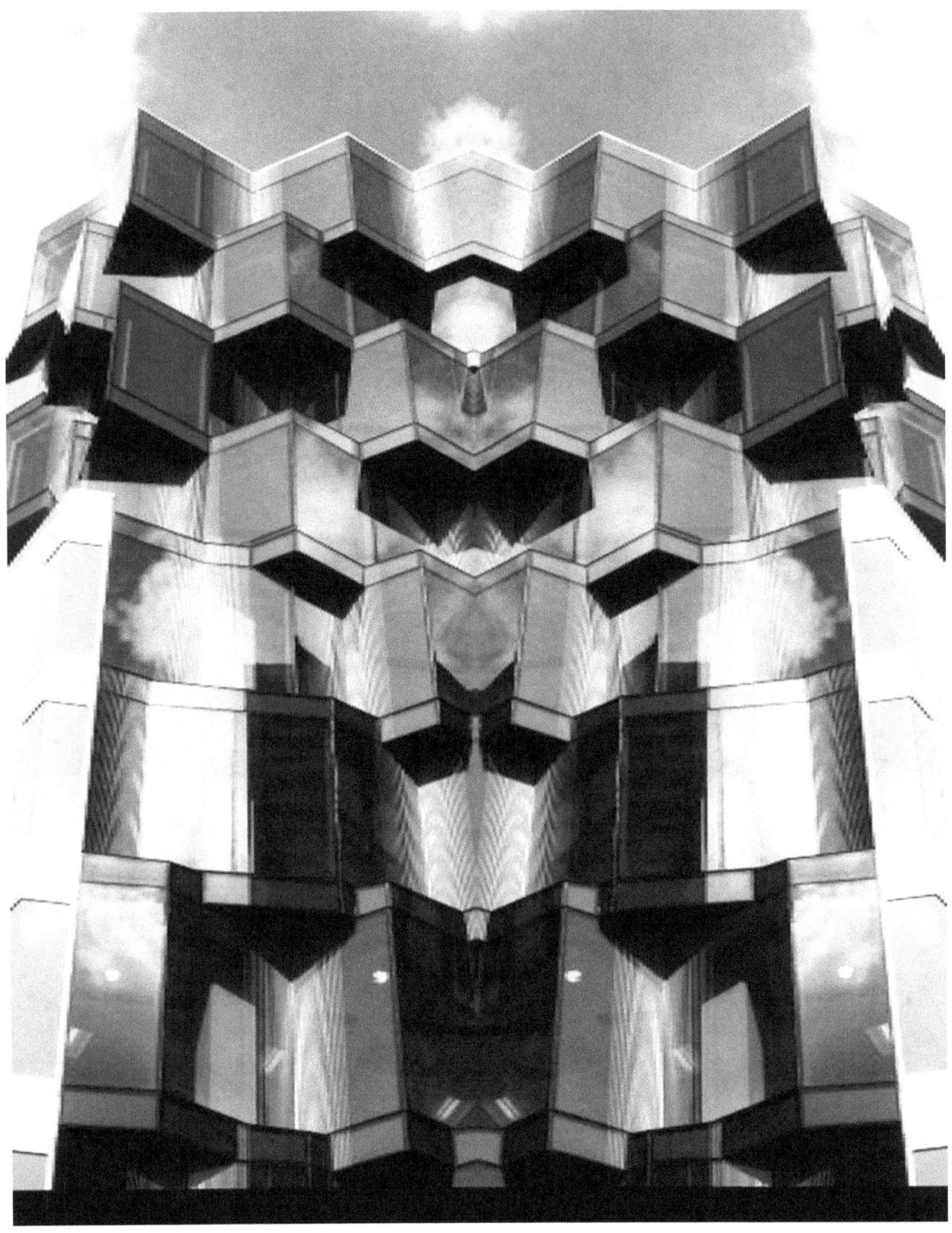

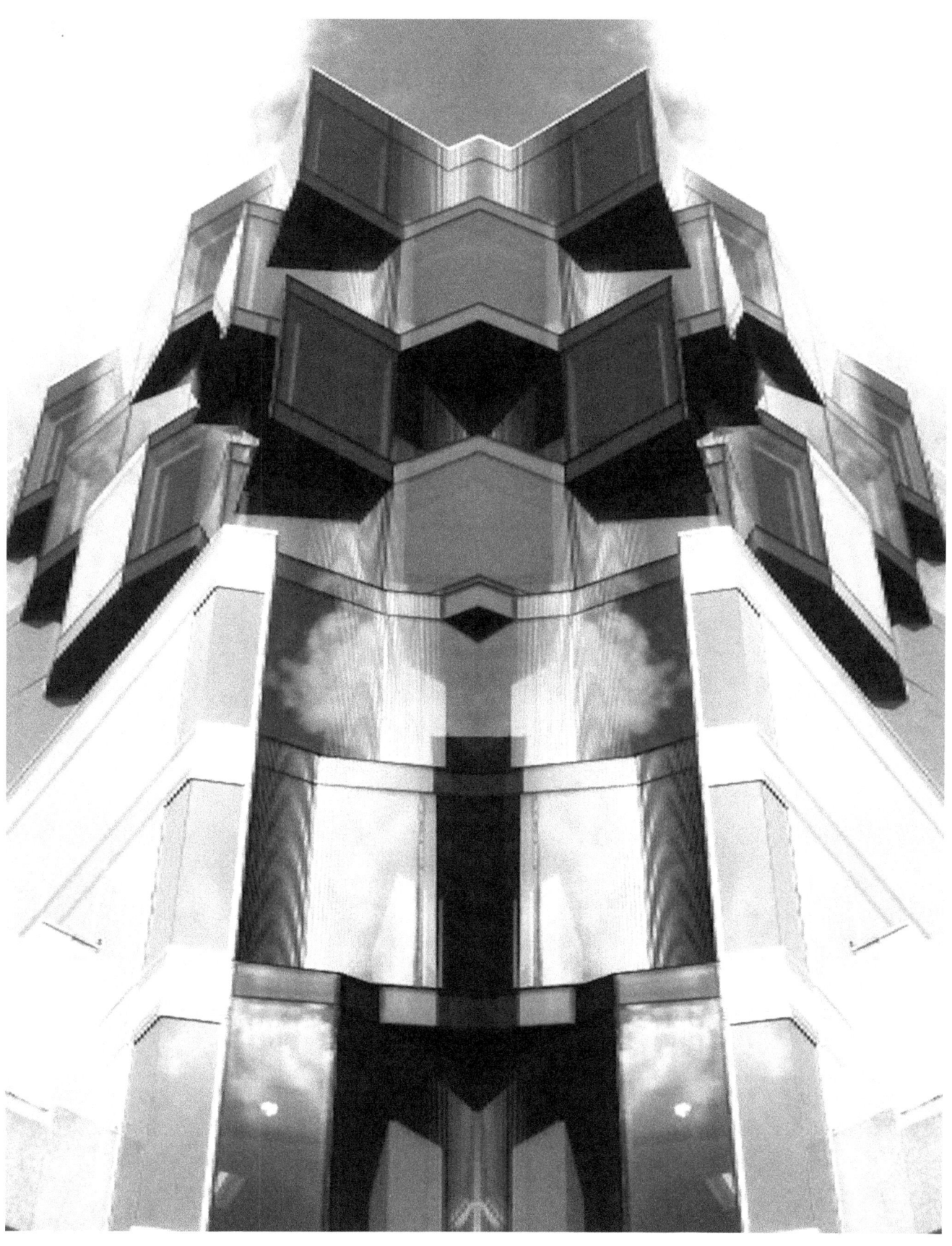

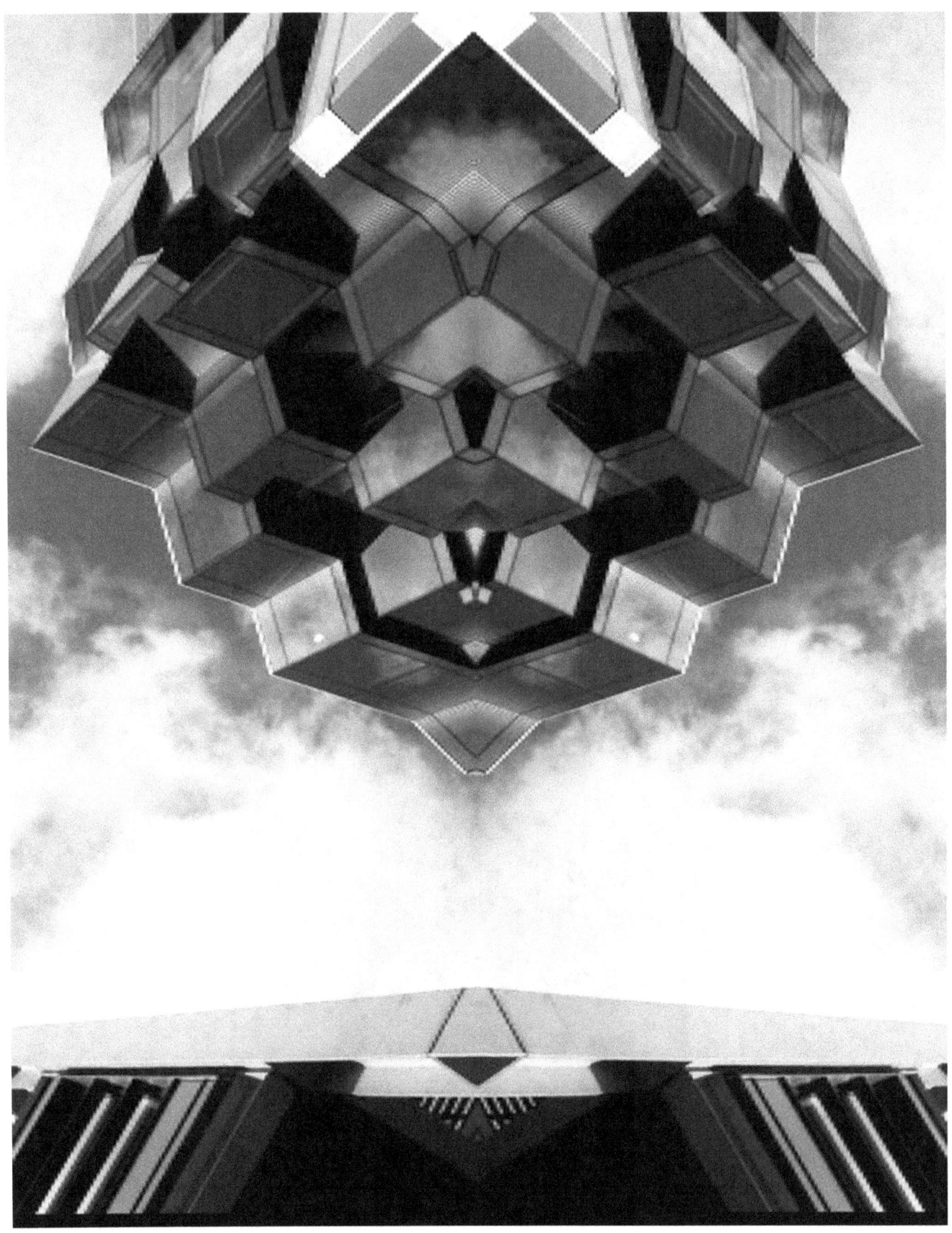

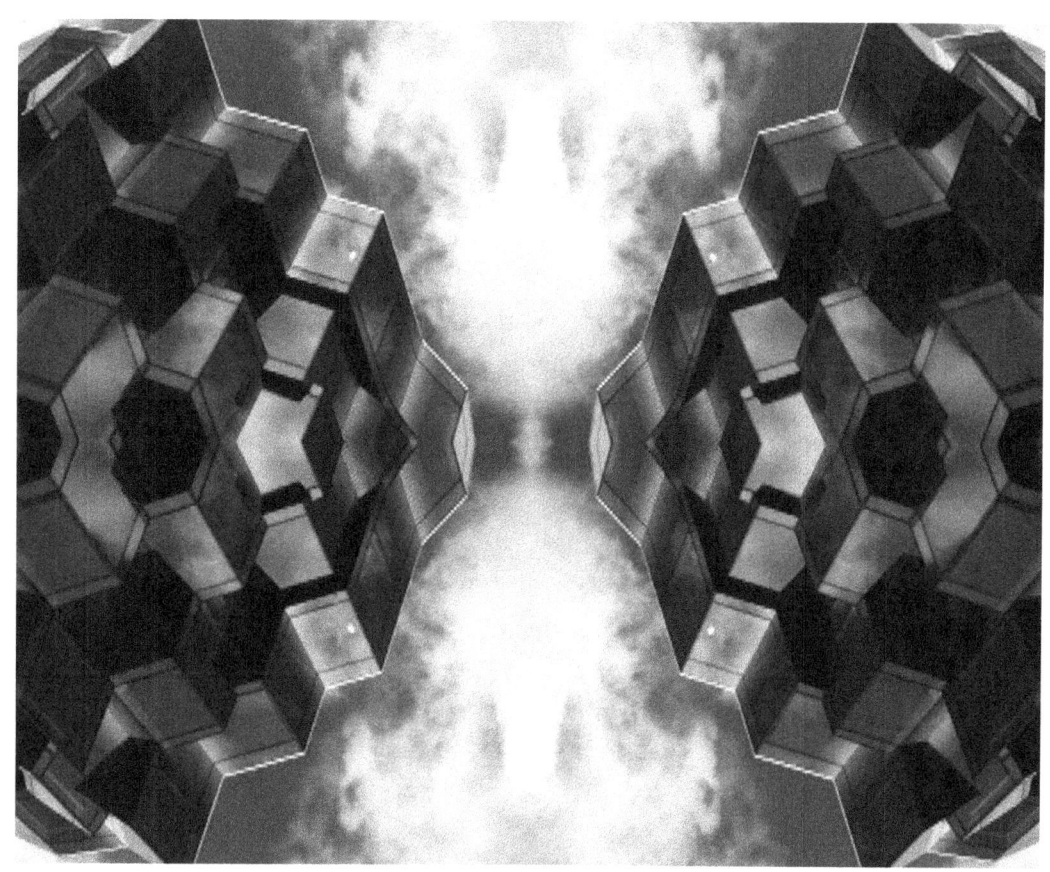

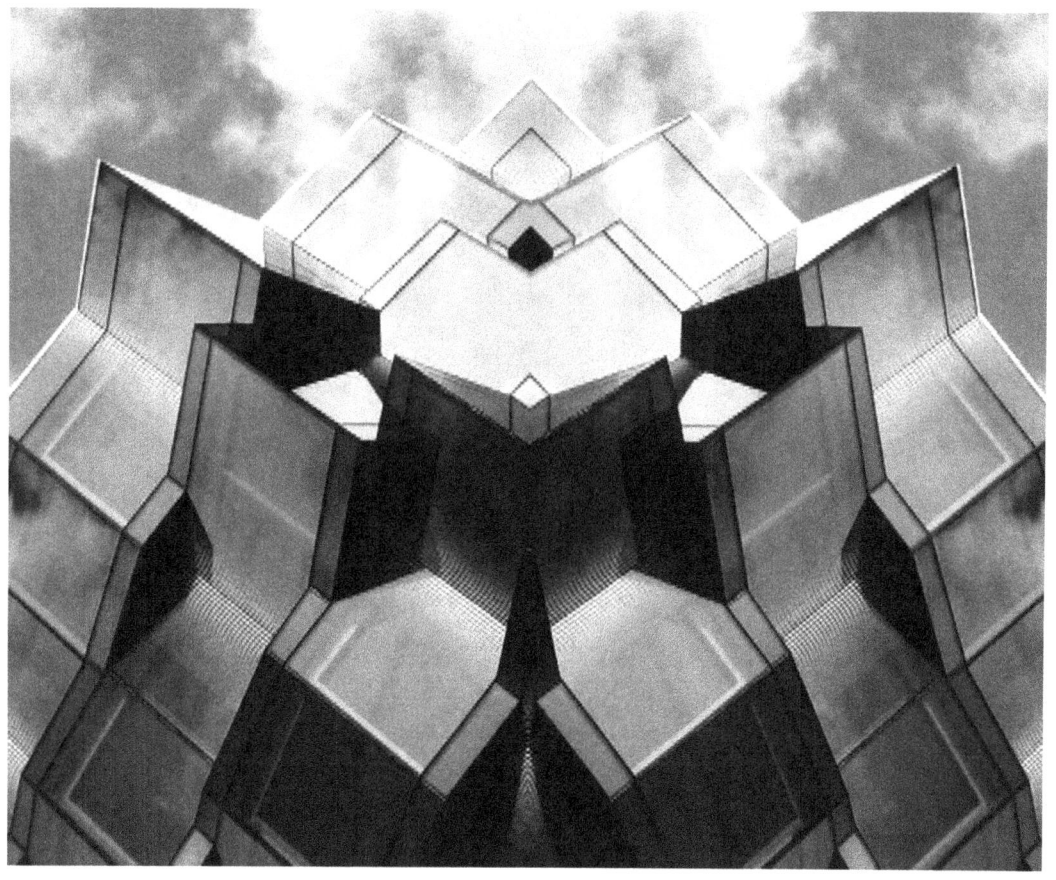

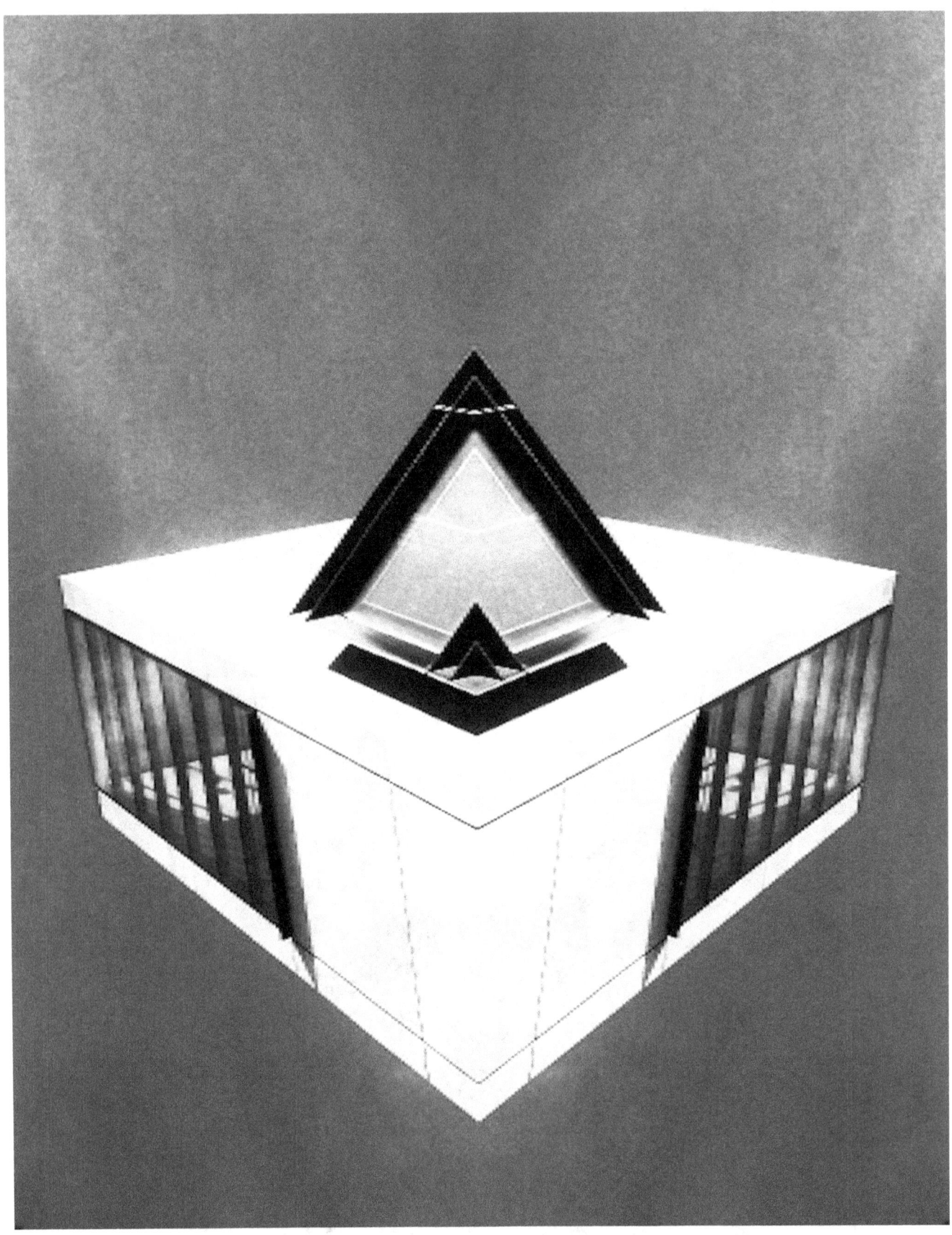

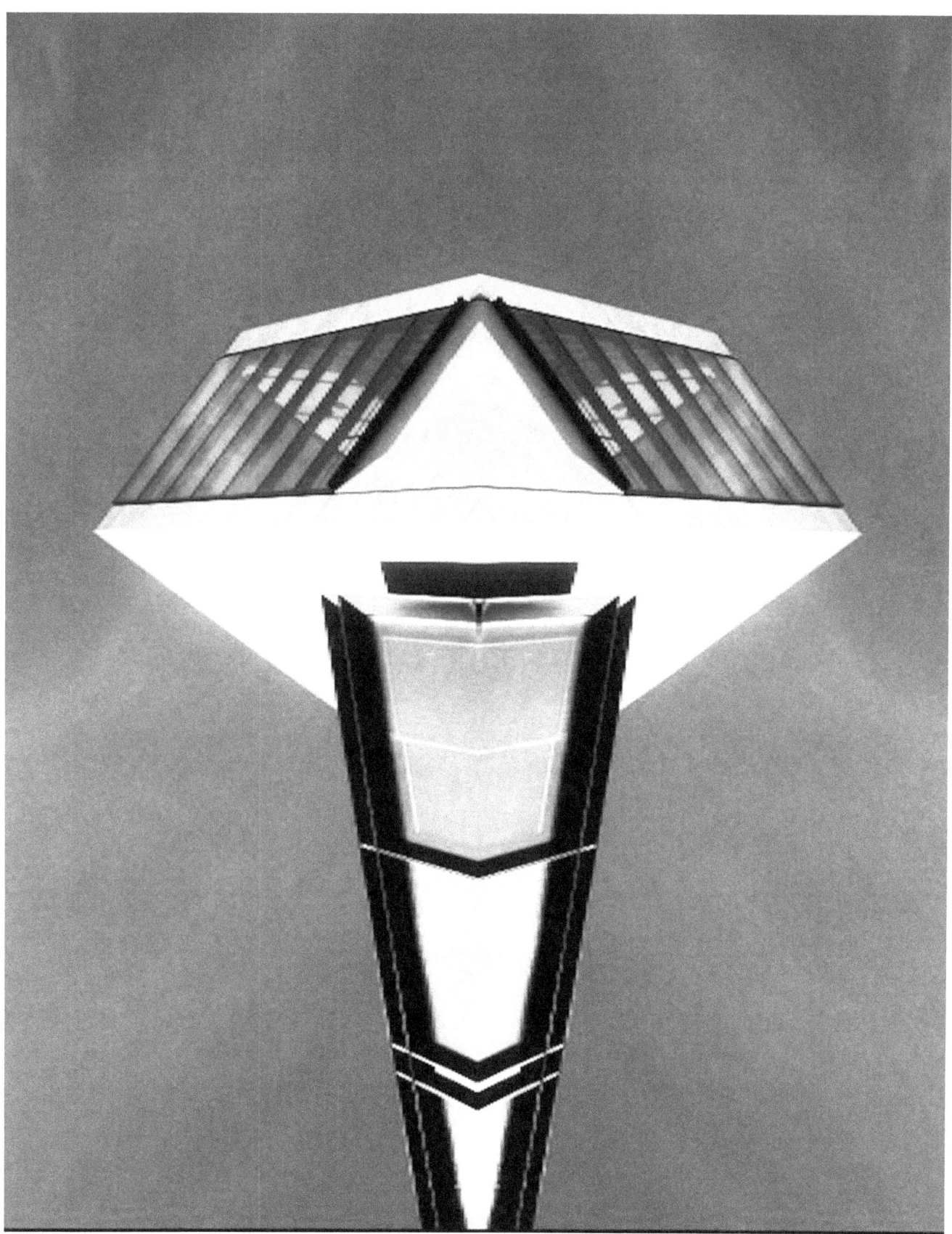

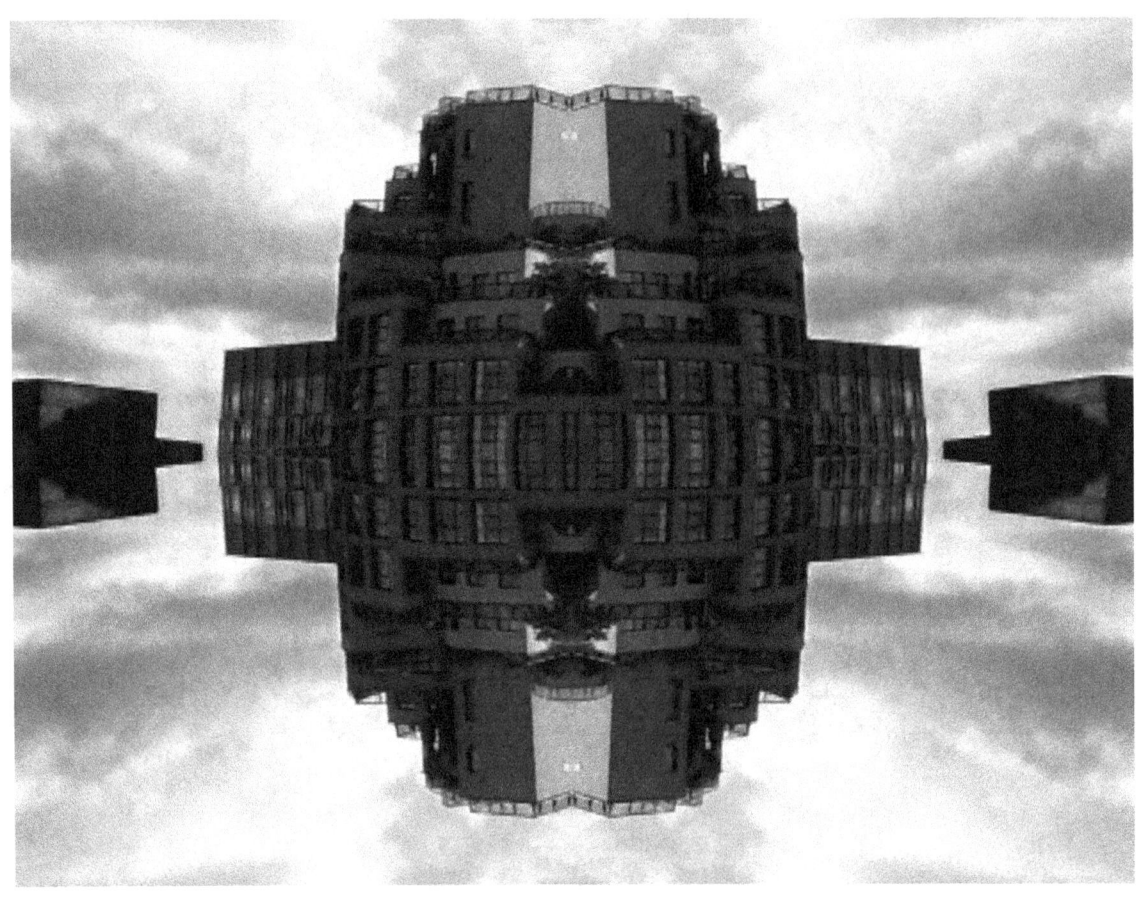

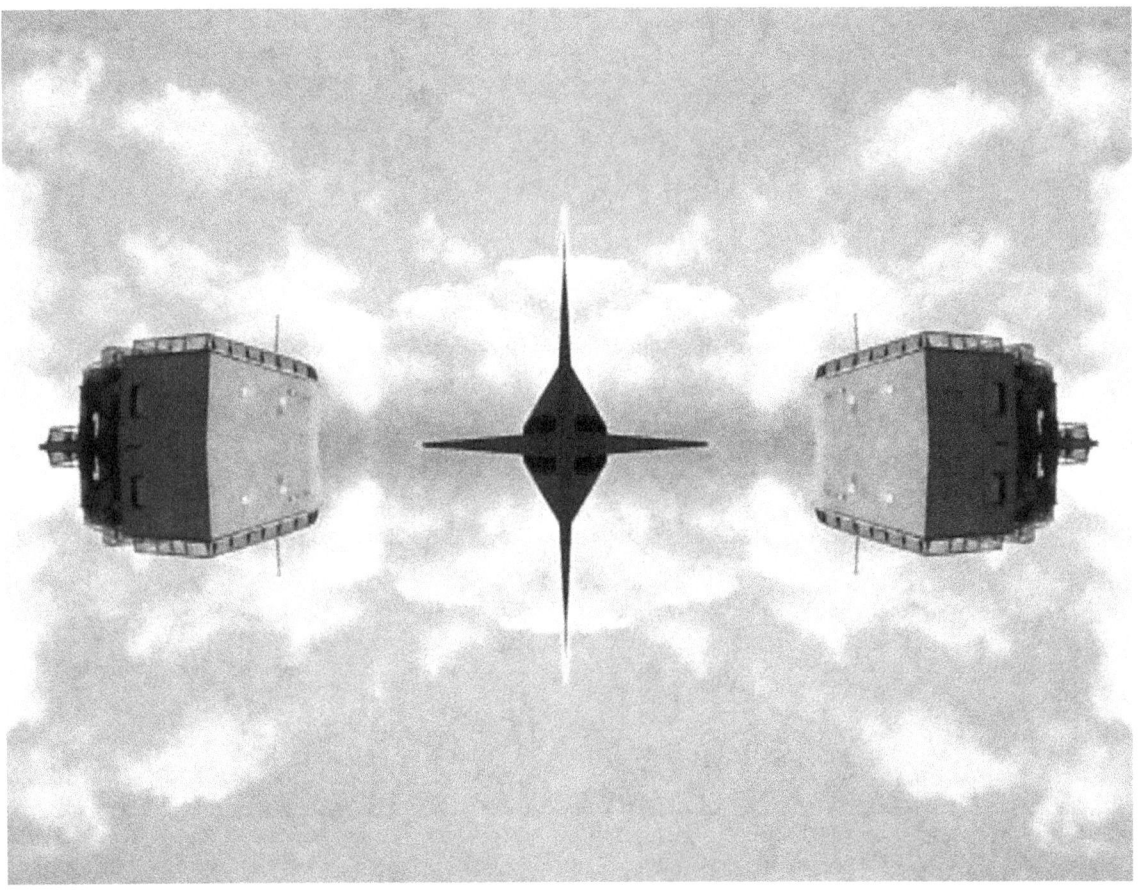

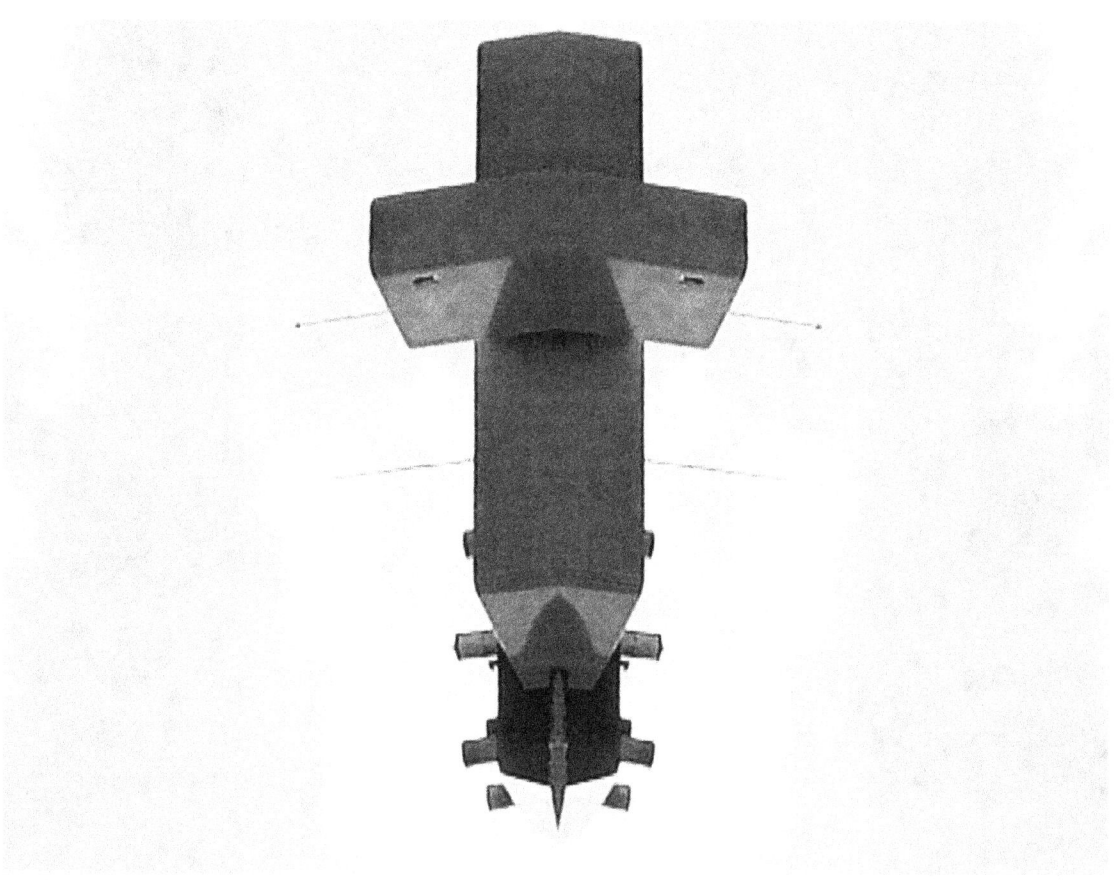

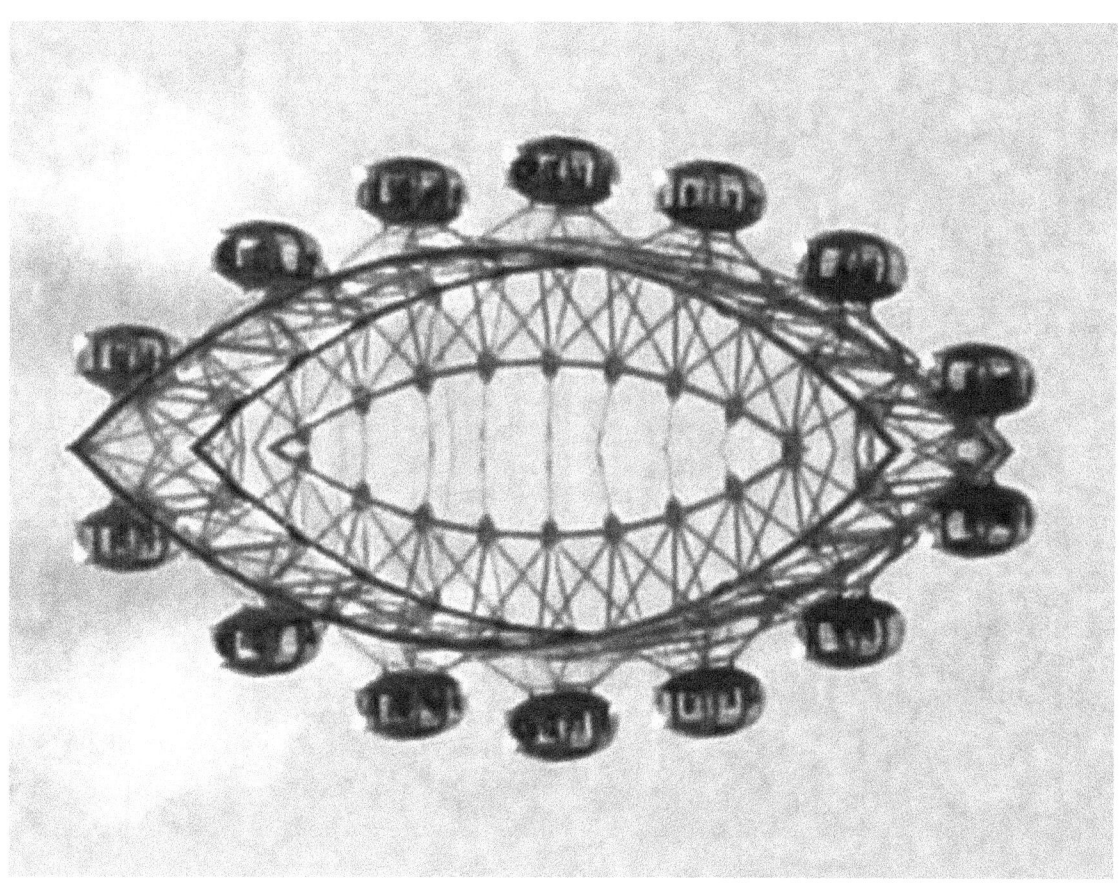

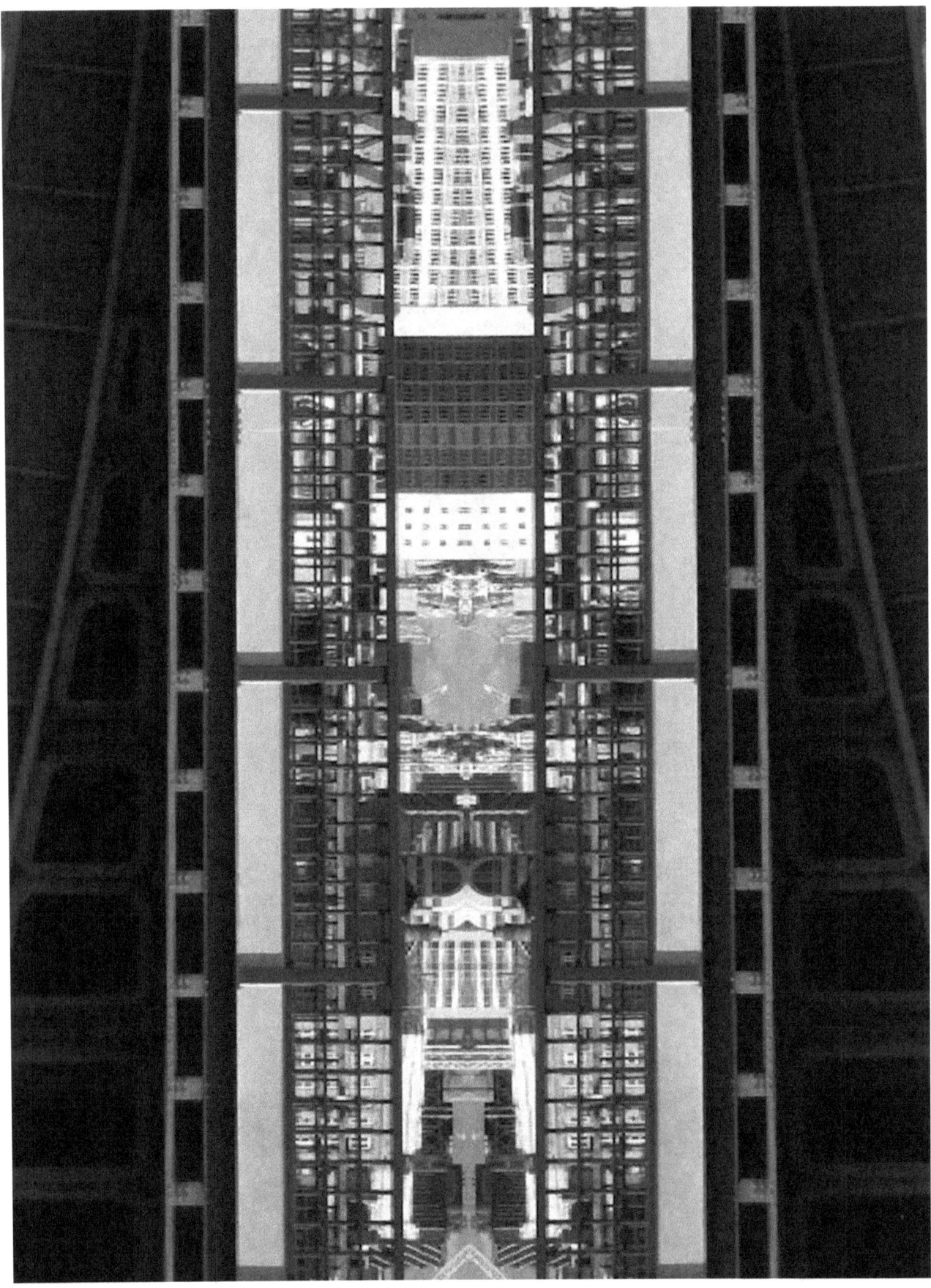

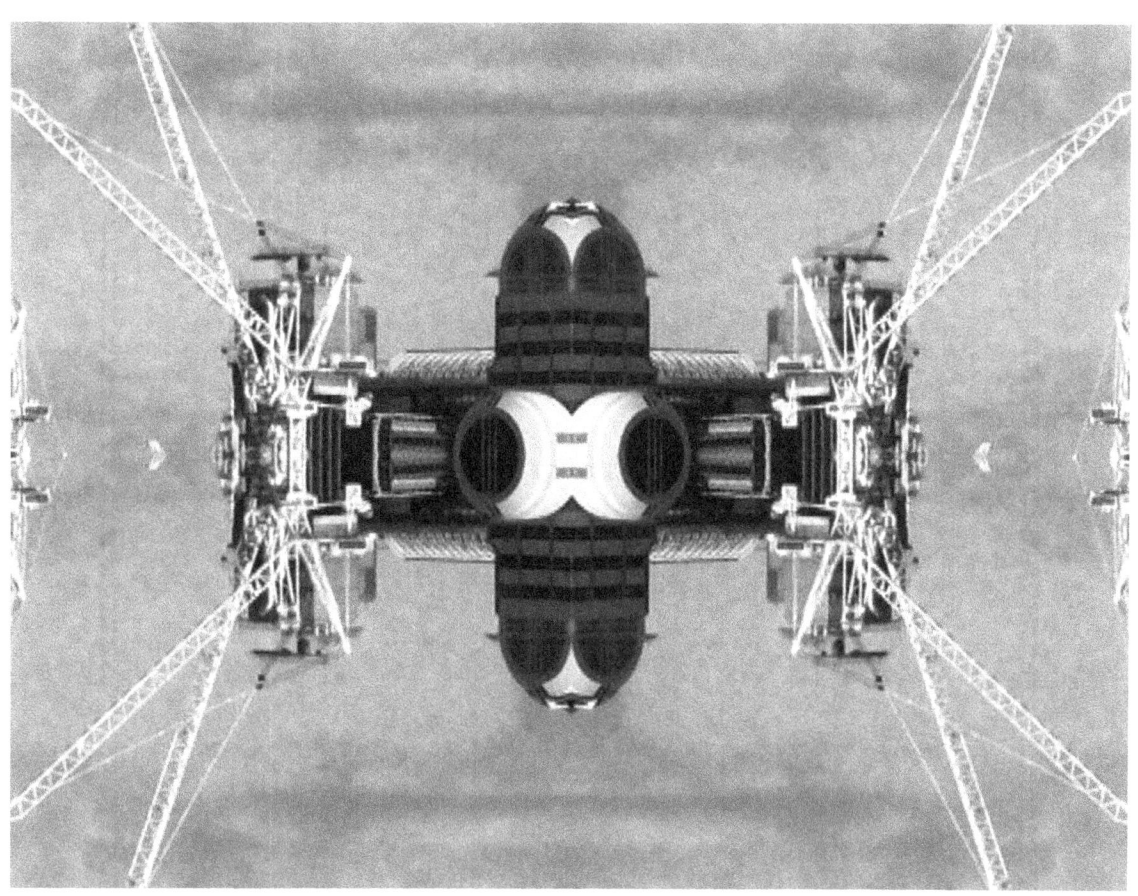

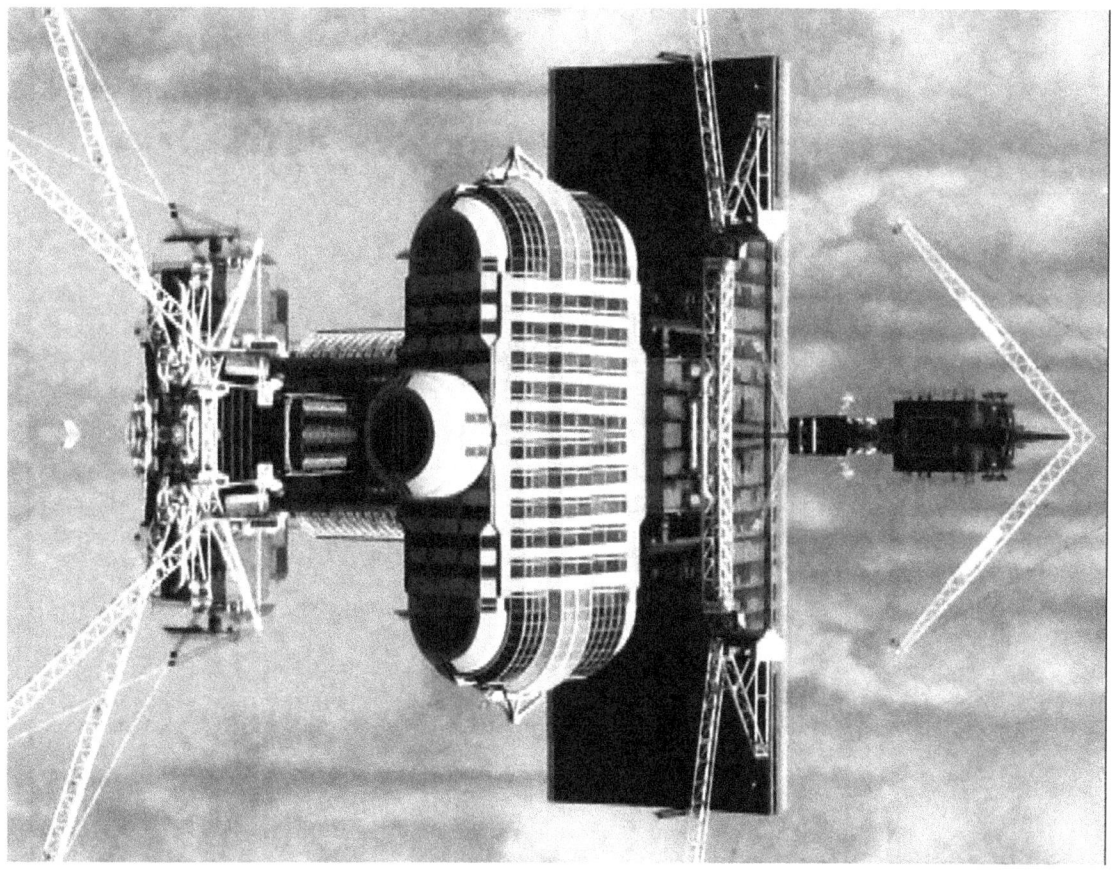

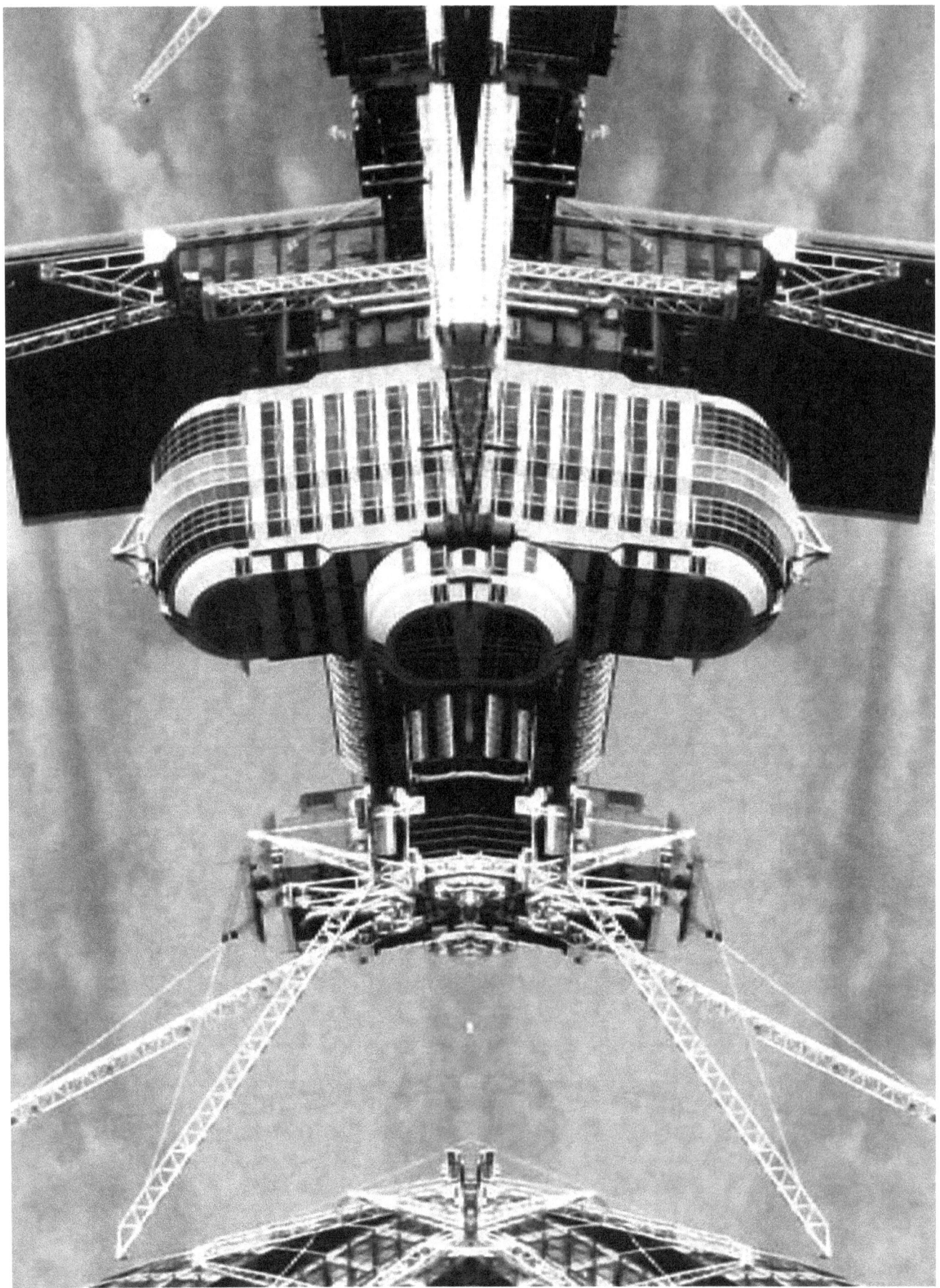

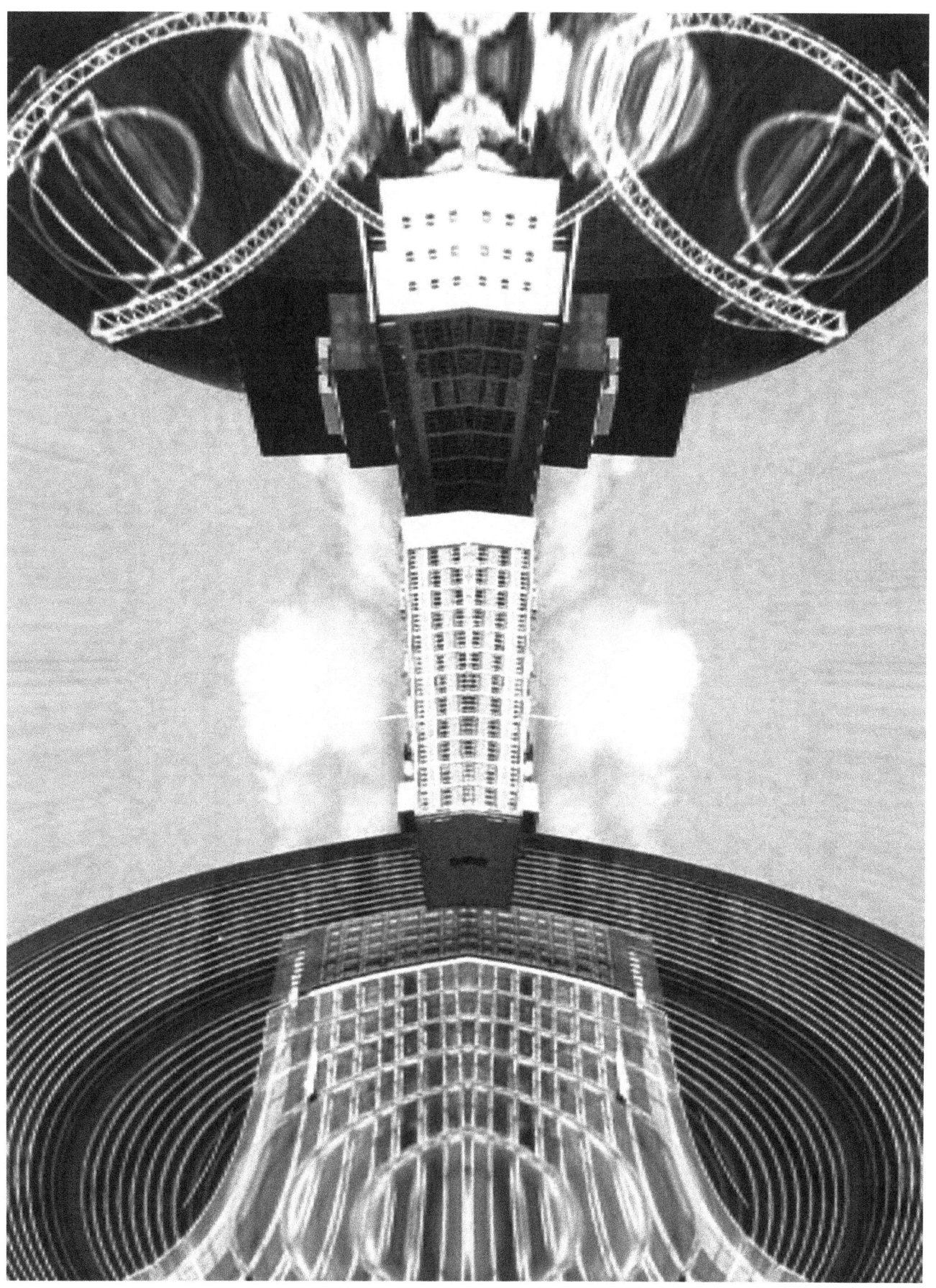

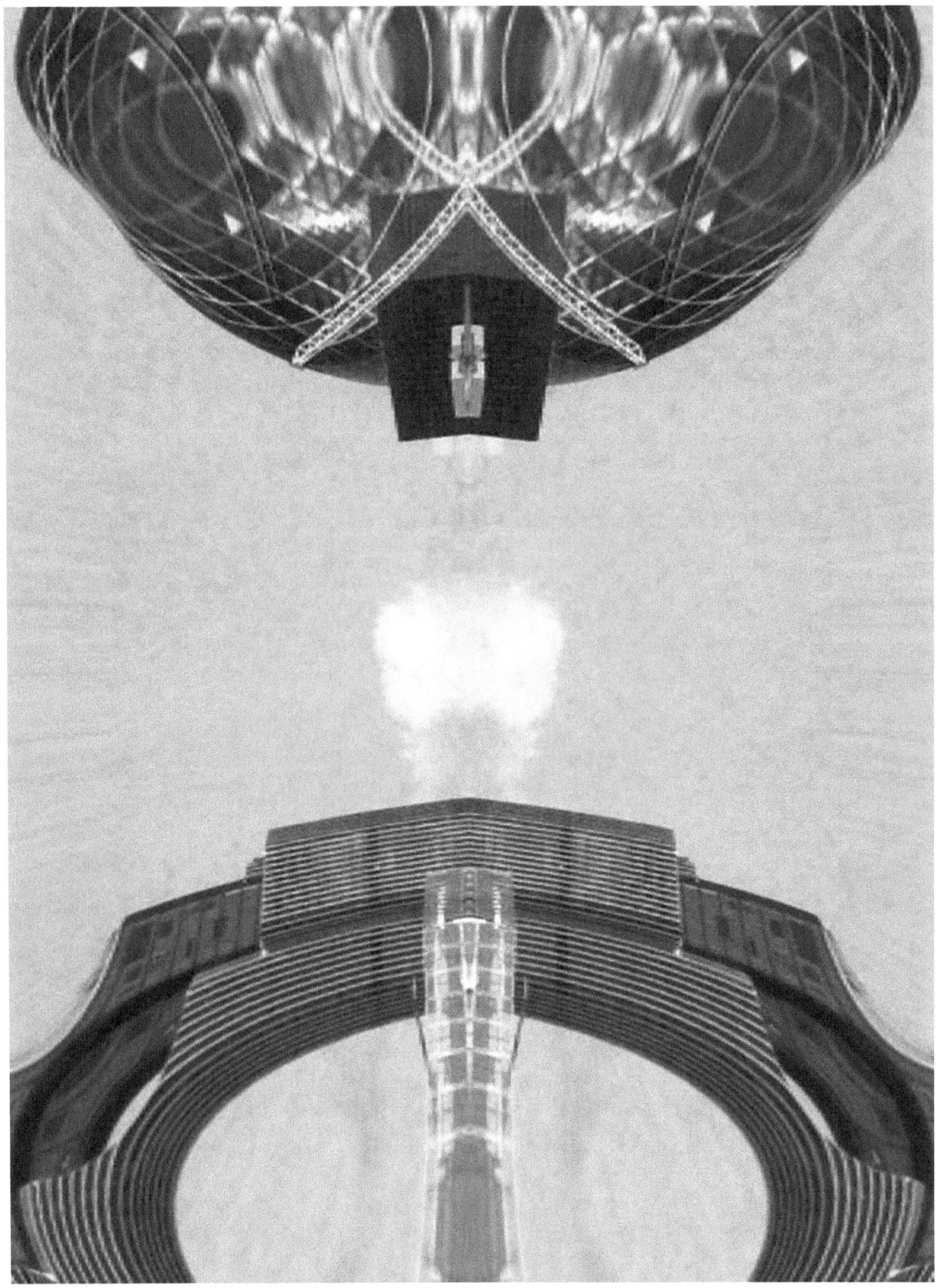

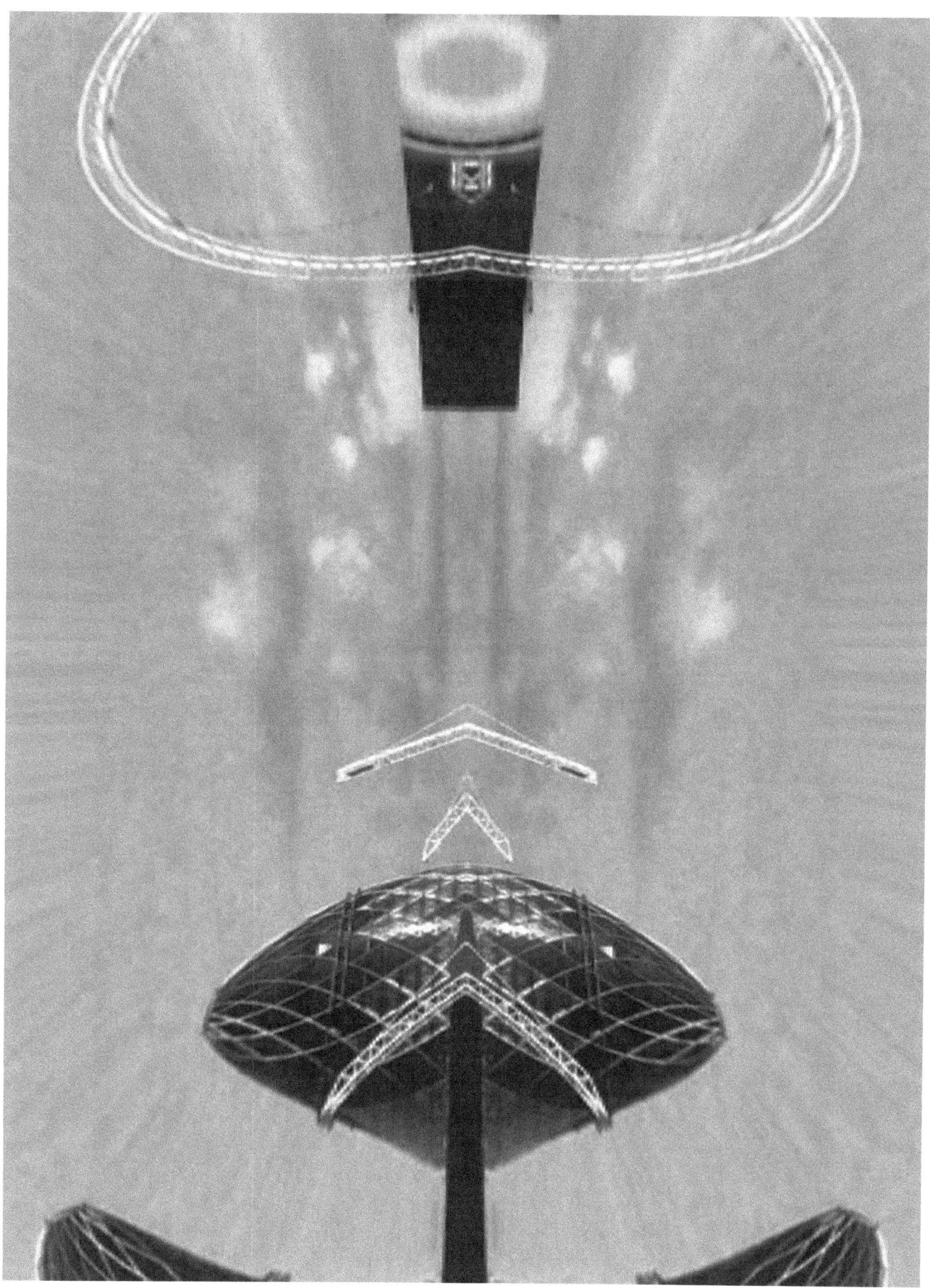

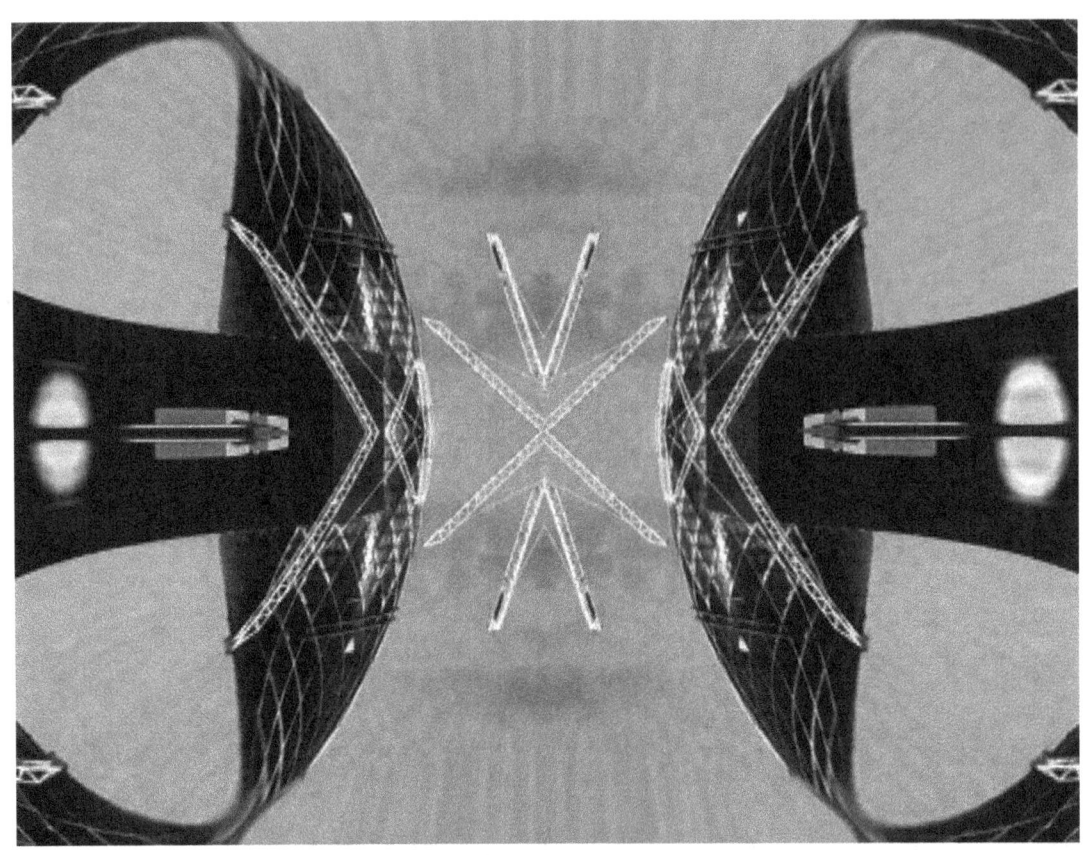

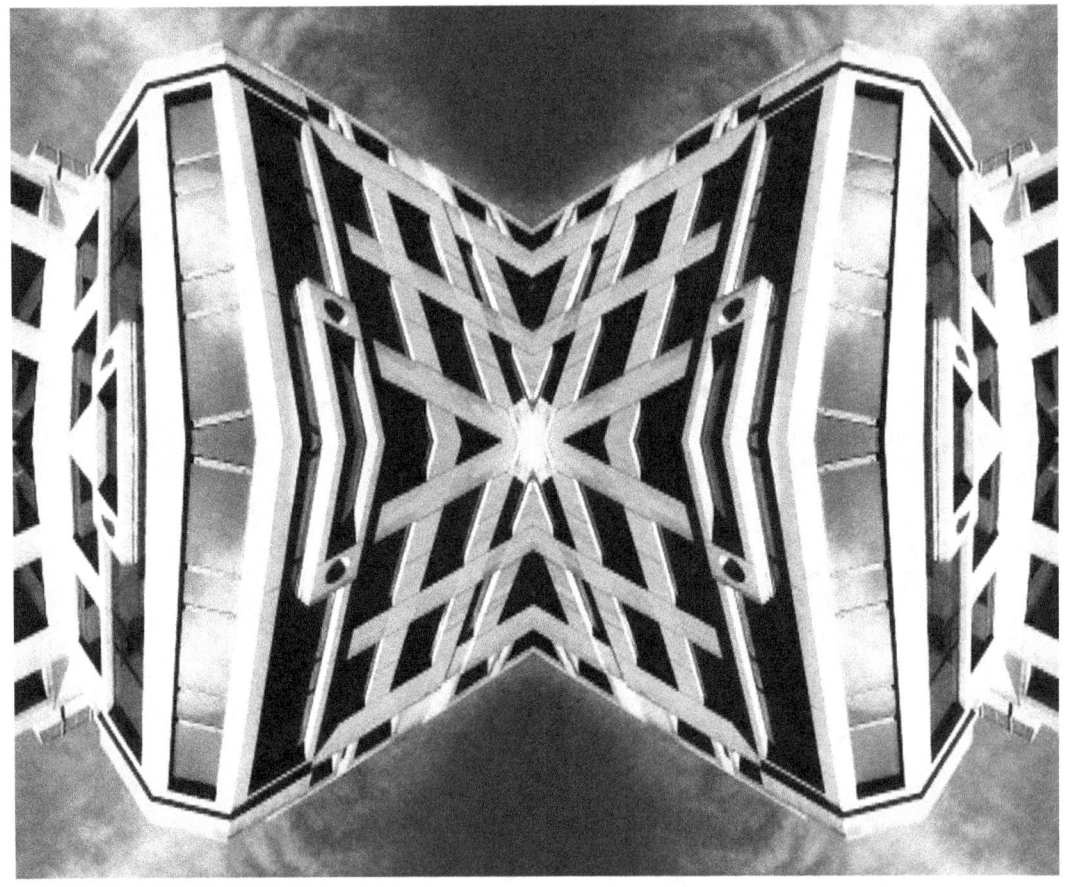

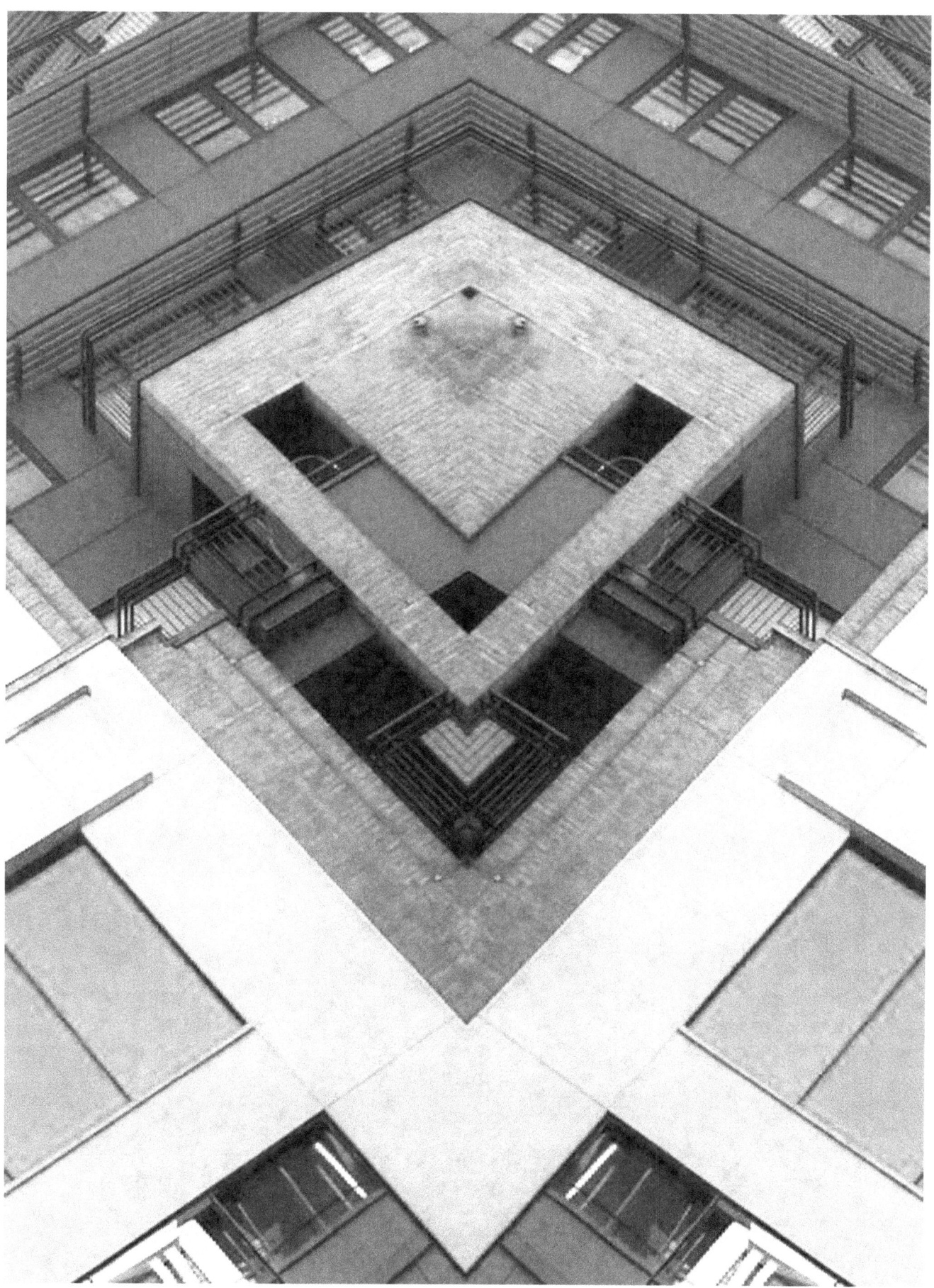

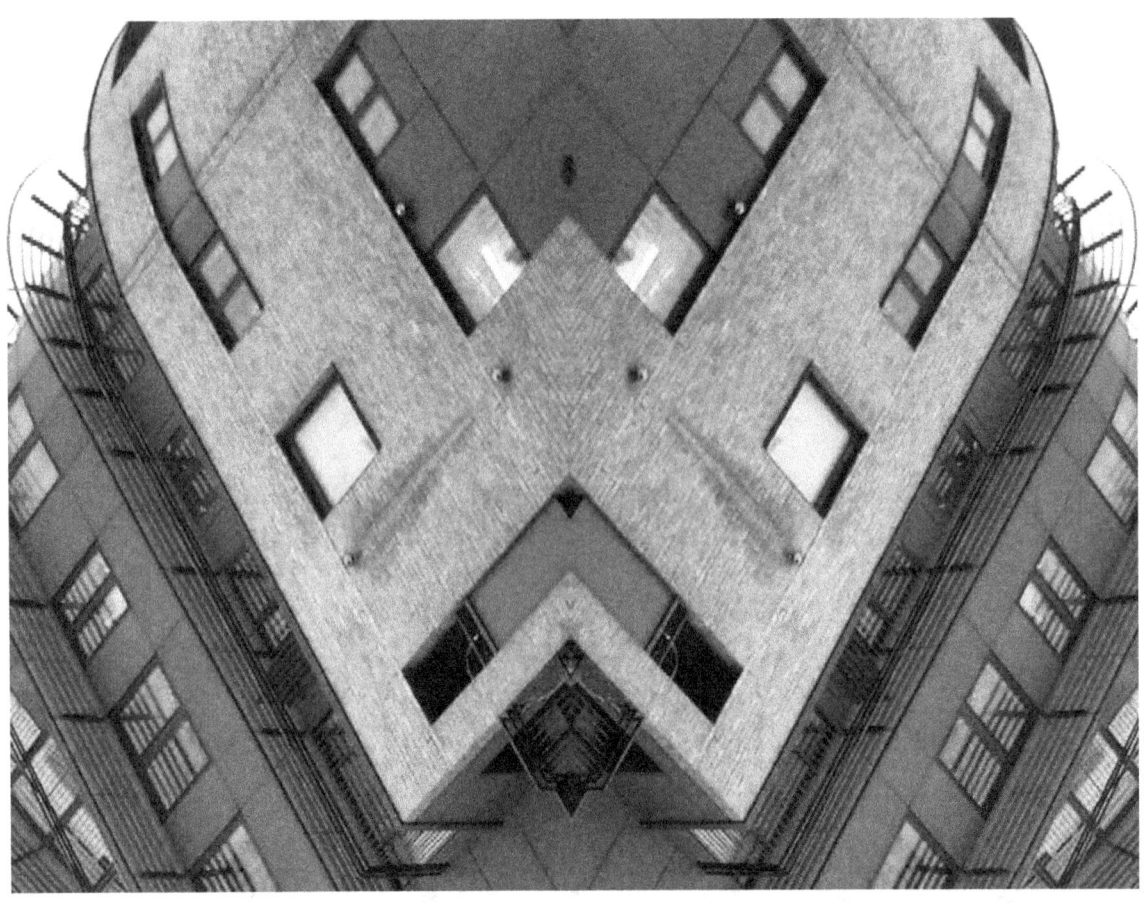

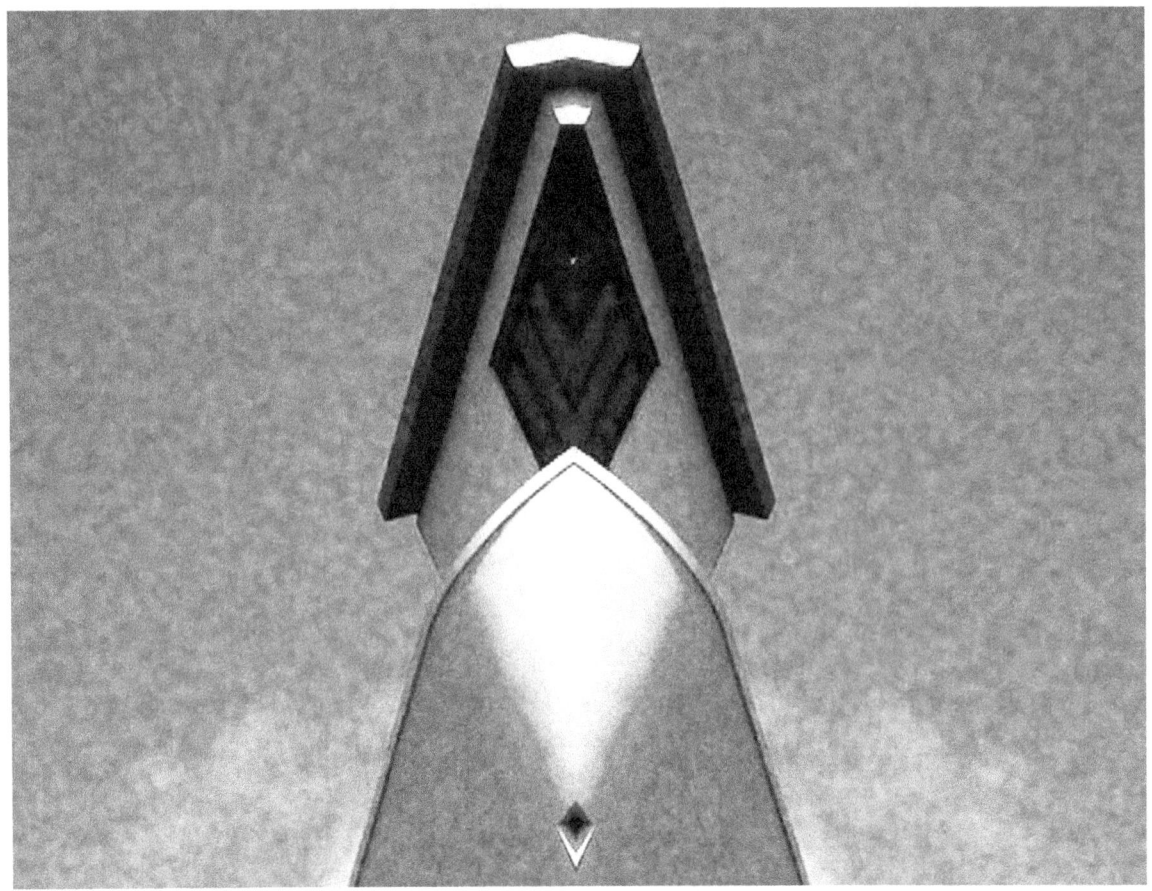

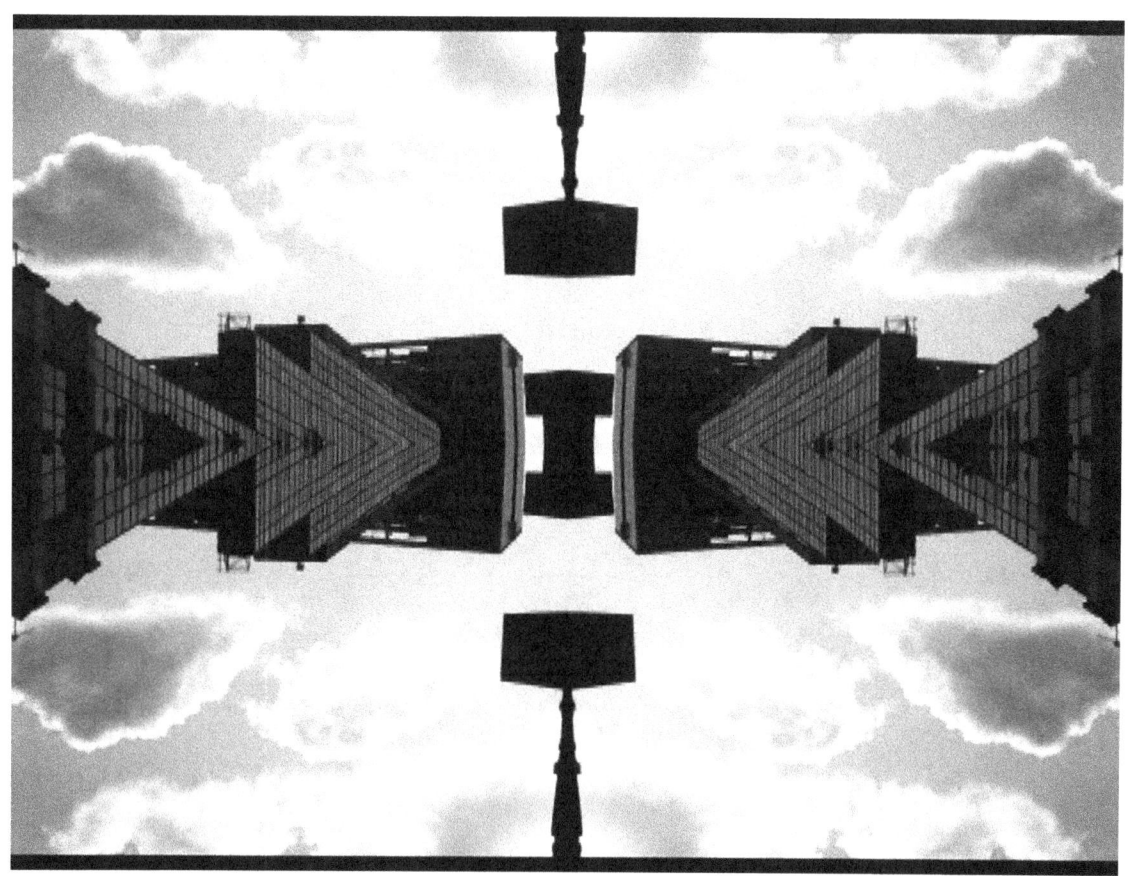

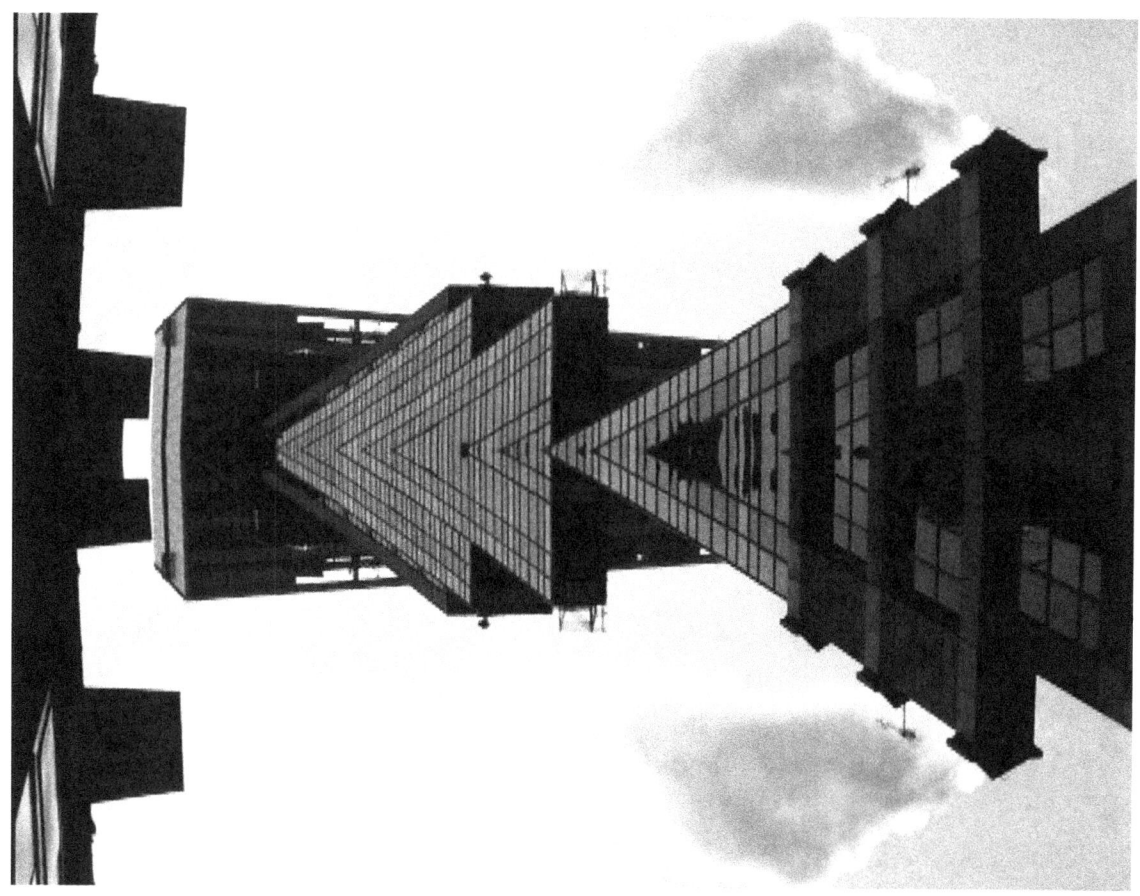

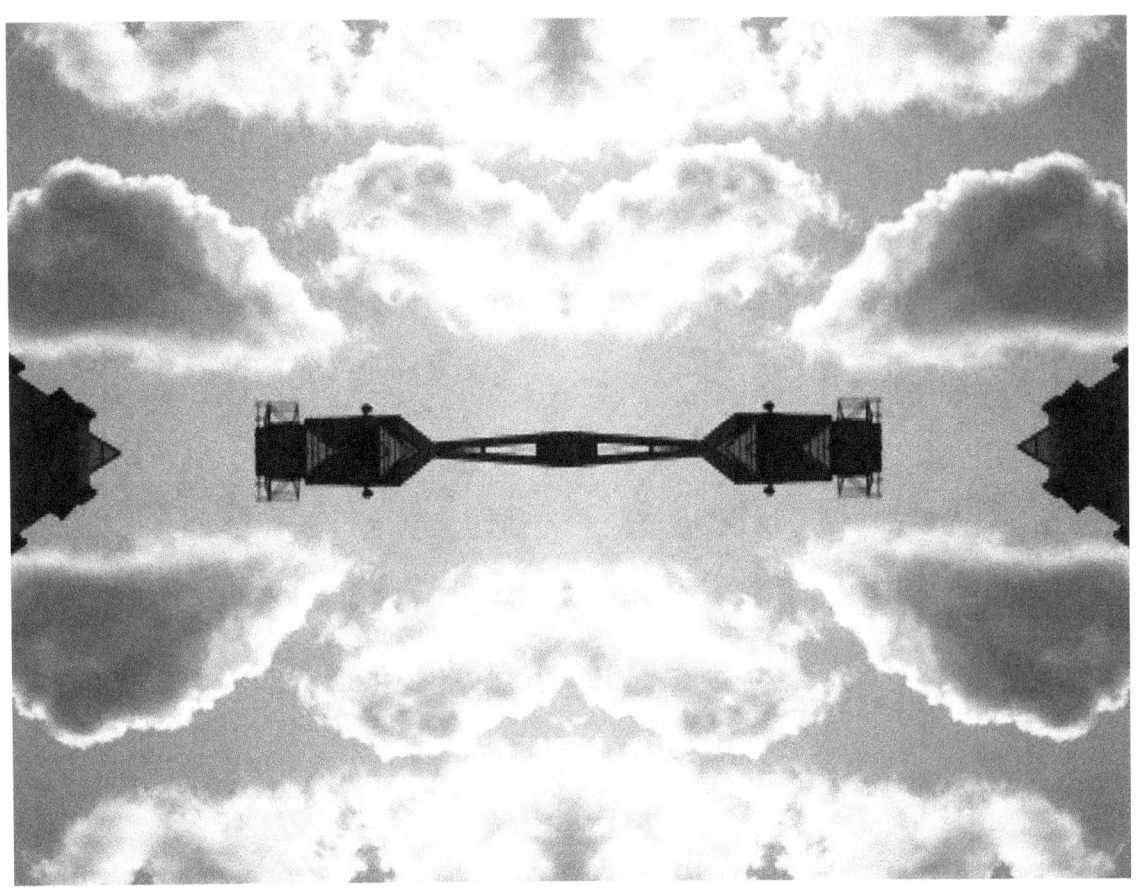

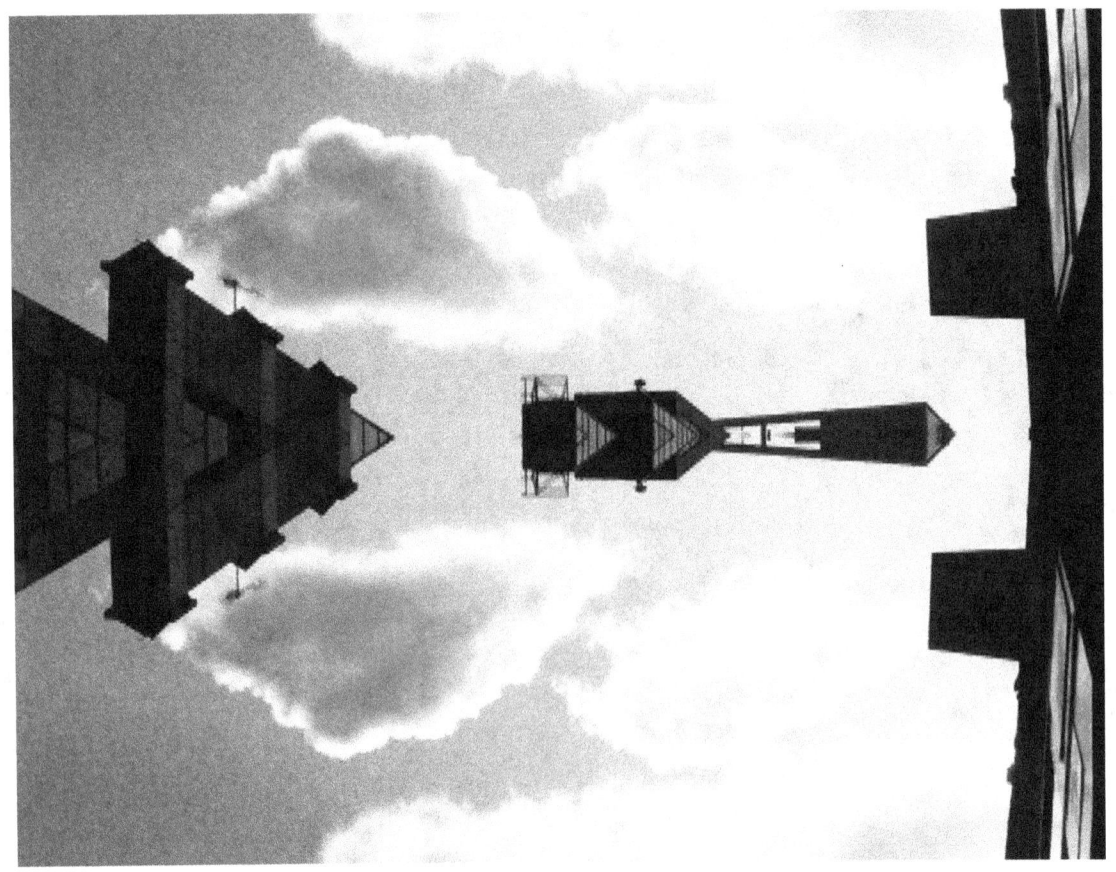

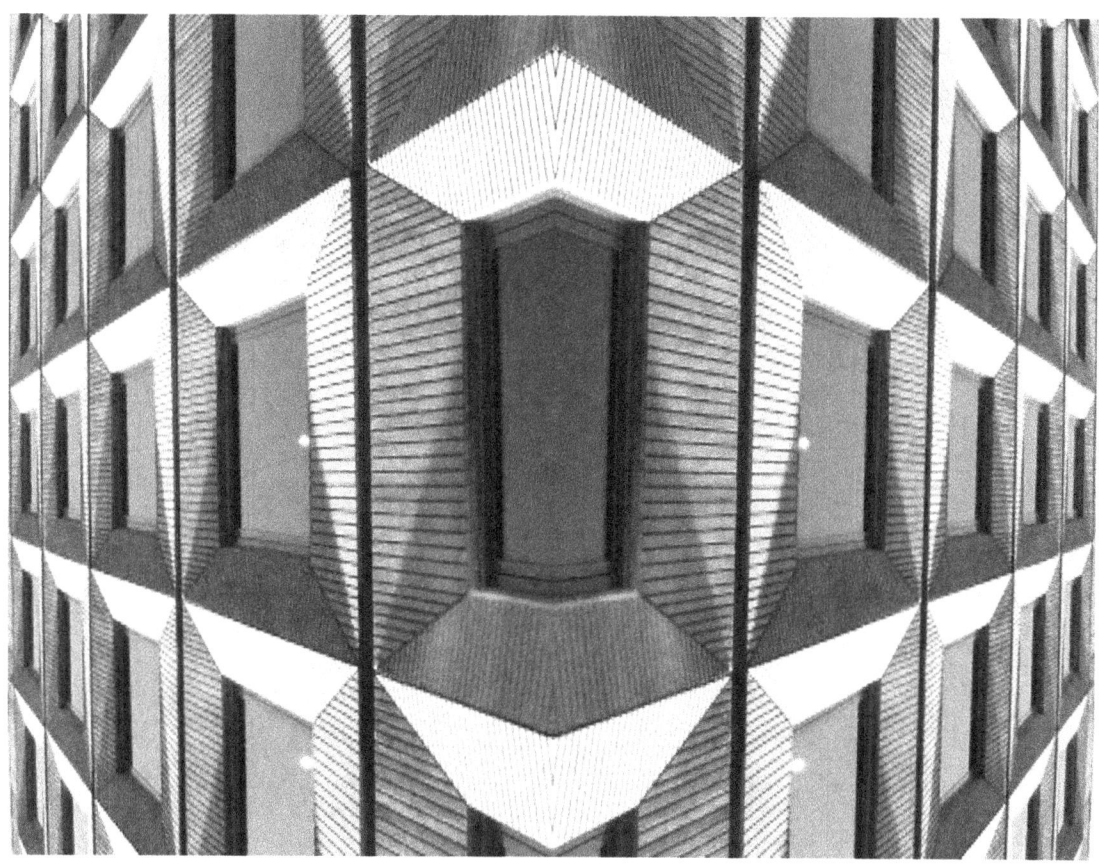

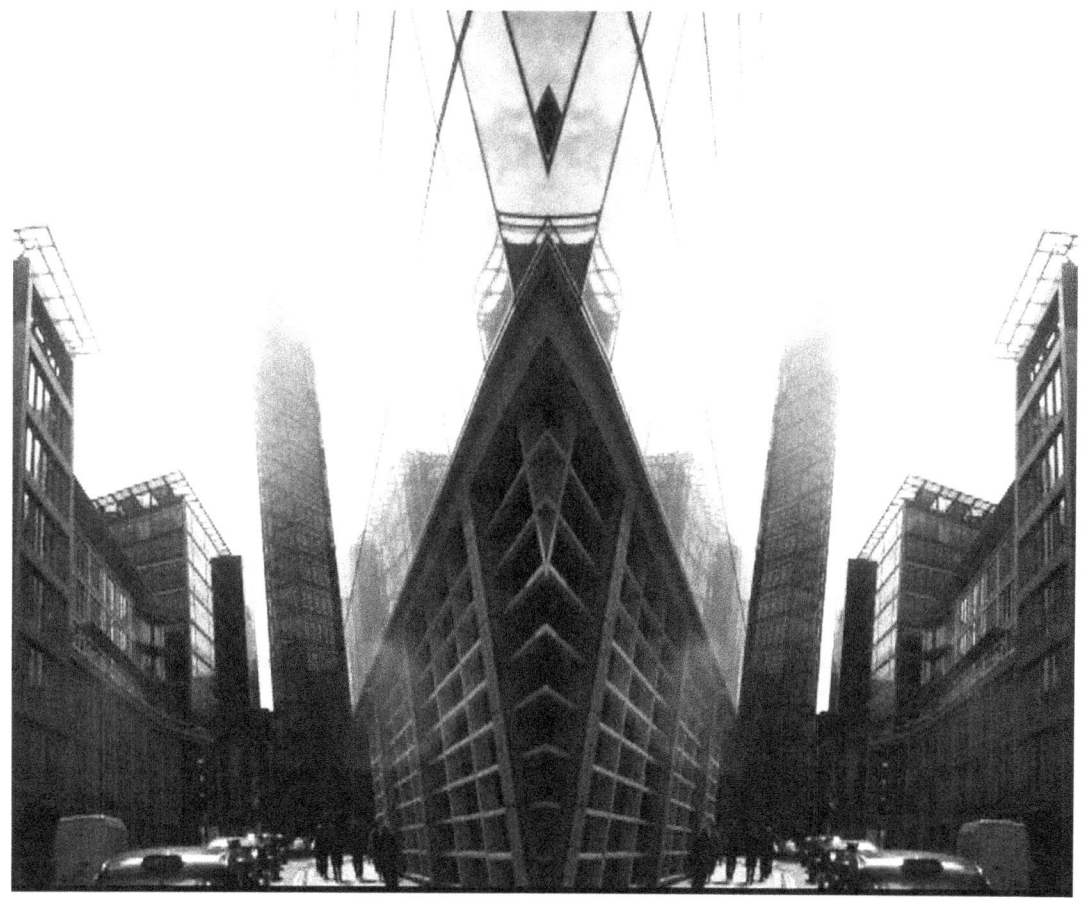

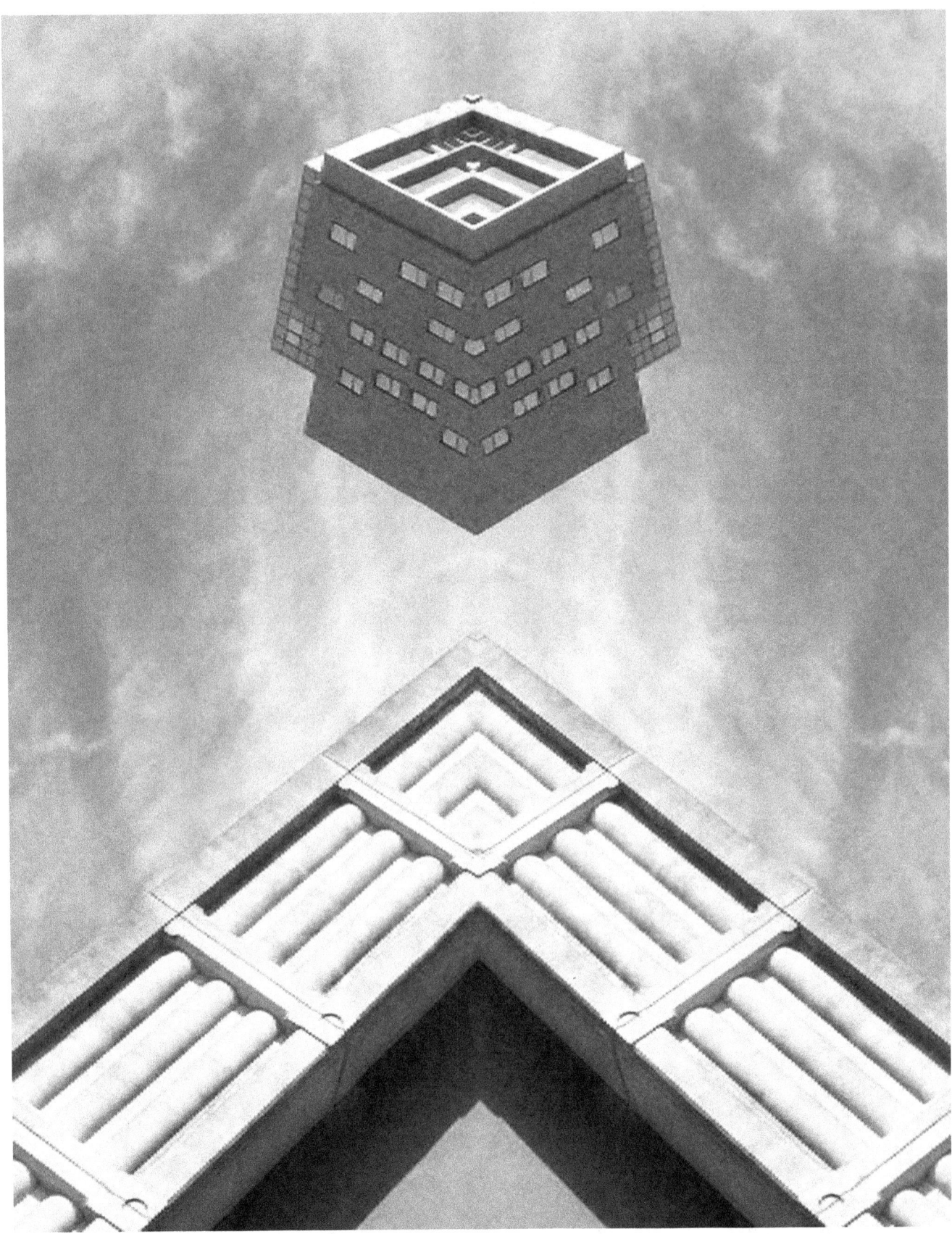

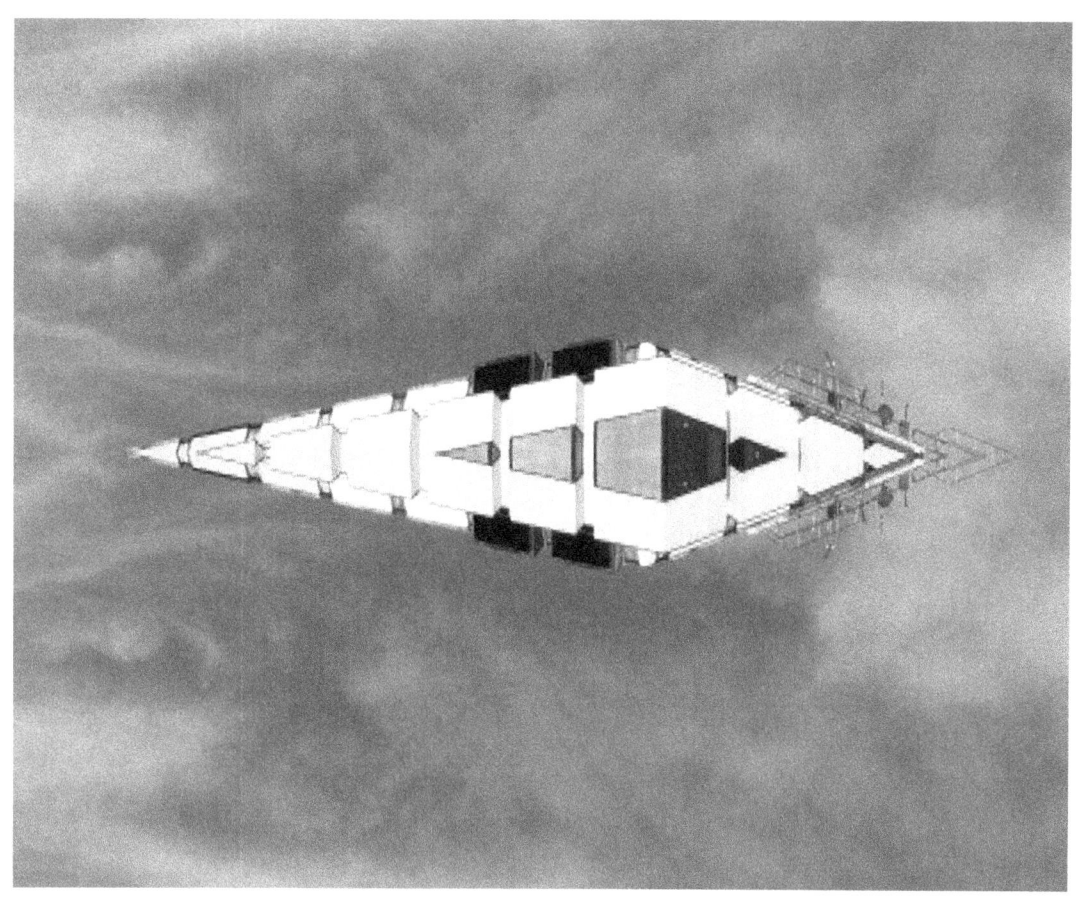

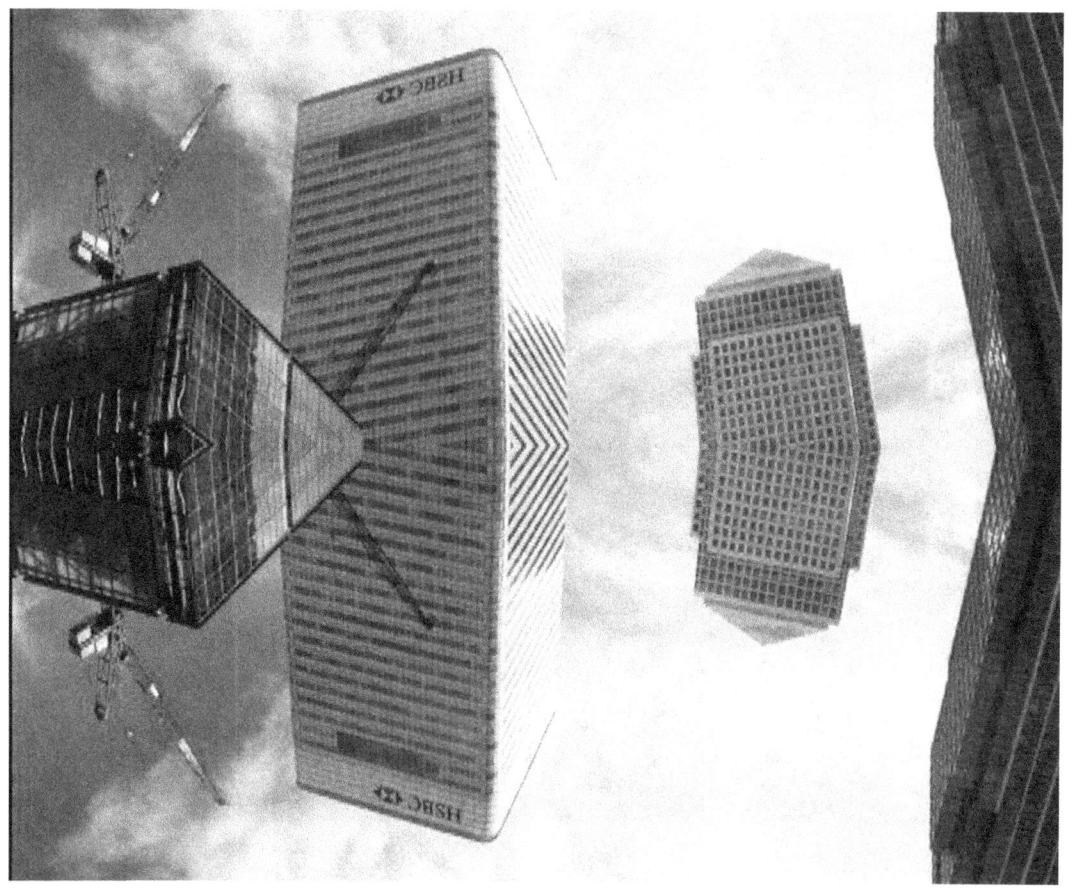

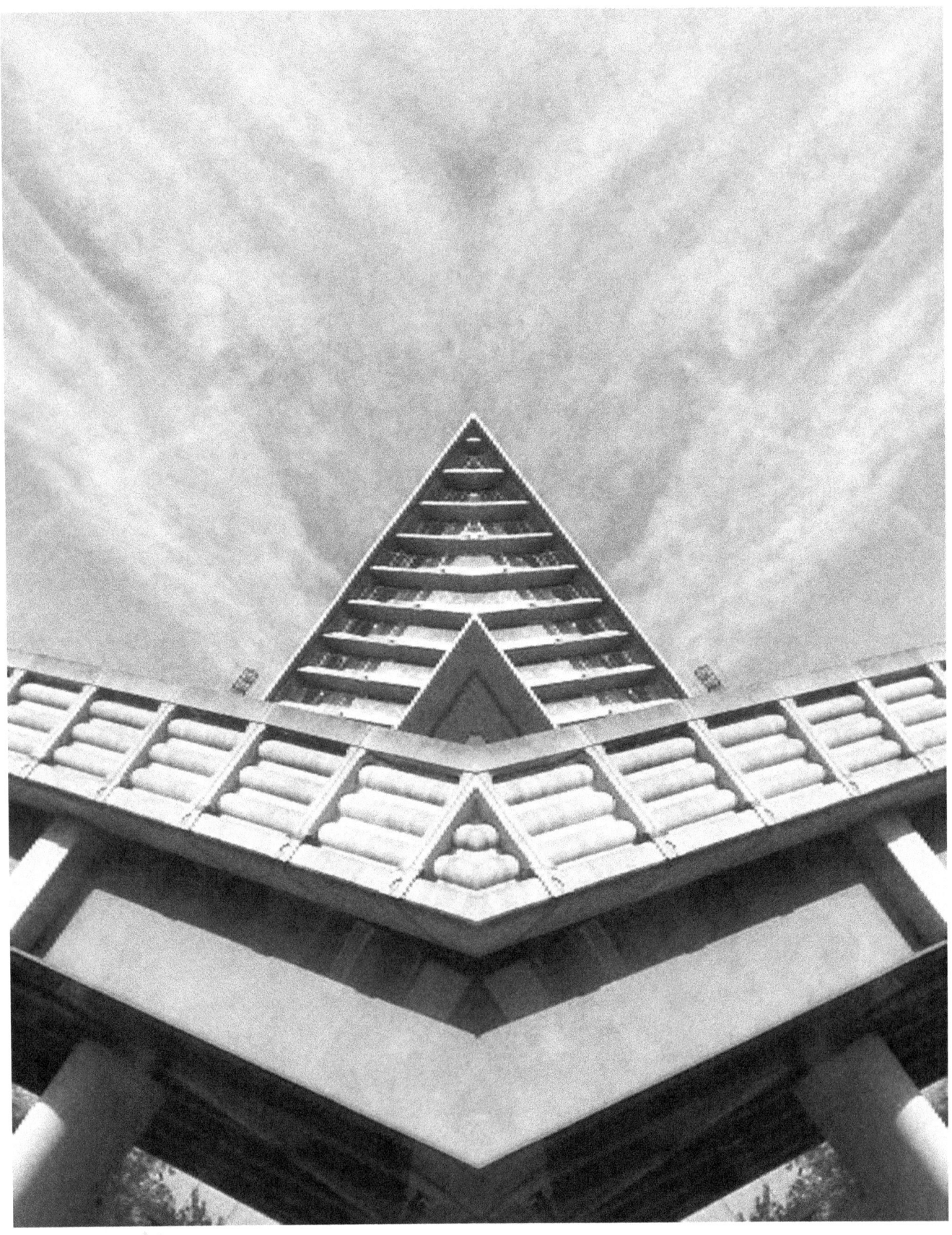

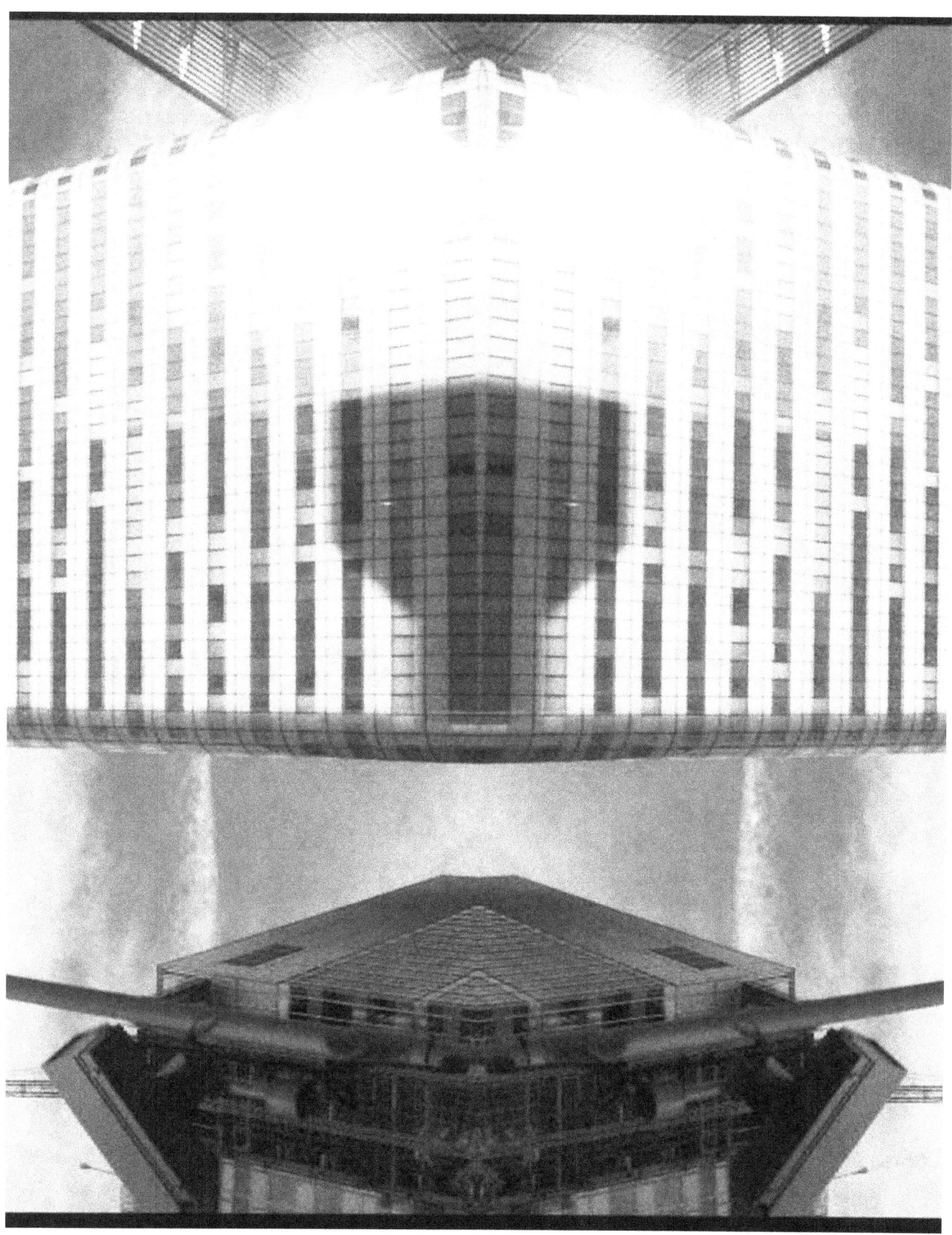

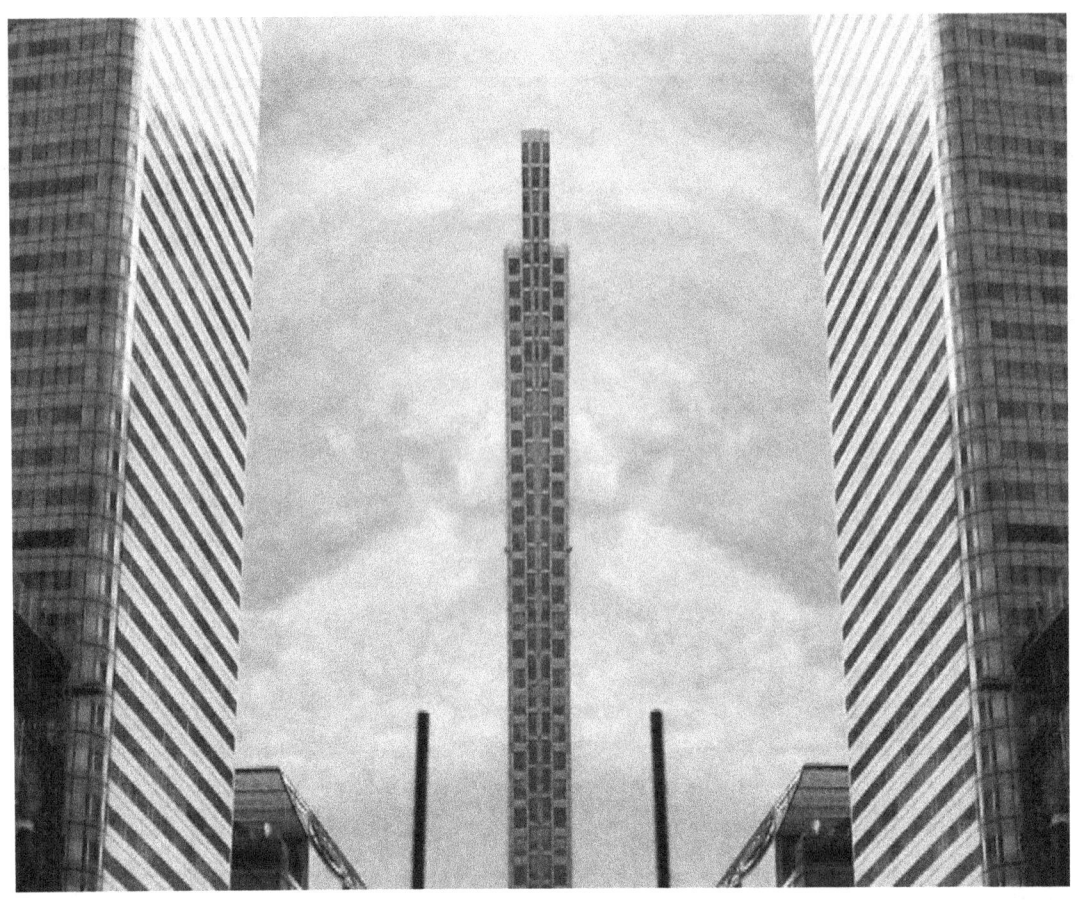

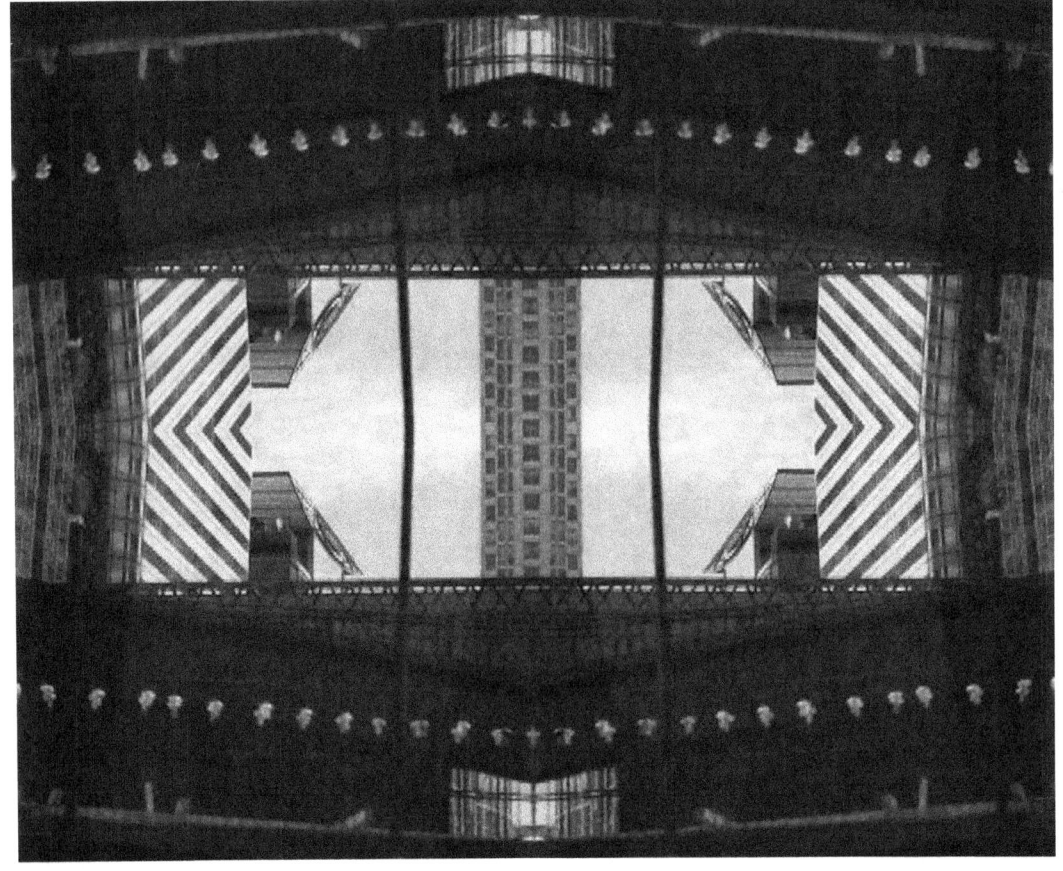

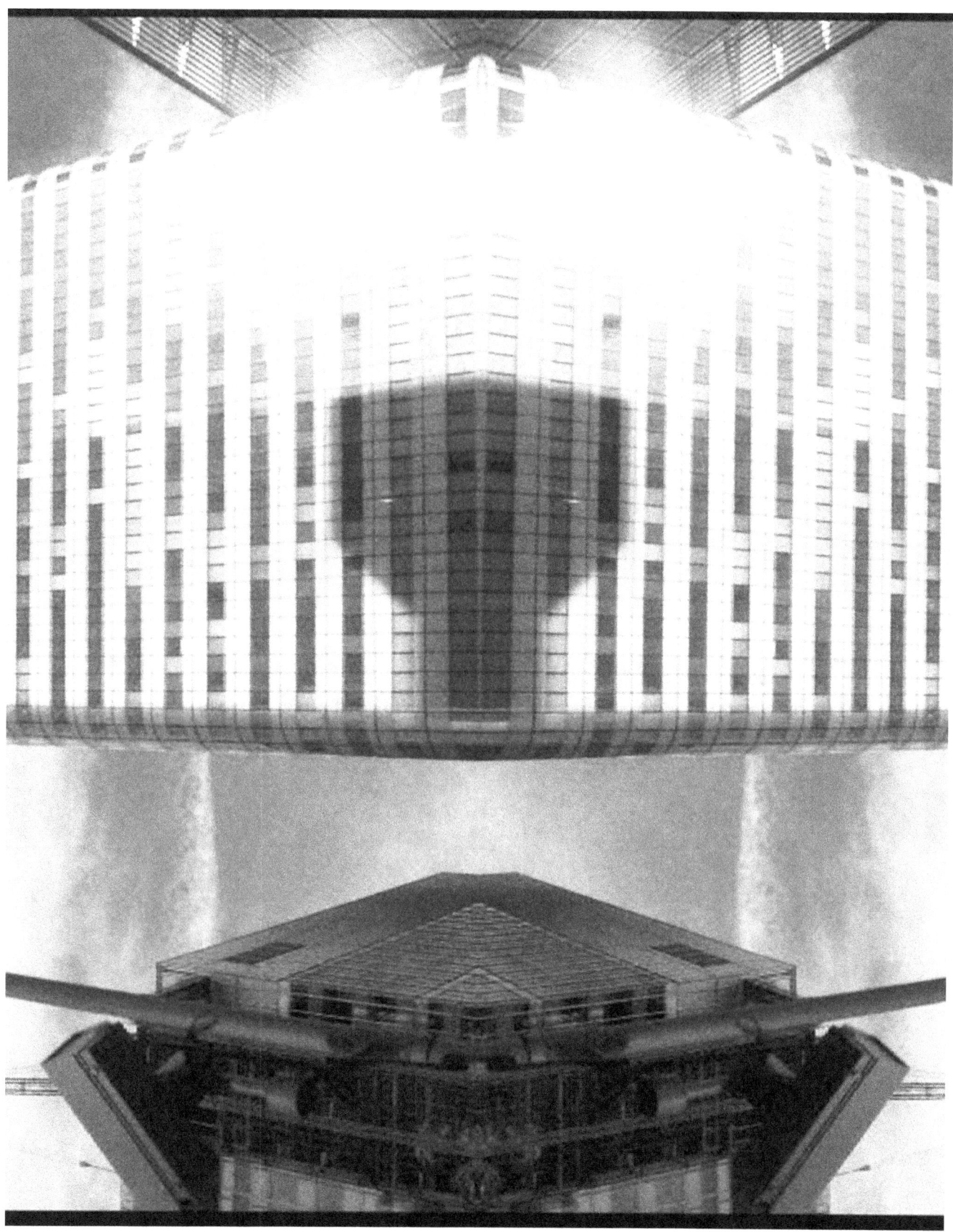

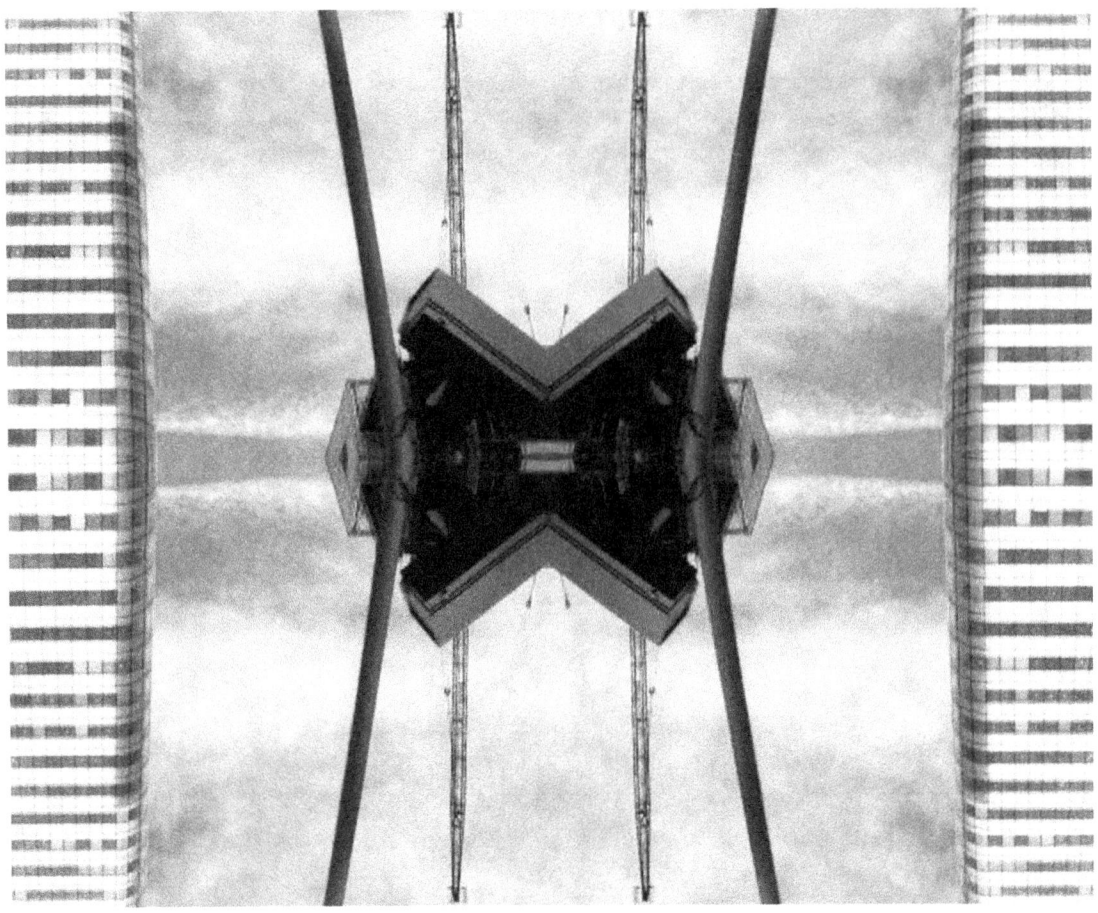

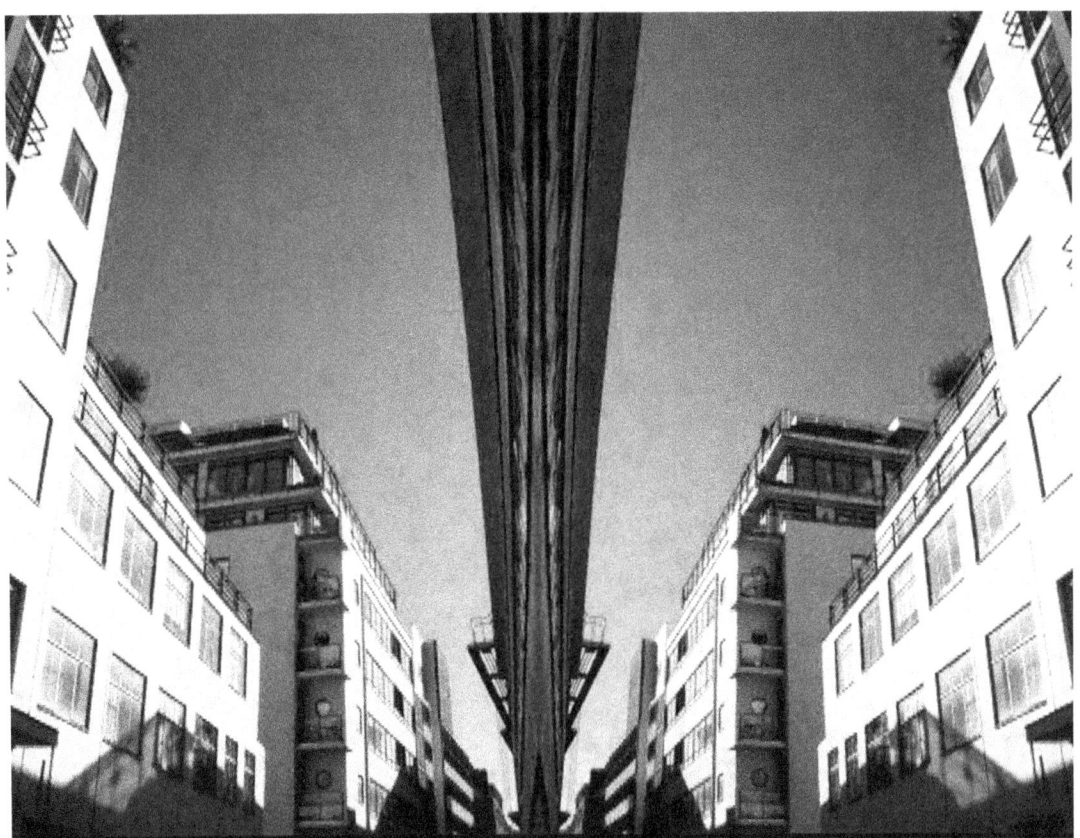

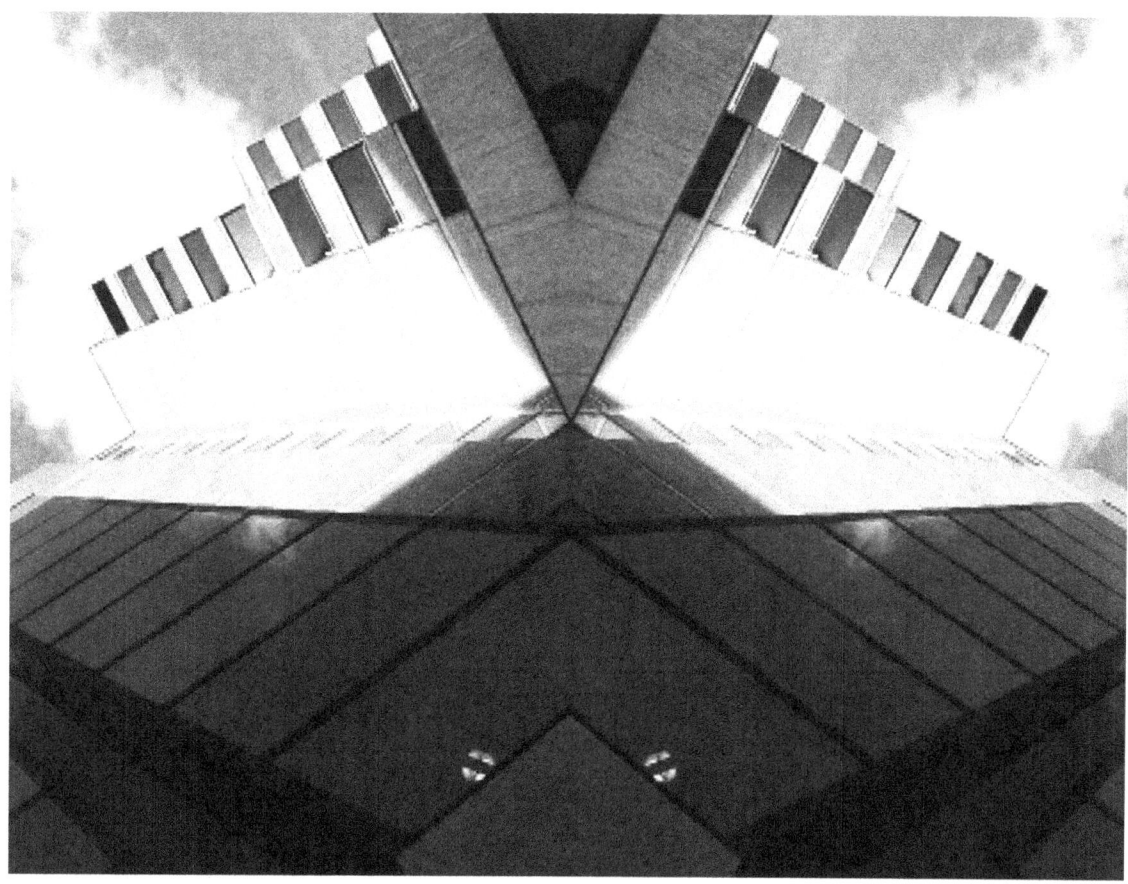

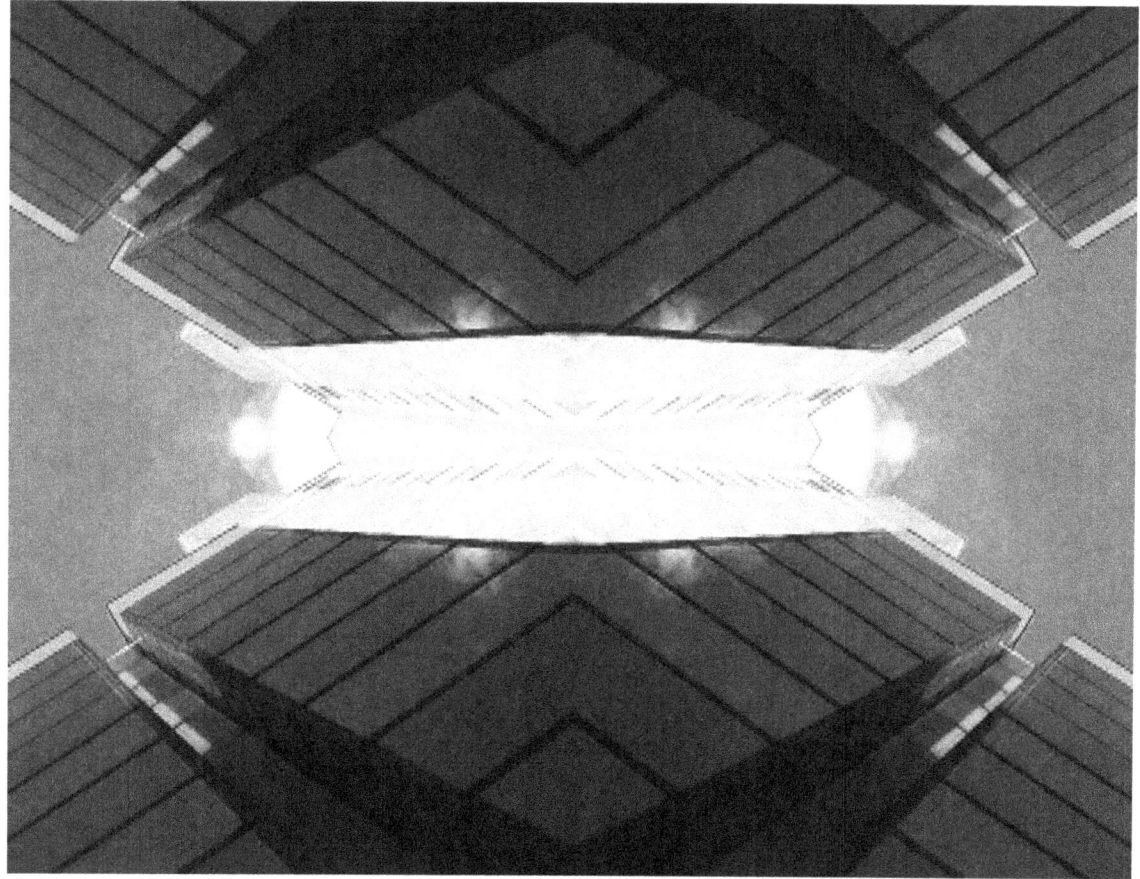

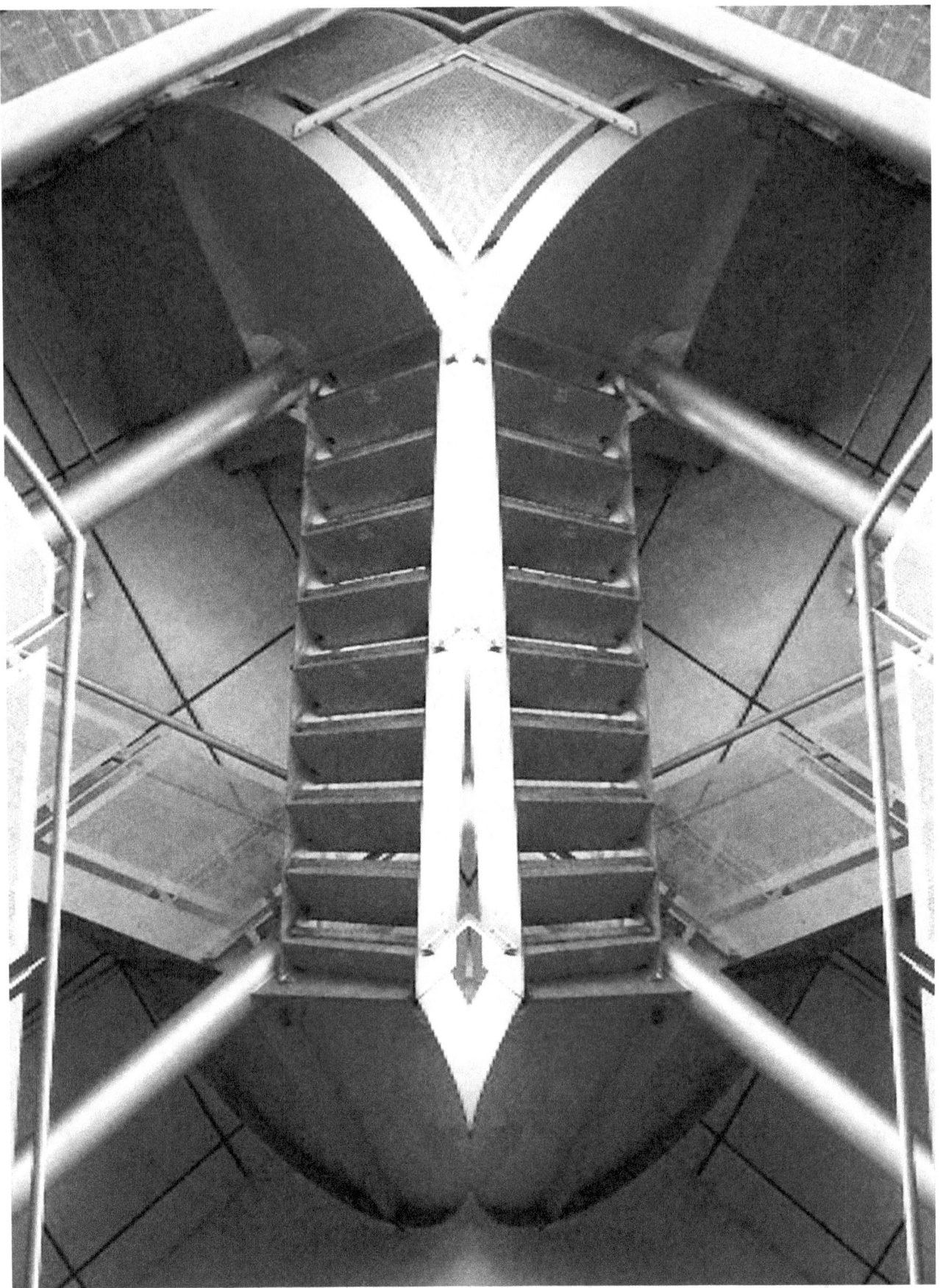

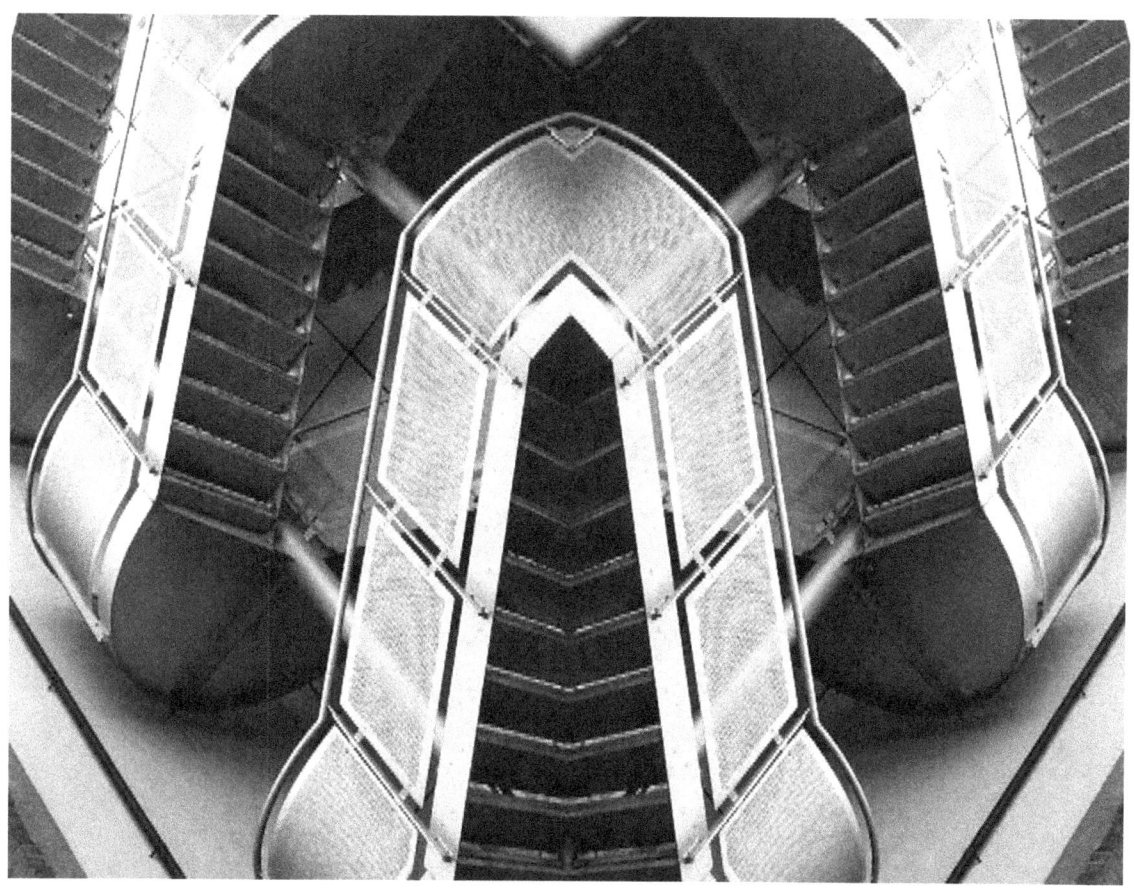

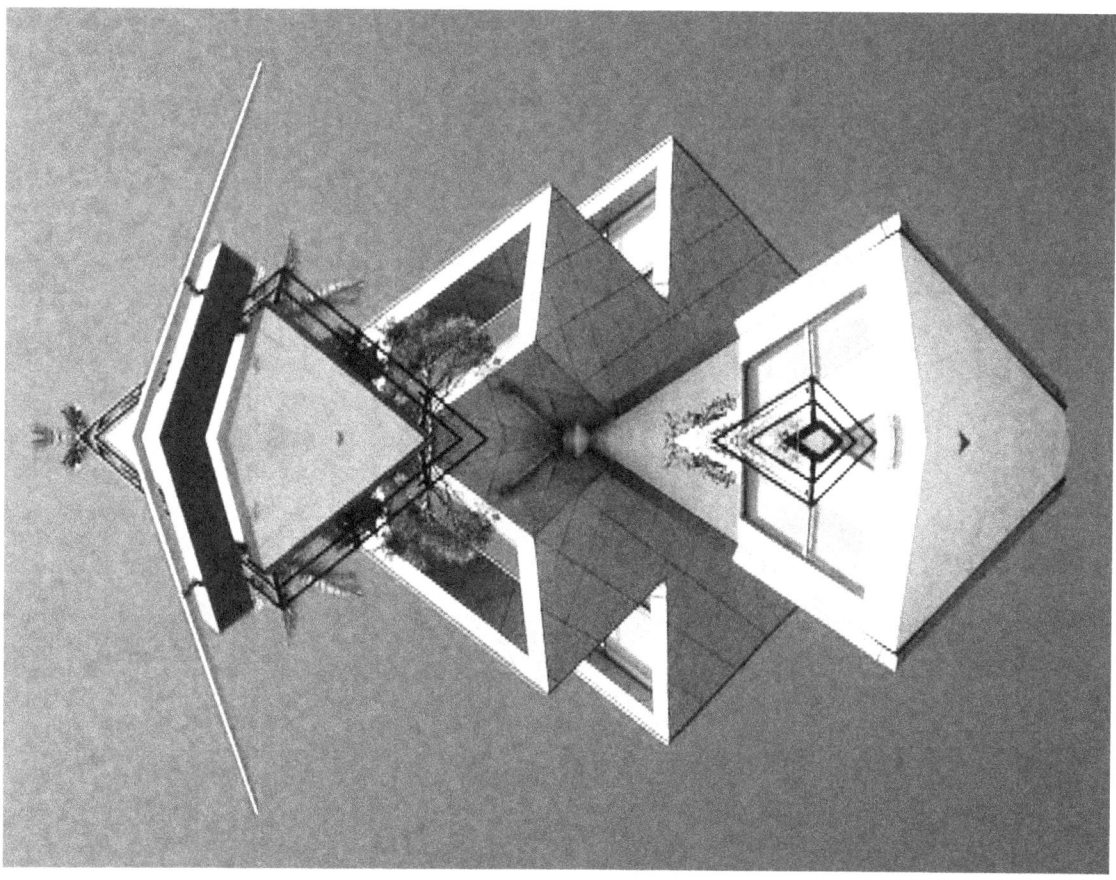

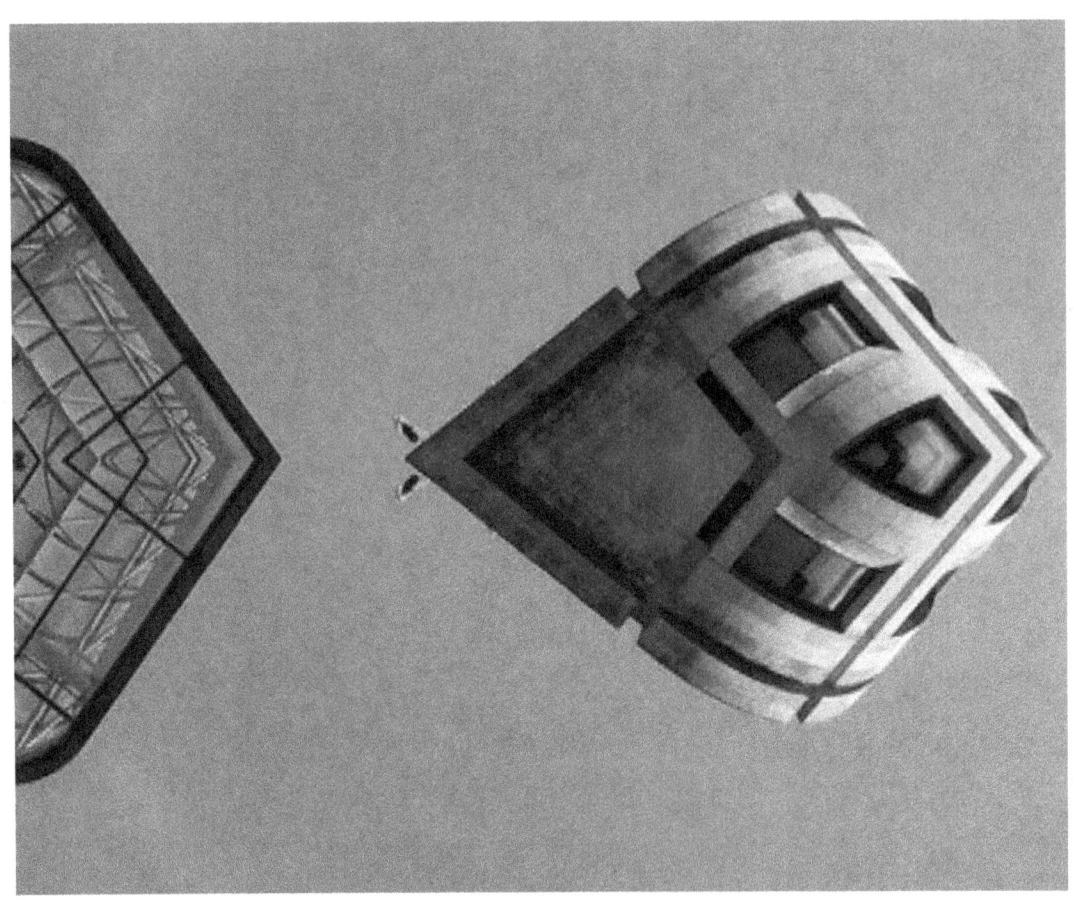

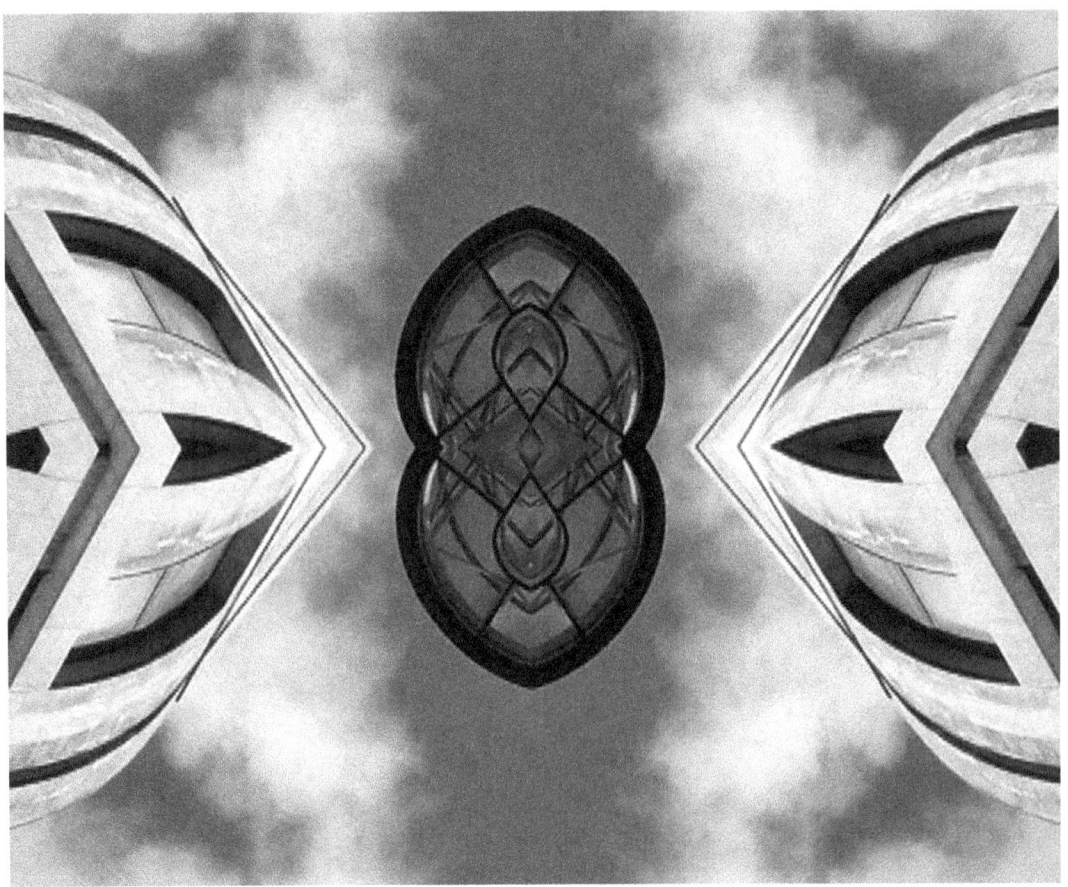

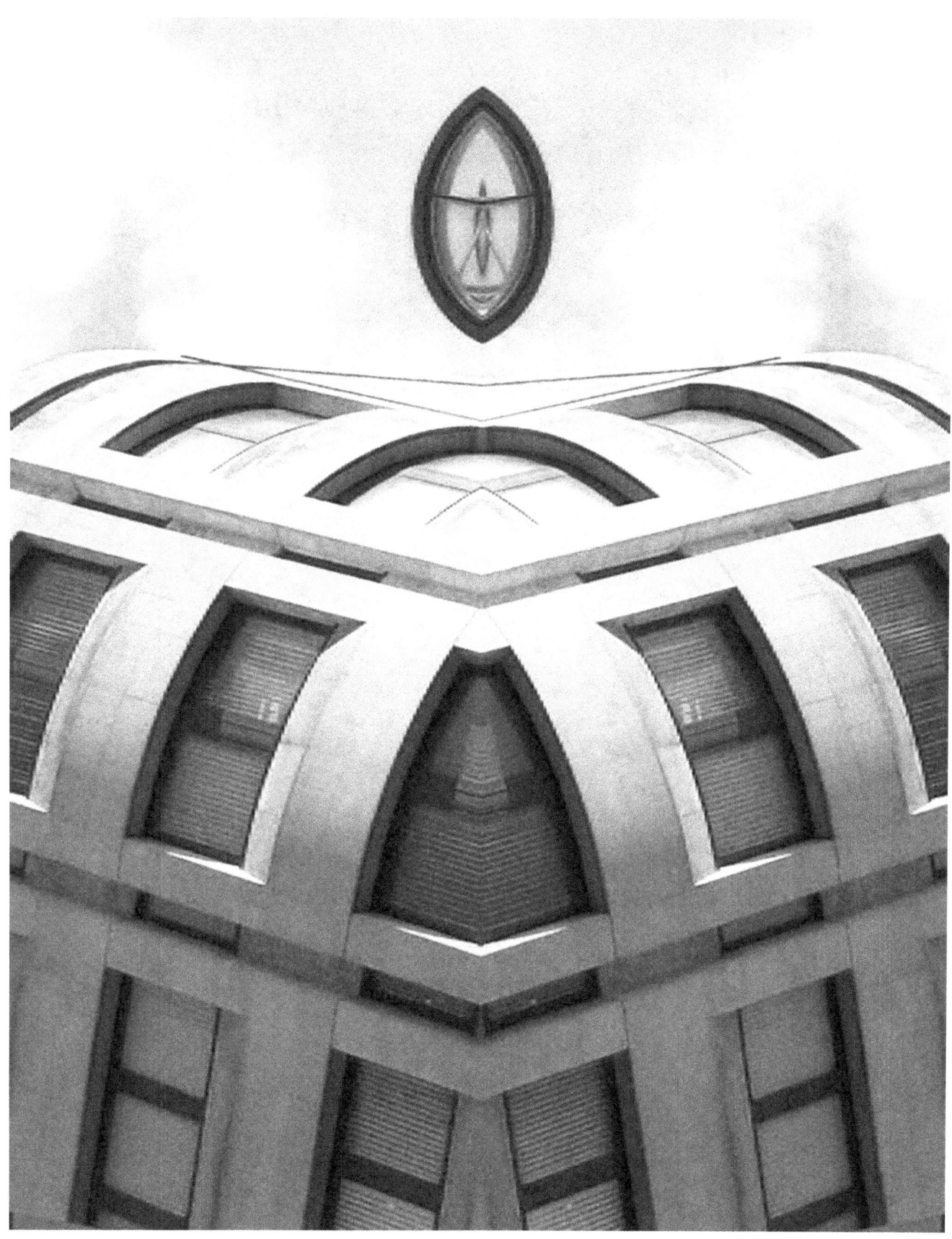

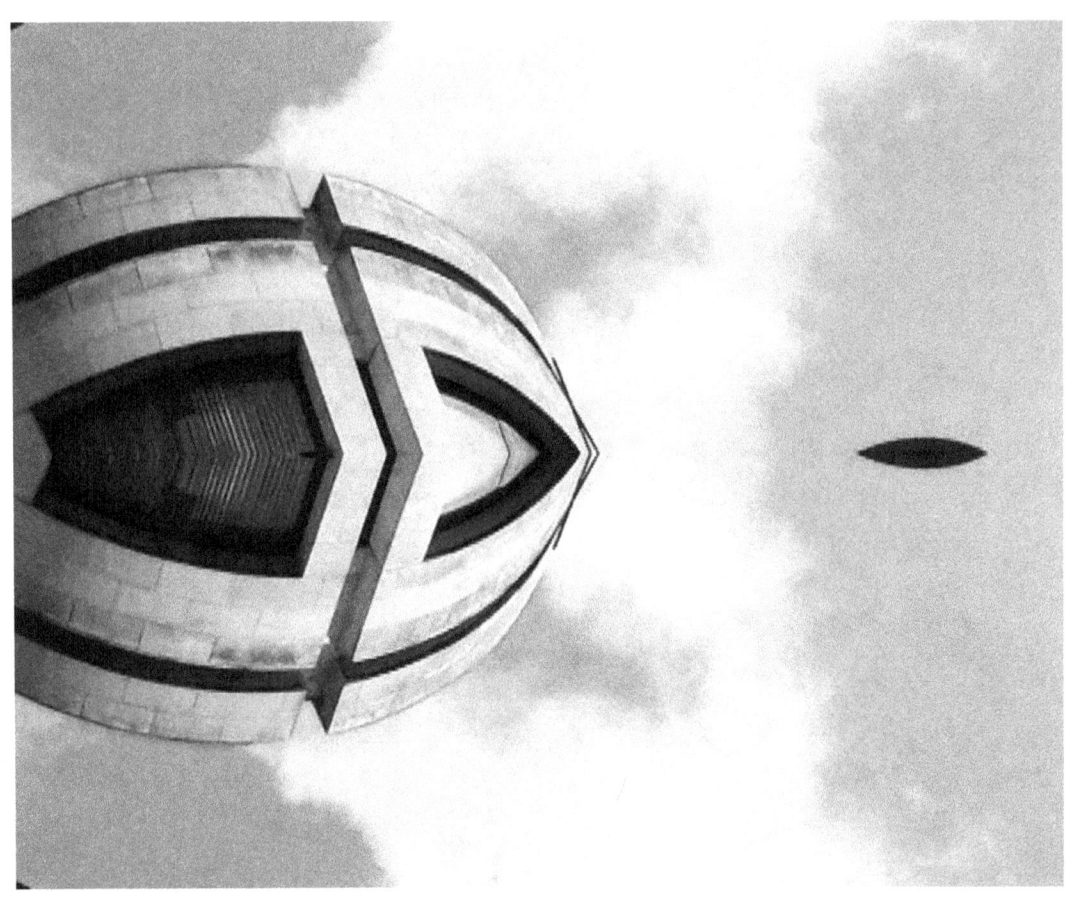

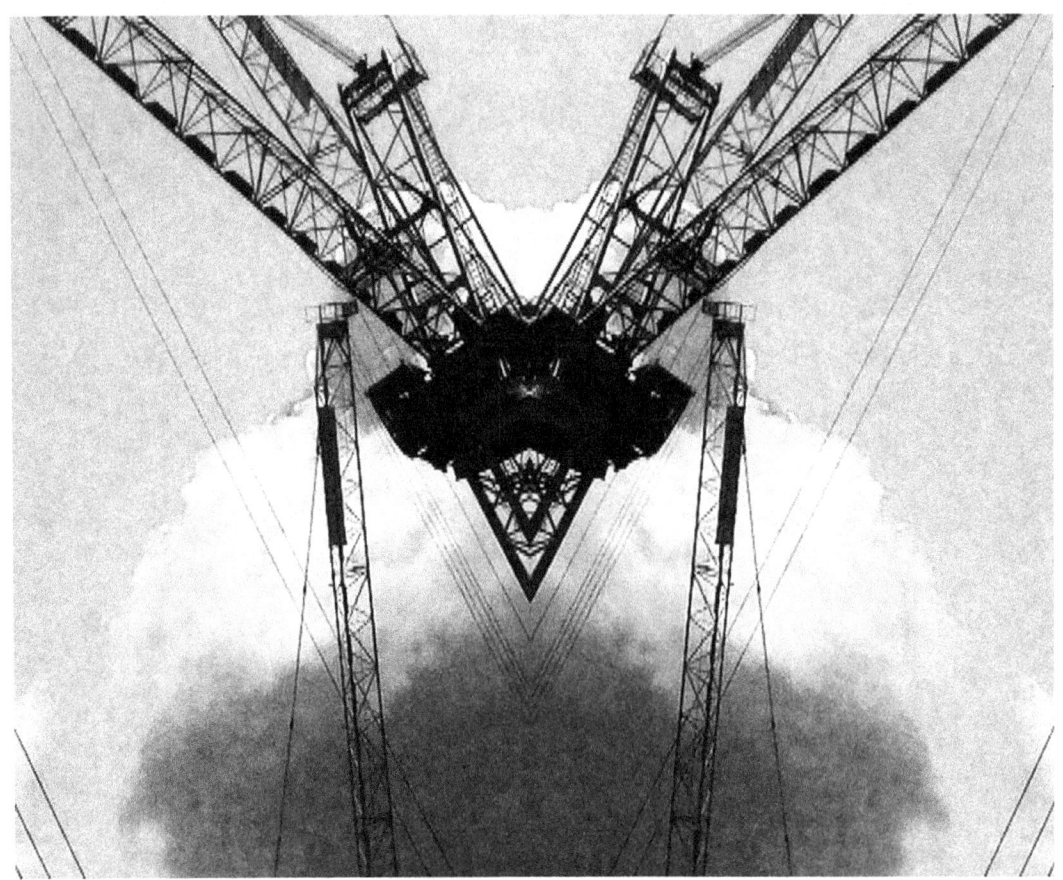

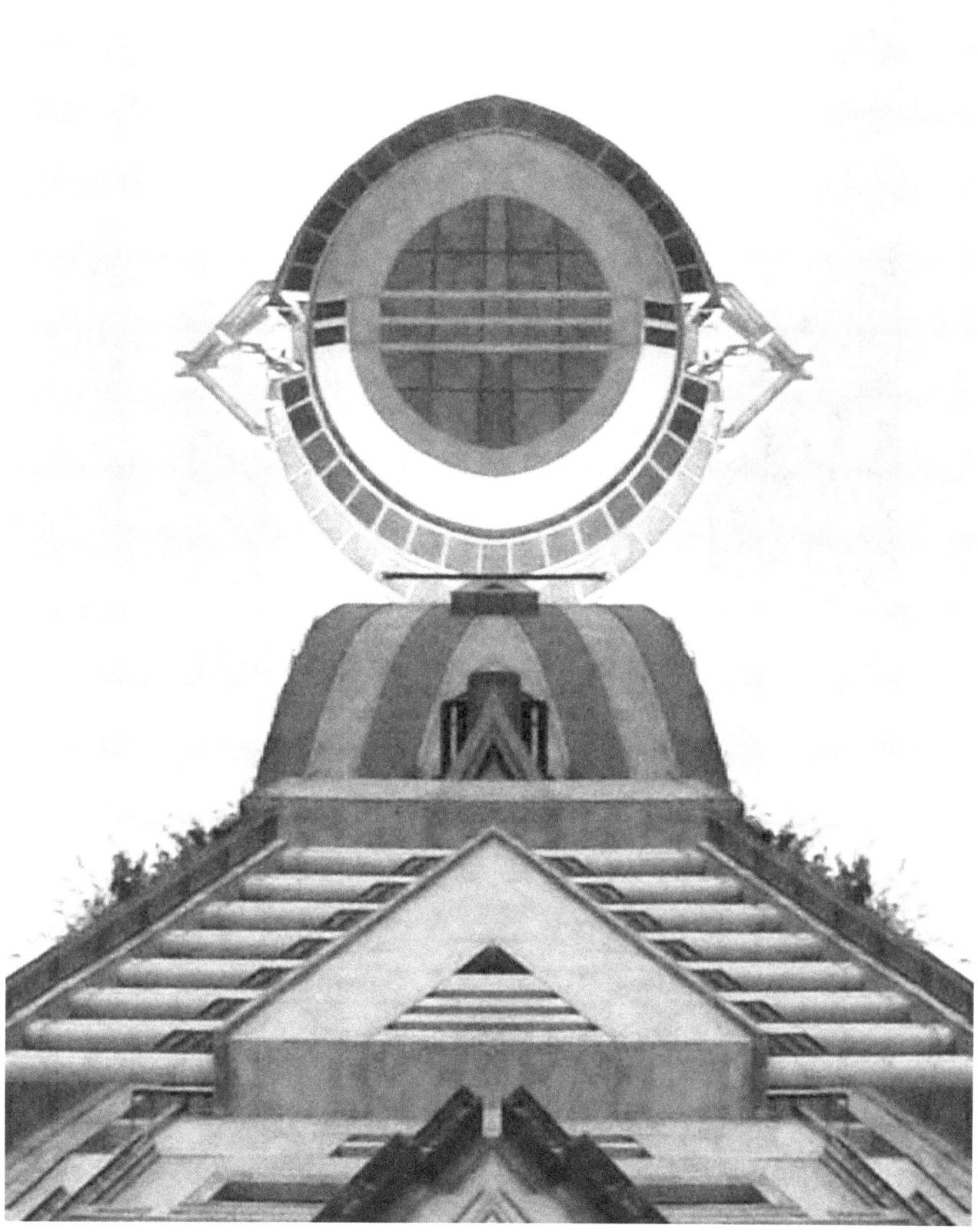

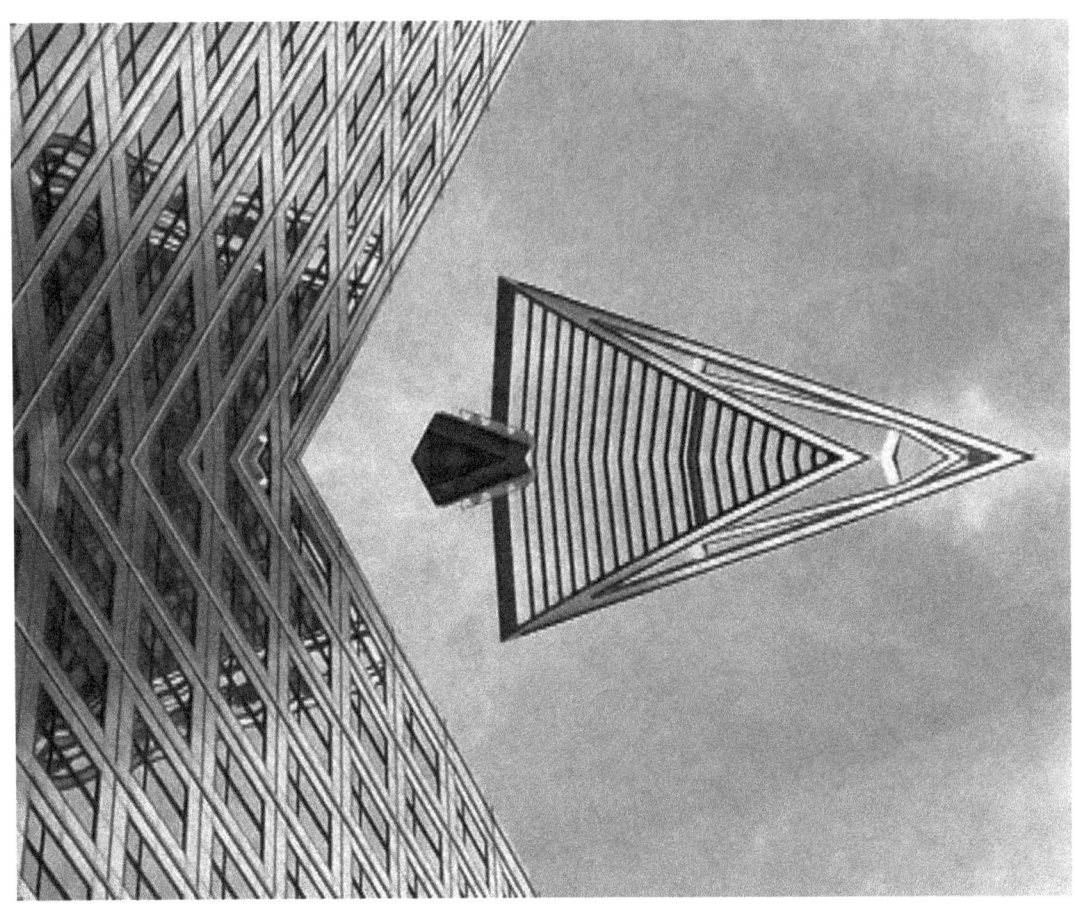

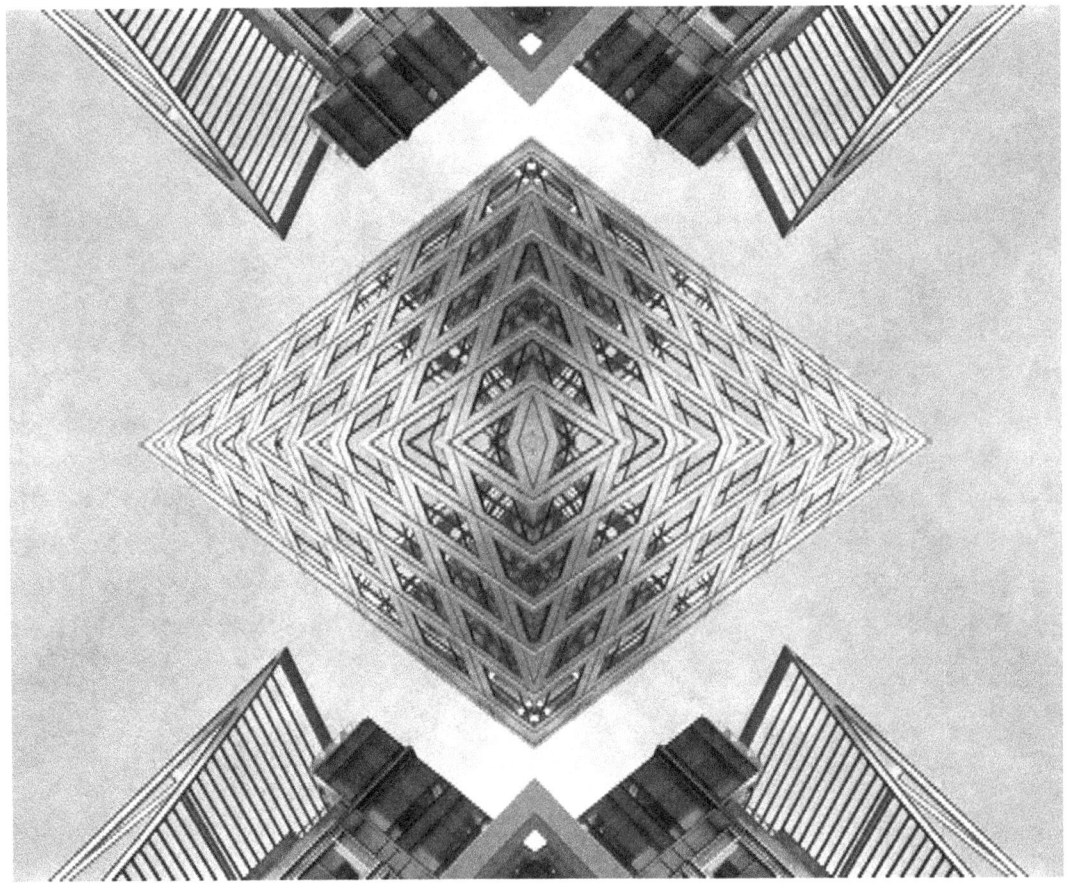

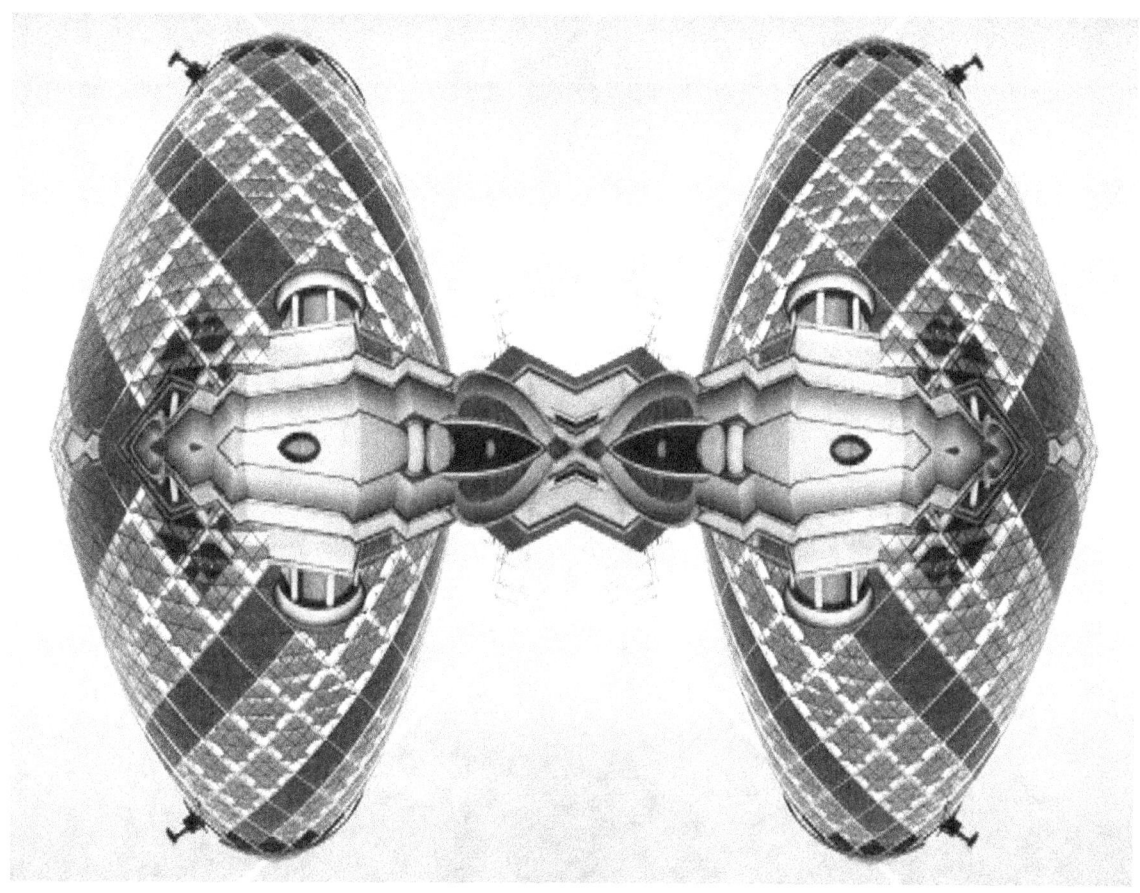

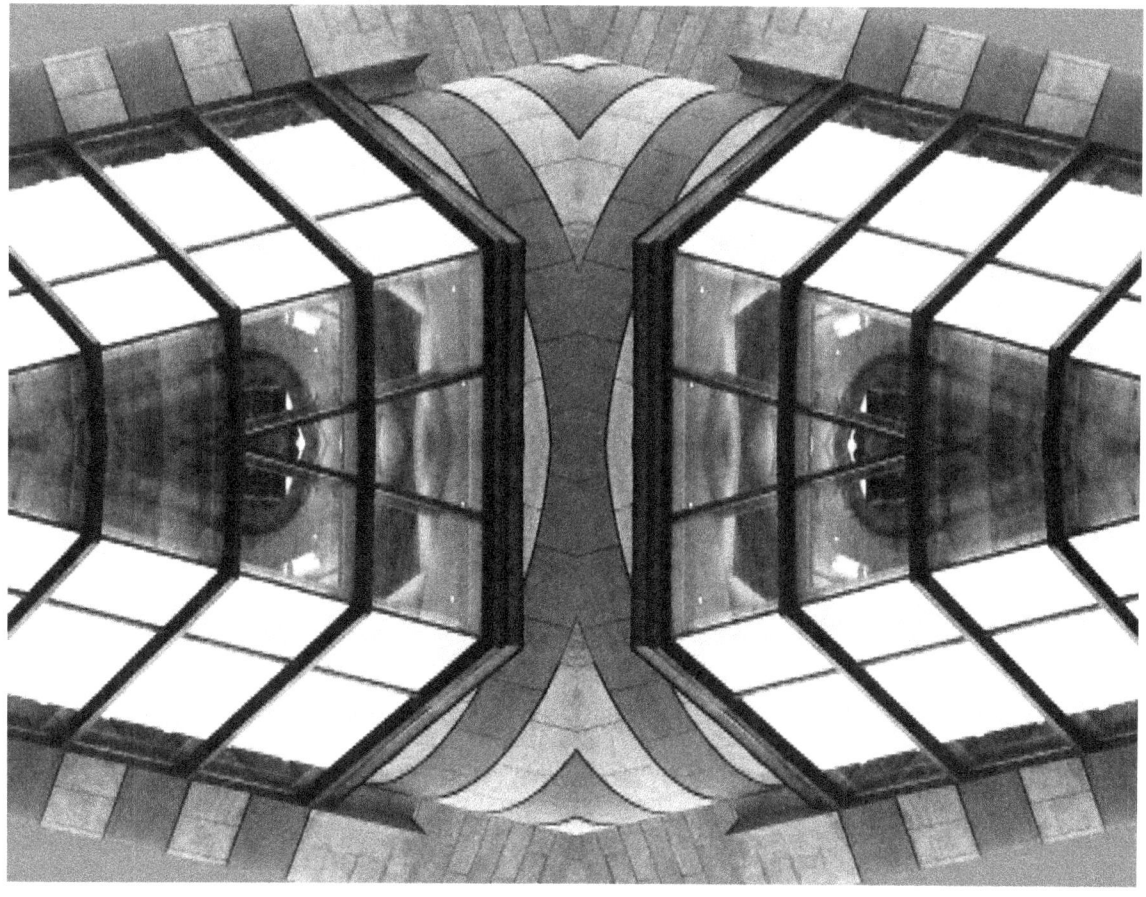

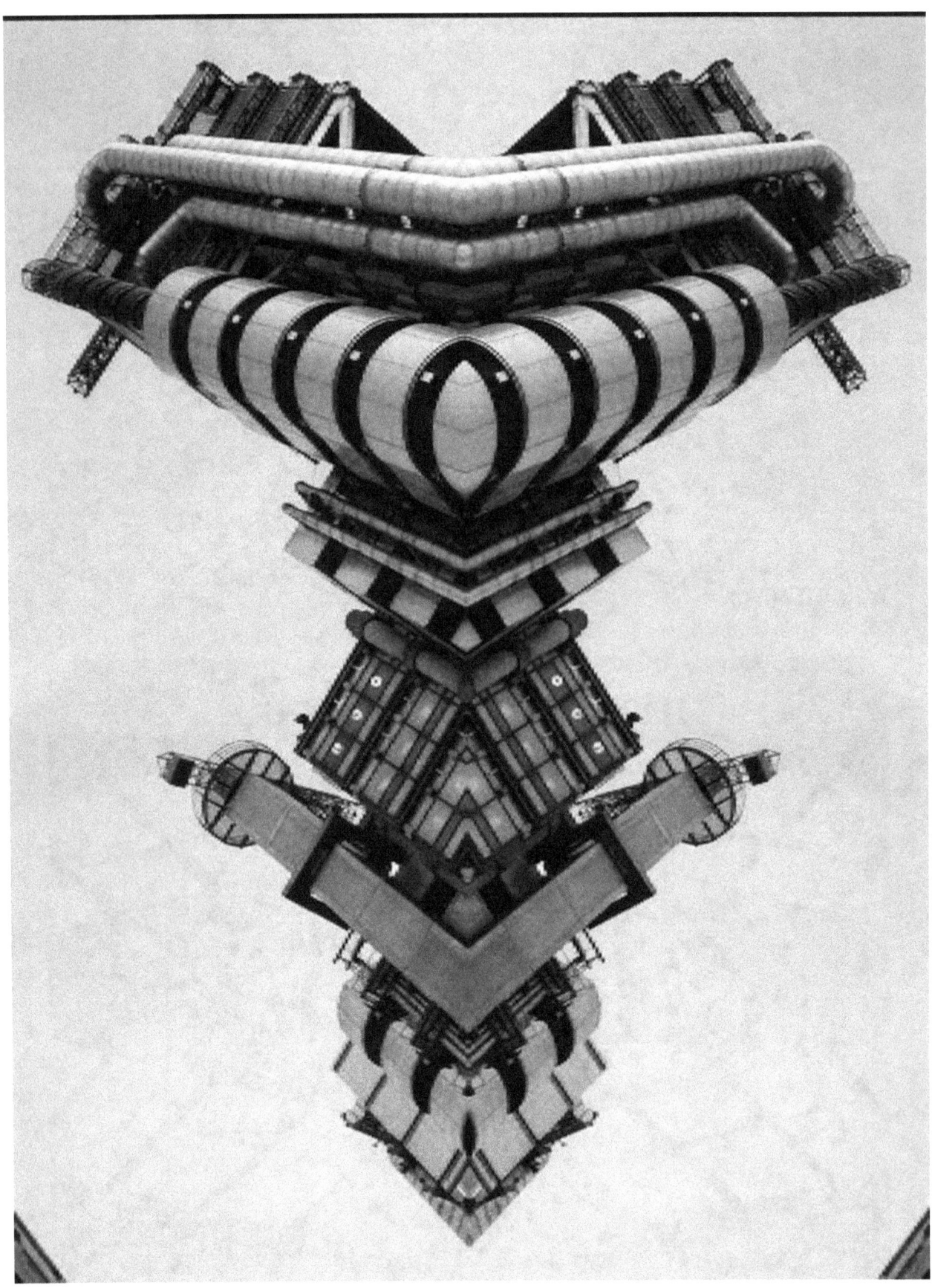

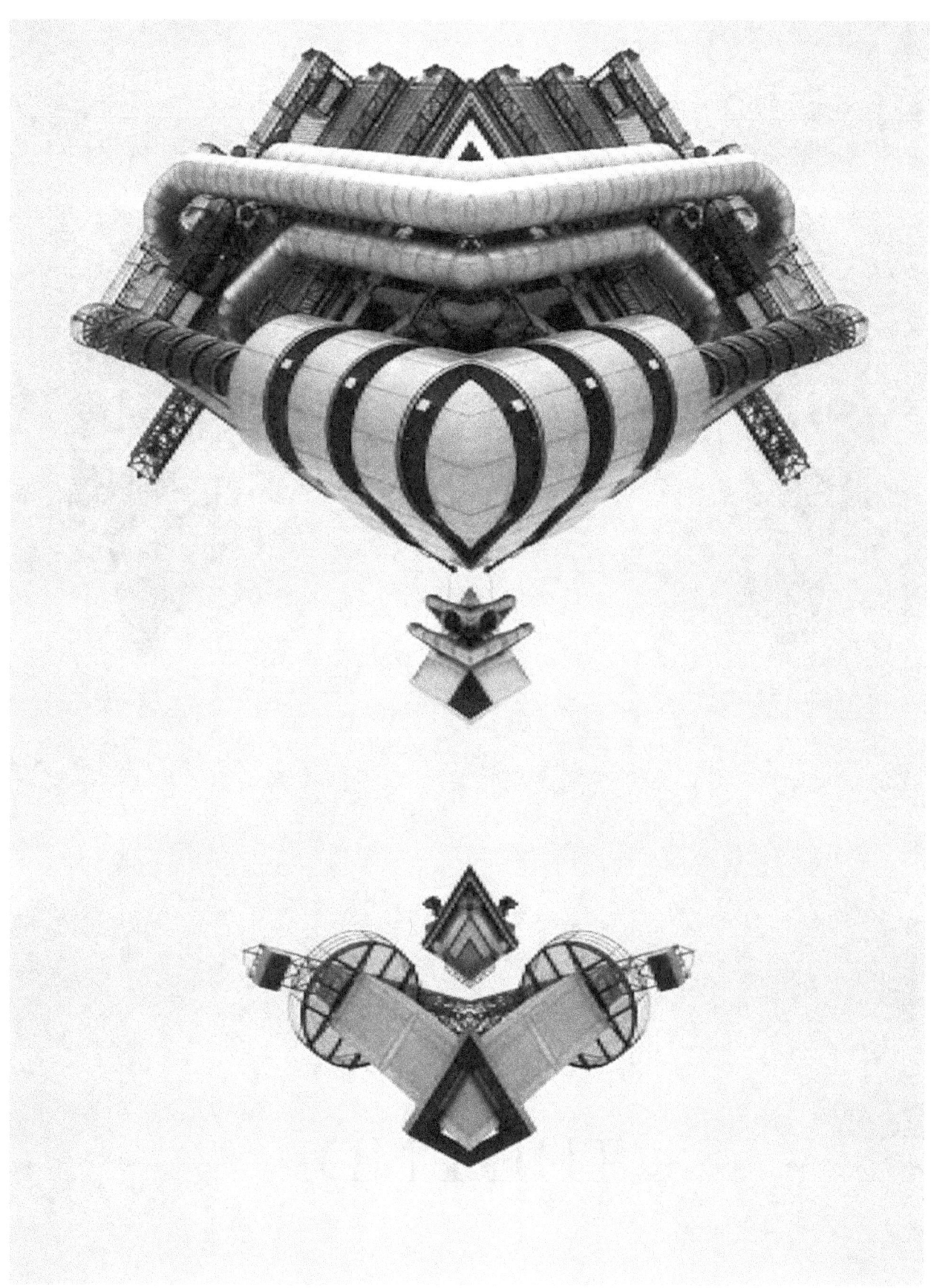

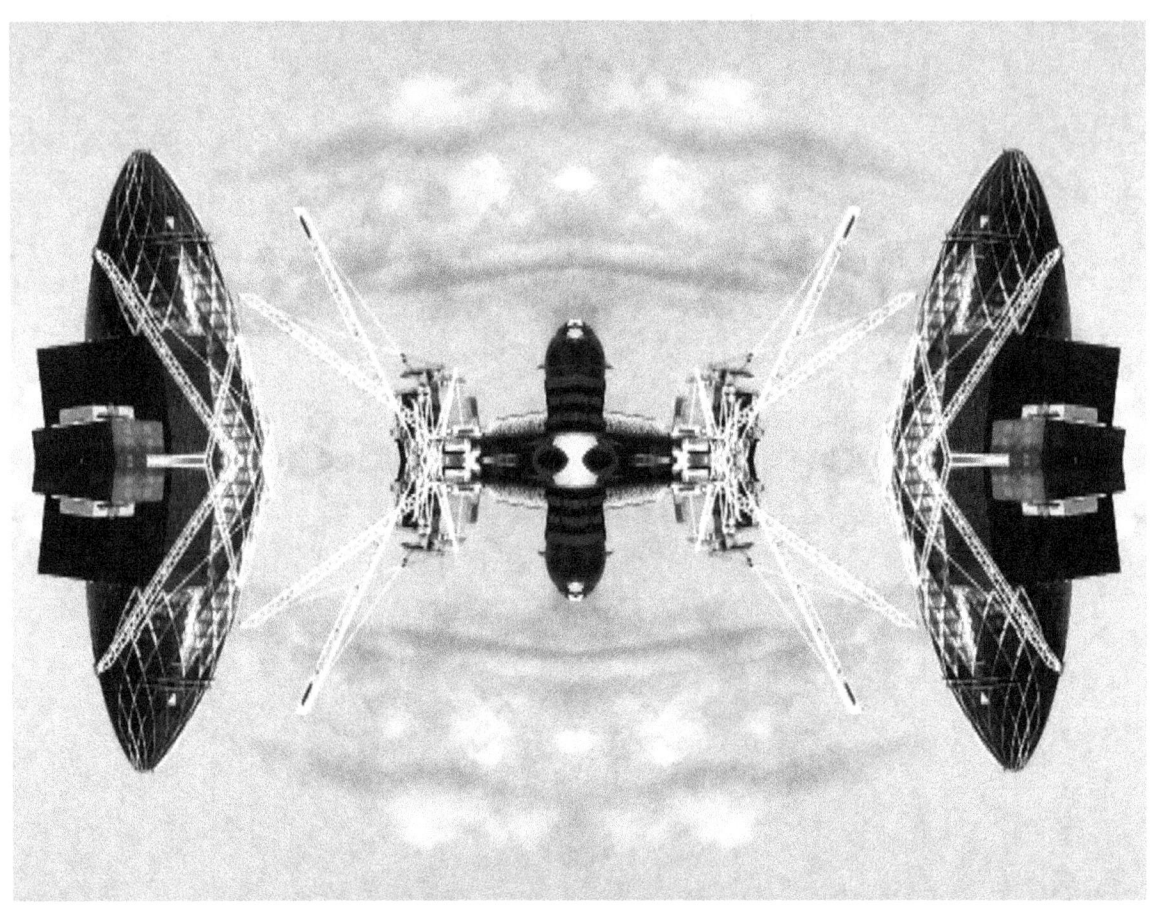

THE END

ABOUT THE AUTHOR

Lee Gibson was born in North-East England in 1962.
He has lived in East London for the past 30 years.
He has written several novels, a punk rock autobiography, a book of poems
spanning three decades, a non-fiction book dealing with comparative mythology
and UFO's, and also a book of his encaustic art paintings.

CONTACT THE AUTHOR:
Lee666gibson@gmail.com